LONE STAR NATION

HOW TEXAS WILL TRANSFORM AMERICA

RICHARD PARKER

PEGASUS BOOKS
NEW YORK LONDON

LONE STAR NATION

Pegasus Books LLC
80 Broad Street, 5th Floor
New York, NY 10004

Copyright © 2014 by Richard Parker

First Pegasus Books edition November 2014

Interior design by Maria Fernandez

Library of Congress Cataloging-in-Publication Data is available.

ISBN: 978-1-60598-626-5

10 9 8 7 6 5 4 3 2 1

Printed in the United States of America
Distributed by W. W. Norton & Company

With gratitude toward
my mother and father, Josefina and James,
who decided I would become a Texan in 1966;

love for my sister Janet,
the only native Texan in the whole original bunch;

thankfulness to my West Texan former wife, Laurie,
who helped me raise Olivia and Isabel;

and with great hope for these two women
—and the Texas they will inherit.

CONTENTS

FOREWORD

G rowing up in Texas left me with lots of memories but one
clear-cut impression: Nothing much ever seemed to happen
here.

Admittedly, the places in which I grew up—first Laredo and
then El Paso, both on the muddy Rio Grande that demarks the
United States from Mexico—probably heightened that sensation.
El Paso, in particular, felt isolated, like a place at the end of the
world. When I considered the things I saw, say on television, or
heard about on the radio or glimpsed in the occasional newspaper
it seemed as though life was happening not here but instead somewhere out there. My father traveled a lot for work. His plane tickets
read: Chicago, New York, Miami, Port-au-Prince, Mexico City,
and Santiago. What was going on definitely seemed out there.

By the time I had reached high school, I was quite sure that nothing of note ever happened in Texas. I rode the bus to school and on the radio heard snippets about Jimmy Carter and Ronald Reagan, the Soviet invasion of Afghanistan and the death of Pope Paul VI. The bands of the era—a bizarre concoction of pre-punk, longhair, glam rock, southern rock, and Canadians, like Styx, Journey, Sammy Hagar, Loverboy, and 38 Special—occasionally played but seemed to prefer the air-conditioned Pan Am Center, up Interstate 10 in little Las Cruces, to the dusty cow palace that was the El Paso County Coliseum. Social life was stratified into the popular kids, who were as often as not well off; the athletes, who were as often as not popular; the cowboys; the stoners; and the Mexicans, who clung to their particular cultures. Oh, and then there was the band. The whole thing seemed to revolve around that great West Texas ritual: High school football.

That was something I tried by the time spring training rolled around at the end of my freshman year. Having played before coming to my 5A high school, a place with over 2,000 students, I realized the currency of being on the team. You were somebody. You fit in. You got to wear your game jersey on Fridays. Yet that grueling spring training in the soaring heat, frequently spent face down in the dust, being screamed at by coaches and gulping salt pills instead of water—as was the practice of the time—was probably a good lesson in the importance of the sacrificial devotion to sport itself, regardless of the outcome. It also left me with a shoulder injury after being hit by a varsity lineman who outweighed me by twice as much—I knew this as he fell on me—that would mark my return to the hard metal seats of the stands. Watching was enough; it was tradition, after all, to devote a Friday night to the game and the spectacle, even as a spectator instead of an adolescent gladiator.

And the spectacle was large. Everybody wore cowboy boots and puffy down vests and jackets to those games as the temperature in the desert fell with sunset. El Paso was over 3,000 feet in elevation and cold at night, even in the early autumn. In the wake of the film *Urban Cowboy*, there was an informal but furious competition for the most exotic animal skin boots, the most exotically feathery band on a cowboy hat or the most jacked up pickup truck. Odessa Permian was always the dreaded opponent in the season opener and only a few years later its football program would be chronicled by H.G. Bissinger in his classic, *Friday Night Lights*. And, of course, our hushed high school crowd of kids and parents alike held their breath at halftime on the brisk night of Friday, November 21, 1980 when the announcers told us what CBS had just revealed on television to 83 million viewers: Who had shot J.R. Ewing on *Dallas*.

Returned to the assembly of nerds to which I belonged, the land of speech, debate, drama, and newspaper clubs, I pleaded with my dad, ridiculously, to move the family. Out of boredom, I would join a small group of other nerds hanging by the edge of the bonfire at some party in the desert, skulking around the beer keg at the home of those luckless, out-of-town parents or slipping through the shadowy streets of Ciudad Juárez, on the wrong side of the Mexican border, in the darkness, where the bartenders didn't care how old you were and the cops just wanted to shake you down.

My high school guidance counselor informed me that my choices were limited: college in El Paso or maybe the U.S. Army. I had already gotten into Trinity University, a liberal arts school, in San Antonio. So, I thanked him for his time and attention all those years. And as much as I liked college, it tended to reinforce my perceptions of Texas: a fairly conservative order, both socially and politically. Then, my perception met practicality. When the savings-and-loan bust hit, followed soon by the collapse of oil prices, there were no jobs to be had in Texas for a new college graduate.

So, in the late summer of 1985, I packed up my 1974 Volvo, hugged my mom and dad goodbye and drove east on Interstate 10, out past Van Horn and Fort Stockton, across the Trans-Pecos and the Edwards Plateau. There was so little traffic I read a magazine much of the way to San Antonio. There, I kept right on going, headed for New Orleans first and later, New York, and Washington, D.C. By dawn I had made it out of Texas and awoke to a Louisiana state trooper tapping on my window with his billy club. I couldn't sleep here in this rest stop, he informed me. I had to keep on going. So, I wearily obliged.

I write this not so much to provide a memoir of life in Texas in the 1970s and 1980s but rather, to make a point: Texas is now the epicenter of dynamic and potentially radical change in America. That's something most people would have never imagined then and may scoff at now but I have spent a lifetime—give or take—observing, and observing Texas, in particular. Texas today could not be any more different—whether viewed in social, economic, or political terms—from the Texas that I knew nearly 30 years ago. Following a pattern that stretches back not just centuries but millennia, this scale of change in Texas will have a major impact on America and the world in the years to come.

The story told in the ensuing pages is mostly one told as an observer, certainly, but one who has a long, personal history with the state which helps to form both a larger context and, hopefully, a richer backdrop than that of an observer who claims to be entirely detached from the subject. I spent nearly two decades growing up in Texas. Later, living on the East Coast, I visited briefly now and again. In 1999 I returned with my young family full of hope and with a bit of buyer's remorse and made it my full-time home. I am, unabashedly, a Texan. I got to collect Texas in snapshots over many years.

I have tried to bring a mix of tools to this project, some of them quite sharp and a few of them with a little rust on them. I have tried to bring as accurate a viewpoint as possible to bear in the following pages; as a journalist, I believe in owing that to the reader. I have brought my academic training in political science to bear as well as my decades of experience in journalism.

The individuals you will find quoted here in the more contemporary accounts are either respected experts or just everyday people; the famous and the powerful tend to get more than their fair share of attention, anyway, though they are chronicled here, too. Every day people, however, tend to get less than their fair share of attention, though their insights and experiences are valuable. I have added my analysis, too, which ultimately is an opinion. This is not to be confused, though, with the ideological hectoring that defines much opinion journalism today. It is intended, instead, to be a judgment, more akin to analysis, of facts, history, and resultant trends to the very best of my ability. I neither favor one political party or another. Without these tools, I would be unqualified to present a brand new thesis with which to understand Texas—one that challenges many of the recent books about Texas, among the thousands of books previously written. Instead, I hope to build on a handful of the great books written about the state and say something entirely new.

In my view, much of what we think we know about Texas is dead wrong. Texas isn't some calcified, reactionary place, trapped in centuries of history. Instead, it is the very epicenter of change in America in the 21st century. As a result, Texas holds out hope of an American renaissance—but only if Texas itself will change parts of its very nature, setting the pace for the rest of a country now in the grip of economic malaise, social unease, and political gridlock. Texas is the American crucible in the 21st century.

★

In mixing the impartial fact-gathering with analysis and occasional personal anecdote, writing this book has reminded me of my work as a correspondent many years ago. I am reminded that the anecdote often encapsulates or even synthesizes an event or experience better than a litany of facts and figures or a complex, smarty pants analysis.

As a journalist, I spent many years looking for stories out there, in places that were far from home, which for many years was Washington, D.C. I had moved east and traveled abroad. I reported on the horror of guerrilla conflict and government retribution in Chiapas, Mexico in the 1990s, and the repeated American crises with Iraq afterward. Always, it seemed, the story was out there. And yet each time, I recall thinking upon my turn toward home that I was mildly disappointed in the nature of the subjects. I felt the same thing at the end of the Kosovo War in 1999, the third, and final, armed conflict I'd written about.

I had gone to write about war and all its sweeping themes but the conflict itself proved to be an exercise in limitations: From the diplomatic stalemates to the limited application of airpower to the way that the regime in Belgrade, accused of horrific atrocities, remained in power for a while as a carefully brokered ceasefire took effect. In the end, there seemed little point to having dropped 6,000 tons of munitions over 77 days in a war that served only to create over 1 million refugees. As it ended and the peacekeeping force arrived, I hitched a ride on a helicopter from Albania to an American amphibious assault ship, the USS *Kearsarge*. The *Kearsarge*, in fact, had been my floating home away from home, where the officers and crew treated me kindly whether I was headed east or, now, west. I hitched another ride toward Italy, eventually making my way to the airport in Venice where I would catch a flight to Washington. Home was a picture-perfect, red-brick Cape Cod in Arlington, Virginia, the Washington suburbs where my lovely wife, at the time, and two equally lovely young daughters awaited, one six years old and one born just that March in the midst of a surprise, spring snowfall.

Arriving at the Venice airport, however, I realized I had hours to kill before my flight so I hopped on a bus and traveled to the half-sunken city that had once ruled much of the world; I had never seen it. Soon, I traversed it on foot, glancing at the map I'd purchased in the Piazzale Roma, at my watch, and at the architectural marvels that slid by—and then glancing nervously at my watch again. Before too long I was immersed in Venice and vowed to return and bring my wife. And I realized, too, that I was lost. As I crossed yet another bridge a kind of panic set in at the thought of missing the water taxi back to the airport and the flight home. Passing through three arches I emerged into a great expanse of light and beauty. Waiters in white jackets served lunch to beautiful women in the print dresses of spring. Flocks of pigeons filled the air, passing in front of Saint Mark's, the Byzantine-era cathedral. My heart finally slowed. I was precisely where I was supposed to be—to catch the water taxi. And I loved being in this place after spending weeks and months out there chasing a story that was ultimately disappointing both in its revelations of human cruelty and the fecklessness of the politics of nations, as well.

Upon arriving at that little Cape Cod home early the next morning, I quietly let myself in and dropped my bags by the door.

Everyone in the house was still in bed so I made my way to the kitchen and brewed coffee, switching on the little television set on the counter. There were the U.S. Marines in Greece now, their trucks headed north. I heard the polished wooden steps creak. Olivia, my first-born daughter, crept downstairs, all wide eyes and rich, dark curls of black hair. I hugged her and she plopped herself in her chair. I poured myself black coffee and her a bowl of Cheerios, her favorite, which she proceeded to munch upon, her eye catching the images of the television screen.

"So you're home, daddy," she began. "That must mean the war is over." I affirmed that it did. She crunched thoughtfully and then asked the next obvious question: "So, who won?" It was an excellent question. I thought that I could explain the use of airpower and its limitations. Or I might describe the complicated tension between humanitarian crisis and geopolitical ambition in an era of globalization. Or the limited gains of limited wars. But she was six. So, I cut to the chase: "I guess we did." I could nearly hear the gears in her little mind turning toward the next question. Her big, dark eyes then peered up at me. "So," she asked, "what do you get if you win?" I hadn't seen that one coming, actually, but it was a simple and brilliant question all at once. One wins or loses if one plays a game, after all. Again, I wanted to be truthful—every moment with a daughter was a teachable one. But reciting von Clausewitz wasn't going to do either of us any good.

So I said, "I guess that means you get to clean up." It had the added value of being true, after all. She munched and thought for a moment and said: "Well, that's not a very good prize now, is it Daddy?"

Her analysis proved more succinct—and insightful than mine. Dissatisfied with the decision to always be chasing the story—out there—I realized then and there that it was time to stop. Instead, it was time to turn toward home, a simpler place, a time to make a little money, a time to raise these girls, an opportunity to finally be closer to family.

So, in the summer of 1999 and much to the disappointment of a boss I never wished to disappoint, I quit my job and drove across the country in our black Mitsubishi Montero. Arriving in Austin and surfing the couches and spare bedrooms of friends while helping lead a startup, I realized I was no longer acclimatized to the unbroken string of 100 degree days that settled over this part of Texas in July.

In early October, we sold the house in Virginia and I bundled my little flock onto an American Airlines flight for our family migration. Migration, of course, is the most vulnerable time in the life of any creature. I packed a wife, baby, a six-year old girl, three cats, and what seemed like five tons of luggage into that airplane and we arrived safe and sound at our new home in the middle of the night: Austin, Texas.

Nearly 15 years later, much has transpired. But now, over 1,000 people a day are following our trail to Texas with no sign of letting up. This story is for them and the millions more who will follow, to Texas.

PART ONE

"If I had to divide the population into classes today, I should characterize a goodly number as Texians, a very large number as Texans. And finally all too many people who just live in Texas. The Texians are the old rock itself; the Texans are out of the old rock; the others are wearing the rock away."

—*J. Frank Dobie, 1936*

1

★ ★ ★

TEXAS

The old, black-faced doe is grazing in the front yard again.

I know her on sight. For all the years I have lived here on this hill, high in the cedar brakes and oaks above the Blanco River, she has appeared here.

In May, 2007, I had found one of her newborn fawns lying in the grass down by the creek. She stood off a little way, as I approached. I was simply drawn to the young, spotted life lying there, newborn and vulnerable in the buffalo grass. Unable to resist the temptation, I jogged down the slope and carefully scooped the fawn up in my arms. It was far lighter than I expected, as a mature deer's bones are dense like iron. Without a trace of fear, the fawn craned its neck forward to sniff me with its big, shiny, black nostrils.

Its eyes shone like big, dark diamonds in the midday light. Its nose touched mine, for just an instant, reminding me of the

Buddhist saying: Consciousness wishes to know itself in all its forms. Cradling it like a gangly child, I carefully laid the fawn back down in the grass and returned to the house. From there, I watched and soon the fawn was up on its spindly, unfamiliar legs headed for the old-black faced doe, waiting in the shade of the tree line.

I recall the old doe and her babies now because they first drew my attention to the very story that surrounded me: Contemporary Texas. My decision to settle in a small town in the Texas Hill Country was really based on a desire to be nearer to the land and a kind of idealized notion of Texas. Divorced, I had decided to trade in my leafy suburb of Austin for small-town life. I indulged my passion for fly fishing and my daughters got a good dose of both living in the city and of country life: Hot, lazy days on the cool river, fishing, dirt-clod fights during the lulls of dove hunting in the corn fields, small-town rodeos, warm fires on cold, winter nights. However romanticized, this, to me, was life in Texas the way it should be, a way in which I'd never experienced it until now.

Living in the country drew the eye, naturally, to the details of the land. You noticed the little, everyday things: When the cattle tanks were full or that the wildflowers would be late if spring stayed long, cool, and rainy. But the blooms of the Indian paintbrush, the bluebonnet and the Mexican hats would be bountiful. The flower of the redbud tree marked the switch from winter to spring, when the white bass would run upstream of Canyon Lake, and the other Highland Lakes, into the rivers that fed them to spawn. In the fall, the rut was on when the deer—particularly the males—were seen on the move in broad daylight. In the early years, from about 2005 through 2009, there seemed to be plenty of water. On the weekends we would leave a car upriver and float two miles in inner tubes down to the other car. Kayaks and canoes could navigate the river with relative ease.

But in 2010, that started to change. The cattle tanks ran dry before summer. The river became far too skinny to float for any length at all. The cruelty of the drought was inescapable. The white tail does grew so skinny their ribs showed. Desperately hungry, they started to raid my garden and chew on plants that were supposed to be resistant to deer, like lantana, or even toxic—like the esperanza. At the hardware store, I heard of a doe and fawn that had been found dead on Ranch Road 12 but had no obvious injuries. Autopsies revealed the green, spear-like leaves of oleander in their stomachs—a plant which is deadly poisonous to deer and that they normally avoid. But the drought brought desperation.

Yes, Texans love to talk about the weather. We are some of the few people on earth who consider a gloomy, overcast, drizzly day a beautiful one. We'll ask on a gray, even morose day: "Are you enjoying this beautiful weather?" It is as if the sunshine is just too common to note. But by 2010, the changing climate—not just the weather—became an inescapable fact of every day life. That year a terrifying and historic drought uncoiled like a long rattle snake in the tall grass, a natural disaster in inexorably slow motion. Life itself slowed down, faltered, and began to fail.

The ground under my boots split and cracked by early May, even before all the wildflowers had gone to seed. The old doe had appeared with another fawn in the spring but by summer the baby no longer trailed her. The creek below the house, upon whose banks I'd once collected her earlier baby, turned dry and bone-white. By July, even the Blanco River—usually cool, fed by millions of tiny springs percolating through the limestone bottom—grew warm and increasingly still.

Then, as 2010 turned into 2011, it was more than the weather that caught my attention. Powerful forces were converging. The drought intensified to levels I had never seen—nor had anyone—since the 1950s. At the same time, the economy in Texas felt the effects of the Great Recession, though far less so than other places. Indeed, economic refugees from California—hit far harder by the collapse of home prices and the rise of unemployment—began to stream into Texas; the population swelled. On August 3, 2011 Governor Rick Perry, claiming credit for the relative economic resilience, launched his bid for the presidency, promising to export this purported miracle of conservative policy to a sluggish American economy, while brandishing his affection for Tea Party politics.

Yet unemployment in Texas, and foreclosures, increased rapidly in the ensuing months. Indeed, unemployment rapidly approached the national average. Perry's state government had been caught unaware by the recession and simply resorted, as a result, to slashing already underfunded services to preserve rapidly dwindling state coffers. Even as cattle died, crops were plowed under, and foundations and streets cracked, no one could do anything about the drought, though it underscored a decided lack of planning, not to mention an earnest analysis of years of demonstrable climate change in the already arid American Southwest.

Much of the state was dying of thirst, on fire, and running out of water even as newcomers streamed in like refugees and Texans lost jobs and homes at increasingly alarming rates. For a brief time, it seemed that all these things would catch up with Perry on the campaign trail in a kind of political conflagration. Instead, his own differences with his party over immigration and his humiliating ineptitude on the campaign trail caught up with him first. By early 2012, he had mercifully dropped out of the race and returned to Austin.

Yet Perry's new narrative of the resiliency and the subsequent rise of Texas only gained in intensity. It was clear, however, that the convergence of economic, social, and political forces was far more than the mere sum of its parts and something too large for a politician to claim credit for, as if he had parted the sea or raised the dead. For years, Texas had been largely immune to change. It had been a state dominated by Anglos with a smattering of Hispanics and a sliver of African Americans. Its economy had rested on agriculture, first, then oil, second, and everything else, third. In political terms, it was a conservative state, one that had been run by conservative Democrats, nearly unbroken, for more than a century, since 1872. In 1994 it became a conservative state run by conservative Republicans, many of them Democratic defectors.

But now, just into the second decade of the 21st century, Texas was in the throes of sweeping and fundamental change: Economic change, population change, demographic change—almost 200 years of Anglo dominance were yielding to an ever increasing Hispanic population—as well as climate change and even political change. Each of these was important but among the subtle differences was not sheer population growth but alterations to the very fabric of Texas. Texas was becoming more urban. As the country's economy foundered, Texas continued to lure more people needing jobs and affordable housing—which in turn, created still more jobs, which in turn continued to lure more people.

Yet these newcomers were not moving equally to each of the state's 254 counties. Indeed, most rural counties were barely hanging on to their populations—or watching them pick up and move away. Most of rural West Texas and East Texas, for example, was simply emptying out. People weren't moving from Southern California or Michigan to the Trans-Pecos, a land of creosote and dry washes. They were moving to Houston, Austin, Dallas, and San Antonio.

This was a seminal change in Texas. For nearly all of its written history, for instance, the story of Texas has been defined by the land—over 680,000 square miles of it, about the size of France. Even after the wars against Mexico, the Civil War, and the Indian wars most of this vast landscape was largely empty. But in the 19th century Texans, newcomers and natives alike, were spread fairly evenly across the landscape. In 1870, for example, just six percent of Texans lived in towns and cities of any size. A century later, by 1970, the majority of Texans lived in cities and increasingly in the new wide-open space: The suburbs. But beginning only in this new century, the population growth became concentrated in just a fraction of Texas, a 60,000-square mile triangle that includes Dallas-Fort Worth, Houston, San Antonio, and Dallas. Eight out of ten Texans were now calling this area home and it was on track to become as densely populated as Southern California or the Northeast Corridor. The entire story of Texas was changing, from that of a land of big spaces dotted by settlements—farms, ranches towns, suburbs, and a few cities—to a story of people inhabiting one of the most densely urban areas in the United States.

Where economics and population density met, they collided with two other forces of change: demographics and diversity. In a purely quantitative sense, the era of Anglo dominance was rapidly ending. This may not seem like news today but historically it is surprising— even shocking. Anglo Americans trickled into Texas in the early 19th century; then, that trickle became a torrent and by 1830 there were more Anglos than Mexicans and Native Americans combined. The war for independence against Mexico followed just six years later and Anglos remained the dominant ethnic population—fueled by occasional migration from the South and, much later, the Midwest—all the way up until 2004 when they ceased to be outright the majority, or more than 51 percent, of the population. Hispanics became the largest single ethnic group and as the trend continues will become the outright majority among all Texans soon.

But in this new century, Texas society was also changing in a way that—when coupled with density and demographics—would alter its politics, and as a result, those of the nation as well. These densely urban areas of Austin, San Antonio, Dallas, and Houston were more Hispanic and Democratic; all were generally dominated by Democrats in local government and a majority of the citizens in each city voted for President Barack Obama in 2012.

But the swing districts—the suburbs of the big cities—were becoming more diverse, too. Anglos in general were not just older than other populations in Texas but an entire generation of suburbanites who had moved Texas into the Republican column was now aging, giving way to a new generation of Anglos, Hispanics, Asians, and African Americans that more accurately represented the overall population. And their political priorities were decidedly different than those suburbanites who preceded them.

All of these forces were like geological forces—silently but relentlessly butting up against a political power structure that was rigidly conservative, sort of like the shifting of tectonic plates that increases the pressure under the brittle earth's crust just before a seismic event.

Although those who ascribed to the conservative and conventional wisdom vehemently denied it, the once invulnerable Republican Party looked like it was in trouble given the booming non-Anglo population, which was skeptical of conservative politics, if not aligned with Democrats.

Most damning, though, to Republican prospects in Texas was really an increasing failure to govern, to solve practical problems. The public school system was stretched to the limit and politicians refused to fund its growth. Hispanic Texan students, in particular, saw increased high school graduation rates. However, their parents found that they then could not afford the cost of sending their children to college; the state government in Austin refused to control costs or provide more help. The engine of upward mobility—namely a college education—threatened to be out of reach, particularly for the lower-income earning Hispanic population that was expected to fuel the consumer economy and uphold the tax base in the years to come.

Republicans once knew how to govern efficiently; by all accounts George W. Bush, for all his failings as a president, was an effective governor. But he was elected 25 years ago. And increasingly his heirs turned to legal gymnastics to keep the emerging majority from voting and to the futility of symbolic politics—God, guns, and gays—in order to ensure their base, now awe-struck by the Tea Party, continued to vote. Governor Perry was a strong governor but as the years went by that strength waned. Perry dabbled famously in the rhetoric of secession and guns—but to no real results. After he withdrew from the 2012 presidential race, his popularity among Texans, even Republicans, plummeted.

The man set to succeed Perry after he announced in 2014 that he would not be seeking reelection, was Republican Attorney General Greg Abbott, whose politics followed a similar path—long on symbolism and generally devoid of the messy details or subtleties of governing. Regardless of the individual politician's personalities or tactics, the writing was on the wall by the spring of 2014: the Republican Party's days in Texas were numbered. With 38 votes in the Electoral College, these developments will have not just regional but national, and even international, significance.

★

Perhaps most surprising to people who don't know Texas is that it is not a backwater of the past. It is, instead, a living laboratory of the future. Texas is becoming Hispanic, again, decades before its neighboring states and the rest of the country; California, New Mexico, and Texas are becoming majority Hispanic. Never before in American history has an ethnic minority become the majority. This trend, frankly, has scared some Anglos. Yet it holds immense promise for rejuvenating an aging America. It will also require that societies that still hold each other at arm's length—Anglos and Hispanics—embrace one another fully and completely, perhaps helping bring to an end the American fixation with race. Because much of it is in a semi-arid zone, Texas will also need to confront the results of climate change directly in order to continue to grow. Without enough water, the Texas boom will turn to bust.

All of these events have had profound impacts not just on Texas, currently the second-most populous state in the country, but they have reverberated across America. Success or failure in Texas is the seminal test of America in the 21st century, just as it was in California in the 20th century. Sustaining economic growth, revitalizing upward mobility, combating the effects of climate change, and fostering a just and democratically representative society are not just challenges in Texas in the early 21st century.

They are challenges across America. Texas merely has to confront them head on, and first.

★

The writer T. R. Fehrenbach is probably a name unknown to most Americans, but to Texans, he is well known for having defined Texas in his massive history, *Lone Star*. Fehrenbach was not a trained historian—following in a long line of self-styled Texan historians who were just journalists, actually—but a boy born in San Benito, Texas and raised in Brownsville; a soldier in

World War II; a Princeton graduate; a veteran of Korea; a newspaper columnist; and author of 18 books, of which *Lone Star* was his best-known.

The original edition, published in 1968, spanned 32,000 years from prehistoric Texas up until the late 1960s and Fehrenbach's racial and ethnic terminology, today, brings a wince. But to be fair, he wrote of and in his time. That was evident in 2000, when the book was released again. Although 32 years had gone by, Fehrenbach refused to call it a revision. He had found, he wrote in 2000, that his central tenet still held—Texas hadn't changed fundamentally—and so the book was just an "update." The story of Texas he told was the story of an immutable land so vast that people were forced to adapt to it—through ingenuity or conflict or both—or submit to the hands of subjugation or worse, perish. The land was the only constant. When he penned his foreword, Fehrenbach was probably still more right than wrong. On my arrival back in Texas at about that time I found it to be—somewhat disconcertingly— much the same as I had left it nearly 15 years earlier.

Fehrenbach died on December 3, 2013. But now, nearly 15 years after his "update" to Texas history, Texas has changed in a way neither he nor others could have imagined even at the turn of this century, which is not all that long ago. That change was just rumbling to life then as Fehrenbach's immovable subject, the land, met an unstoppable force: People on the move once more but this time filling the cities and suburbs. Historian Randolph Campbell's *Gone to Texas* was published about the same time and paid greater attention to the role of African Americans, Hispanics, and women than did Fehrenbach. But the change taking place quickly outstripped both men's notable accounts. Now migrants came not from a single point on the map—namely the American South—but from every point on the compass, here and abroad. Long sluggish, prone to booms and busts, the Texas economy suddenly seemed, for the first time, astride a longer and fundamentally more sound boom—an unfamiliar phenomena in Texas history. And change begat still more change.

So, I named this volume *Lone Star Nation* because unlike the work of many others—though not all—it is focused on the people as much, or more, than the place. I'd like, in a small way, to honor Fehrenbach's amazing work—but to challenge it, too, with the additional benefit of a decade and a half of perspective, admittedly. The future of the Lone Star State is bright—if it successfully grapples with the challenges it faces now: Namely demographic change, climate change, and upward mobility.

Already, Texas has one of the largest economies in the world. It is the nation's leading supplier of technology to the globe, even surpassing California. Based on current trends, by 2050, Texas will account for one-sixth of all the economic production in the United States and as a sovereign country it would have the fourth largest economy in the world, eclipsing Germany and trailing only the United States, China, and Japan.

The continued geopolitical power of a globally competitive national economy, in turn, would help maintain America's preeminent place in the world. Here at home, Texas may surpass California in population around the middle of this century, and as a result it might wield the largest number of electoral votes for the presidency and deploy the largest congressional delegation in Washington. That would reshape American politics for much of the rest of the century at least. But by then, something more important is set to happen. One in 10 Americans will call Texas by a different and more familiar name: Home.

For me, too, the idyllic life at home in the Texas Hill Country changed. Now, I could hear the increasing traffic noise floating up from Ranch Road 12, bouncing off the hills to the back porch all day long and into much of the night. Only around midnight, as the stars came out, did it become serenely quiet. In my small town, roads were widened, traffic lights started to go up, and home values soared. Suddenly, my desolate, dead-end road was filled on weekends with realtors and eager buyers of home and land alike.

★

On an autumn afternoon, I walk the grassy banks of the Blanco River, a fly rod in hand. A few frisky smallmouth and Guadalupe bass come readily to the fly and dance at the end of the line. Once brought to hand, I admire their patterns and plumpness, the way their skin and eyes sparkle in the sun and then slip them back, unharmed, into the clear water. The air cools as dusk gathers; the sky is overcast; the light is gray and weak, foretelling of winter. So I return home.

With its metal roof and cedar plank siding, the house once was filled with the sounds of my daughters. There was a television here, music playing softly there, a loud conversation growing louder over a boisterous card game. Now, the house is still. One girl is in college, then off to Europe, and the other is off to high school, each developing new friends and interests that have nothing to do with this place, nor with my idealized—indeed romanticized—version of life in Texas. Now, it's just me walking these wooden floors, out to the front porch after writing these words.

And there she is, again, in the gathering dusk: The old, dark-faced doe, staring back at me, still.

2

★ ★ ★

GREAT MIGRATIONS

On an isolated stretch of desert an imaginary line slices the land, separating New Mexico from Texas.

This is a land of boundaries. A few miles to the west, the muddy Rio Grande cuts its way south, separating Mexico from the United States. To the east, the Organ Mountains mark the southern end of the Rocky Mountains and the purple Franklin Mountains to the southeast note the beginning of the harsh Chihuahuan Desert, which unfolds for hundreds of miles. Interstate 10 stretches out across the mesas, a pair of double-wide, blacktop ribbons between the mountains and the river, connecting the Atlantic and Pacific coasts. Eighteen wheelers push on in both directions. But most of the cars are going east. One after another bears the same license plate: California.

Quickly, a bright yellow sign framed by rustic wooden posts

bids them a farewell to New Mexico: "Now Leaving the Land of Enchantment!" A few seconds later, a modest, green highway sign with a red, white, and blue flag comes into view: "Welcome to Texas." A giant stone lone star monument slides into view. For many travelers from California a brief elation will set in. They have crossed 761 miles of desert from, say, Southern California, after all. But that feeling is dashed by the very next mileage sign:

El Paso 18
Beaumont 852

And it is still some 600 miles to the big cities in between East Texas and West Texas. Dallas, San Antonio, Austin, and Houston are all still a full day's drive away. Between 2005 and 2010, some 3.4 million Californians left the Golden State. For many in the middle class the reasons were simple: High housing prices, scarce jobs, and mounting taxes. Housing was expensive and then, when the real estate bubble popped, it took the economy and jobs with it. But taxes remained high. And so, those that could—and those who had to—got out, reversing decades in which California gained more people than they lost.

California once embodied the American dream of orange groves, opportunities, and sunny beaches. Now, the California diaspora dispatched people to neighboring states like Oregon and Arizona. Yet the single largest number, about 1 million in the initial years, went to Texas, with many making that long trek through the desert, past the state line, and onward to reach the big cities of Texas: Houston, Dallas, San Antonio, and Austin.

Yet California was not the only home Americans left behind for a new life in the Lone Star State. Over the same five-year period, nearly 3.5 million Americans arrived in Texas from all points in the United States: California, yes, but also New York, Washington, D.C., Chicago, Miami, Portland, Seattle—and hundreds of other towns and cities. America was in the throes of one of its periodic and epic mass migrations. Among them were the westward expansion and European migration of the 19th century, the Great Migration of African Americans from the agrarian South to the industrializing Midwest in the early 20th century, and the Great Depression migrations from the Dust Bowl to the fields and groves of California.

When these occur, they alter the course of history. Entire economies arise. New social pressures are created. Power changes hands. Texas has seen five such great migrations. This is the sixth. In each case, the migrations to Texas created economic, social, and political change that reverberated across America and, in some cases, around the world. Indeed, Texas may be one of the great magnets of mass migration in human history, given the number of times that millions have picked up and moved here.

Like the current of a strong, new river suddenly carved into the earth, the Sixth Migration has delivered 3.6 million people to the state and deposits over 1,000 fresh arrivals every single day. In the 1970s and 1980s, the collapse of the Industrial Rustbelt drove the first large wave of non-southerners to Texas, the Fifth Migration. These migrants decisively moved the state's conservative politics from the Democratic column into the Republican one, where Texas remains today. No Republican has won the White House in the last quarter century without Texas, nor could they. Early in the 20th century, oil brought Southerners in the Fourth Migration to create an industry that, to this day and for better or for worse, fuels modern economies around the globe.

The Third Migration, the mass arrival of Southerners in the early 19th century led to war, independence, the expansion of slavery and the Indian wars; then it triggered still more war with Mexico and ultimately, after Texas was granted statehood, tipped America into its bloodiest conflict, the Civil War. The Second Migration from Asia spawned the Native American cultures that, in turn, brought with them agriculture, trade and war. The arrival of the first humans, also from Asia, 16,000 years ago constituted the First Migration; for the first time, the pristine natural order of North America met with hunting, harvesting, and the hand of a creature it had never known: Man.

★

In the morning, 150 miles east of El Paso, the sun comes up and the interstate roars across the creosote-studded flats into little Van Horn, population 2,000. The town has a truck stop, a couple thousand residents, and a jam-packed breakfast rush at McDonald's. Everybody here is headed somewhere else, true to form for a town that has been a way station since it was founded as a stagecoach stop in the 1850s in the midst of Apache country. Off in the distance, the Davis Mountains rise.

Back on the road and coming fast, big green highway signs warn drivers that a fork in the road approaches and the time zone is about to change from mountain to central time. A lengthy drive beckons. Soon enough, a fork in the road arises: Bear left and head for the big cities of Dallas-Fort Worth, though many hours away. Bear right and hours from now, Austin, San Antonio and, later, Houston will eventually come into view. I bear right across the creosote-studded Trans Pecos and the hours slip by as slowly as the highway signs: Exits for Balmorea, Pecos, Fort Davis, Marfa, Big Bend. Each remains hours away, hidden from view of the interstate which crossed the middle of nowhere on its way to Fort Stockton. A little south, at Iraan, an exit reveals a back road into the Hill

Country, leaving the big interstate behind for the Llano Uplift. Narrowing to just two lanes, U.S. 377 jogs across the Edwards Plateau. It is afternoon now and the spring light is bright and clear. The limestone remains of a Spanish presidio, established on the San Saba River in 1757, come into view. This is as far west as the Spanish ventured in Texas.

All these towns out here, from Junction to Mason to Llano, wait patiently for fall, when city hunters fill up the hotels, little restaurants, and the bars for deer season. But now, the next deer season is nearly as far ahead in the calendar as the last and the towns seemed empty. The light reflected off the broad, rushing waters of the Llano River bounces off the struts and girders of the big metal bridge, as the road leads toward the town square. It is getting close to fishing time, in fact. The giant schools of white bass are forming up, even now, in the deep water of the Highland Lakes to run the shallow rivers to spawn.

By early afternoon on a Tuesday, the square is empty, the parking lot around the town hall largely devoid of cars. A faded Confederate flag hangs limp over the memorial to the Civil War dead. The plaque reveals the short list of the small town deceased who set off for a very faraway conflict. I turn right on State Highway 16 and, in a little while the road begins to climb, the town slipping out of sight. The cell phone signal falters as the road climbs through a narrow saddle, heads due south and backwards—to the beginning of time itself.

Rocks, big and nearly square, rise up in a ruddy color, as if a giant playing with red blocks had forgetfully dropped them here and there, forming whole escarpments. Off to the right, Enchanted Rock rises, a pink granite dome reaching some 425 feet above the rest of the countryside, the result of magma from the earth's crust bubbling upward as long as a billion years ago. The giant rocks and hills of the Llano country are literally the blocks from the bottom of the world. No younger than 600 million years old, these Precambrian rocks come from the foundations of the very continents themselves, the basement of the earth and the beginning of geologic time.

The ones lying here, scattered, big as whole buildings, are the only ones still visible in Texas, and one of only seven sites where they are visible in North America. All come from a silent vault in time that still encompasses nearly 90 percent of the earth's history. From here, though, history pressed relentlessly forward. A quarter of a billion years ago, this area was bordered by salt water to the east and south. Then the Ouchita Mountains arose, stretching from present day Arkansas across northern Texas. Rivers drained westward into the shallow seas that covered West Texas. By the Permian Period, the sea began to withdraw, leaving only flats and basins. Some 140 million years ago, dinosaurs and flying reptiles roamed Texas.

From here, Highway 16 presses determinedly south, toward the Pedernales River. The land flattens. Thick Spanish oaks and formidable thickets arise. A quick left turn onto Farm Road 1323 deepens the isolation. A solitary sign warns: "Watch for cattle crossing road." Not even a house in sight, cows and calves impassively chew their cud while watching the car go by, just yards away. At the one-house junction at Sandy, the land changes yet again. The exposed limestone, lifted out of those ancient seas, turns the ground white and rocky. Here the road enters the Cretaceous Period: 65 million years ago when the extinction of the giant reptiles brought forth the mammoths, sloths, and the large cats.

The last great Ice Age came and brought with it, as far back as 15,500 years ago, the first humans: The First Migration to Texas as people from Asia crossed the Bering Strait from Russia to Alaska and then headed south, away from the ice, to hunt the giant Columbian mammoth. Predating even Clovis man, once thought to be the earliest Americans, these ancient people settled in places like Buttermilk Creek, in Bell County near present day Waco, for its water and game, certainly, but mostly for its rich supply of chert rock, used to shape trademark spearheads and blades, cut with funnels along the side. The blades not only cut into the animal's flesh but their clever design deftly allowed their quarry to bleed out even as it fled. Once pierced with an arrow or spear point, the more the prey moved, the more it bled. But these people vanished, too, as suddenly and inexplicably extinct as the giant mammals they had hunted.

Yet before the land bridge sank from view, more people came from Asia, arriving in waves 7,000 years ago and making their way southward, too, away from the ice to hunt the ancient bison, twice as big as the modern buffalo. The last great Ice Age concluded, the land bridge sank into the rising waters of the Bering Sea and the glaciers retreated northward. The once lush Great Plains dried out and the sea in Texas conducted its final retreat, sulking into the shallow Gulf of Mexico some 3,000 years ago.

The people of the Second Migration, who would become known first as Indians, and later as Native Americans, were like any migrants. They sought opportunity and moved to find it. Racially similar, they quickly became linguistically and culturally diverse, spreading across vast distances. The Caddoan people of East Texas were close in culture, for example, to the Mound Builders of the Mississippi and showed strong Mexican influences. Smaller tribes, reputed to be cannibals, spread along the coast of the Gulf of Mexico and fiercely repelled any intrusions. Coahuiltecans inhabited the harshest scrub desert and adapted by digging, grubbing, and eating anything from pecans to spiders to undigested seeds harvested from deer dung, not to mention agave bulbs, flies, and even maggots. Before they came to know the horse, the Tonkawa lived on the fringes of bison country on the Edwards Plateau in the forested Hill Country.

A still newer culture arrived from the Rocky Mountains, speaking Athabaskan, the language of the Pacific Northwest. Known simply as Apaches by other Native Americans, they spread out onto the plains and down into Texas, taking on different permutations themselves, Jicarillas, Lipans, and others. After washing ashore in 1529 near present-day Galveston, the Spanish explorer Álvar Núñez Cabeza de Vaca recorded Native American tribes that herded hundreds of deer into enclosures for food, dug up roots, and plucked the fruit of prickly pears as he and a dwindling group of shipwreck survivors battled starvation, the landscape, the weather, and disease, while trying to get back to Mexico City: "One third of our people were dangerously ill, getting worse hourly and we felt sure of meeting the same fate, with death as our only prospect, which in such a country was much worse yet."

Cabeza de Vaca, one other Spanish adventurer, and the slave Estevanico de Dorantes were the only men to finally reach the capital of New Spain. The two adventurers married well. For his trouble, Estevanico was sold back into slavery and killed by Indians, eventually, in what became New Mexico while scouting routes for the return of the Spanish, this time en masse. When the Spanish arrived in numbers in 1540 during the disastrous expedition of Coronado, the oldest living cypress trees in the Texas Hill Country today were young saplings. In 1680, the Spanish horse dispersed throughout the American Southwest and yet another mountain tribe came out on the plains: The Comanche—a Ute word for "enemy"—who mastered the feral mustang. By 1750, the Native American horse culture spread from Texas to Canada. Soon enough, the Comanche and the Apache would struggle over their rights to the Southern Plains, one displacing the other in wars for food and territory. Other tribes migrated to Texas, too, or were pushed across it by aggressive neighboring tribes. In the 19th century, the Kickapoo, an Algonquian tribe of the Great Lakes region, dispersed to regions as far as Texas after pressure from white settlers and other Native Americans.

While the French presence in Texas was inconsequential, the Spanish occupation of Texas and the Southwest was a long but half-hearted affair; a global kingdom had far more pressing concerns than the rough and untamed wilderness of Texas, after all. Paramount among these concerns was Mexico, the Viceroyalty of New Spain. On behalf of Madrid, Mexico City governed a swath of earth that stretched from Cuba, Puerto Rico, and the Cayman Islands in the Caribbean, encompassed all of Mexico and Central America, all of Texas and most of what is now the American West, including California—and then stretched westward across the Pacific Ocean, to include the Philippines and the Marianna Islands. Each year, a Spanish fleet would drop anchor in Acapulco Bay to fill cargo holds with Mexican gold. Then the heavily-laden vessels sailed west, stopping in Manila and Guam, following the setting sun home to the mother country, half a world away.

So Spain invited American southerners from the Missouri territory led by Moses Austin to settle in Texas in 1820, as new citizens of a rough, backwater outpost of their global empire. After independence from Spain the very next year, Mexico, too, failed at sparking a migrant culture of its own to move into Texas. So, by 1830 some 30,000 Anglo settlers—largely of Scotch and Irish descent—filled the void, traveling from the ports of the Carolinas to Tennessee and Kentucky and into Texas, eclipsing in a few short years the Mexican and Native American populations combined that had arisen or arrived over centuries and millennia.

This was the Third Migration to Texas. This period became most infamous for the Battle of the Alamo as well as victory on the field at San Jacinto and the region's subsequent independence. Like all the great migrations to Texas, this one had an impact felt well beyond those early years in the 19th century and one felt well beyond the borders of Texas itself.

★

But why? Why would these people travel to a foreign land which held meager promise but was fraught with risk from Indian attacks, disease, thirst, and outright starvation?

The answer was simple: These people not only had the desire to come but the need to come. Their drive was a perfect balance of ambition and desperation—as it is, frankly, with many people who decide to move, whether across the country or across the world. T.R. Fehrenbach accurately noted that the southerners sweeping into Texas numbered among them a few rich men, certainly, but most were Scotch-Irish from the Appalachian South. Many landed at the port of Charleston, South Carolina. There they had generally found limited opportunity in the settled Carolinas. So they pushed into the wilderness of Tennessee, Kentucky, and northern Alabama only to scratch out small farms on land that quickly played out, fighting recurring Indian wars and carrying the burden of staggering debt.

Like a lot of members of the Third Migration, one Tennessean named David Crockett found Texas a vast and beautiful place, when compared to the broken down plots people like himself had left behind in the East. It was true. Texas was a wide open space that just a little rain, now and again, could turn thick with vegetation, rich with water in some places and promising. "I must say as to what I have seen of Texas it is the garden spot of the world,"

Crockett wrote in 1836. It held "the best land and the best prospects for health I ever saw, and I do believe it is a fortune to any man to come here. There is a world of country to settle."

The records of the original Austin colony showed 776 colonial families, most coming from Louisiana, Alabama, Arkansas, Tennessee, and Missouri. "The vast majority emigrated to Texas for no other reason than economic opportunity: the chance to get cheap land," Fehrenbach wrote. "Some left debts behind in the States, but most brought some form of capital: Seeds, equipment, stock, or slaves . . . For the price of 80 acres of plantation ground in the South, a Texas settler could acquire a square league or 4,428 acres." Even leaders, like Sam Houston, who would be president of the Republic of Texas, senator, and governor, fled the failure of his marriage, the stall of his political career, and a mountain of debt in Tennessee for a potent mix of opportunity and uncertainty in Texas.

The Austin family, of course, was quite happy to extend credit, even to fleeing debtors. Stephen F. Austin, heir to the colony after Moses died, had vacillated over the increasing arrival of slaves with the new migrants; it was one important source of friction with the Mexicans who had abolished slavery in 1829. Ultimately, though, he came down on the side of slavery, declaring, "Texas must be a slave country!" Austin himself purchased a slave for $1,200—for no apparent purpose. The Mexican government then cracked down, banning immigration from those in the United States who might bring their slaves into the region..

The Mexicans, in turn, called on European Catholics, namely Germans, to settle and balance out the new and largely Protestant migrants from the American South in the hopes that fellow Catholics and Europeans might not be eager to join the United States. A few initially answered the call and settled an arc that stretched from Galveston on the coast to Kerrville out in the western edge of the Hill Country. After war and independence from Mexico in 1836, more European Catholics followed: Germans, Czechs, and Poles, though they were still a decided minority among the settlers and they were culturally, linguistically and religiously different from the Scotch-Irish from the American South. There were political differences, too, namely over that original American sin: Slavery.

Texas joined the Union on December 29, 1845 and the Third Migration now birthed global consequences. War against Mexico in 1848 had a devastating effect on the Mexicans who ceded what became the American West, including the gold fields and Pacific ports of California. Mexico would descend into political tyranny, economic privation, and eventually the chaos of revolution. America would become a rich power, its ambitions spanning two oceans. The gold of California would fuel the industrial revolution, the Indian wars, the settlement of the American west and reach across the world to remove the remnants of the Spanish empire in the Caribbean and the Pacific at the close of the 19th century, replacing it with an American one.

A vague concept in the early 1800s, Manifest Destiny was the belief that the American people alone possessed both the virtue and God's will to remake the continent in their own image; its ideological heirs would include present-day American Exceptionalism. President James Polk and his supporters created the concept of Manifest Destiny to justify war with Mexico and realized its birth with expansion to the sparkling waters of the Pacific Ocean. But Manifest Destiny was midwifed in Texas first.

★

In 1850, new Polish settlers joined their European counterparts on that arc that stretched from Galveston to the Hill Country. A small settlement, christened Panna Maria, grew up in the mesquite country at the confluence of the San Antonio and Cibolo creeks, east of San Antonio. The dusty cattle track that led through it would soon enough become the Chisholm Trail. And the town would become the oldest Polish settlement in the United States.

In Texas, slavery divided European Catholics and Mexicans from the American Southerners. For Mexicans, the issue had been settled in 1829 when Mexico forbade slavery and gave Texas a one-year extension to abolish the practice. For the Germans, the trade in human flesh was an abhorrent throwback to the Middle Ages. The *Sachsenspiegel*, the most important German legal code of that era, shunned slavery beginning in the early 13th century.

But the practice of slavery in Texas reached far beyond the Sabine River into Washington, D.C. The issue delayed the accession of Texas into the Union because of the well-placed fear that it would expand slavery; so the impoverished Texas Republic floated in the limbo of independence at the fringes of the Union. John C. Calhoun devised a scheme in which Texas would be divided into six states to give it more power on behalf of slavery in Congress. Debates over slavery in the Midwest dragged—often because of Texas. And as war approached, Texas inadvertently also strengthened the inaccurate perception of Southerners that Texas would strengthen the Confederacy to the point of invulnerability, opening a new Manifest Destiny to the south this time, expanding an empire of plantation servitude into a conquered Mexico and Central America.

These calculations and miscalculations about Texas helped to trigger and then prolong the deadliest conflict in American history, the American Civil War. Already much has been said about the Civil War and nearly as much has been said about the Civil War and Texas. But this tragic conflict was proof positive of how the great migrations to Texas had consequences of national and international scale. While the Third Migration of American Southerners became legendary for its battle against the Mexicans, less understood was how the Third Migration played a crucial role in the American crucible over human chattel. The men who followed the heroes of the Alamo and San Jacinto helped tip America into a war that left as many 750,000 Americans dead, according to a recent estimate— more than in any other war.

Because of weather and topography, plantation farming could only thrive in the southeastern quadrant of Texas, where the land was rich with alluvial soil and and rivers and bayous allowed for the easy shipment of crops to market. And these were no subsistence crops. Plantation crops like sugar and cotton were just about the only cash crops in nearly 700,000 square miles. There had been just 20 Africans in Texas out of a population of 3,000 in the late 18th century, according to the 1777 Spanish census. By the end of the 1830s, around 5,000 slaves toiled in Texas, despite Mexico's ban on the practice.

The plantation economy, originally centered near present-day Houston on the Colorado and Brazos Rivers, greedily demanded more and more free labor. "We want more slaves," wrote Charles DeMorse in the Clarksville *Northern Standard*. "We need them." Independence from Mexico and statehood in the United States actually accelerated the spread of slavery, north and west on to the blackland prairies, a grassland east of San Antonio and Austin stretching north toward the Red River. On the eve of war in 1860, the slave population had increased 40-fold since independence from Mexico to 182,000 men, women, and children.

Texas had far fewer slaves than many southern states and large slaveholders were a decided minority—though with their wealth a disproportionately powerful one. Out of a population of 600,000 people in 1860, only 20,000 white males owned slaves. Of these, half owned fewer than three. Only three men owned more than 200 but they also owned nine out of ten cotton bales bound for export and the cash that came in return. The Knights of the Golden Circle, a secret society established by Kentucky plantation owners to spread slavery westward, now engulfed Texas, encouraging secession as the fear of a Republican presidency in 1860 was realized with the election of Abraham Lincoln.

By early 1861, southern states were leaving the Union and on February 1, 1861 an unruly mob disproportionately dominated by slaveholders was convened on the question of secession at the capitol in Austin, despite the determined opposition of Governor Sam Houston, who fumed, as he said, at "the mob upstairs." Houston disliked abolitionists but foresaw that leaving the Union would prove disastrous. As former president and part of the original American wave of migrants, he held no special love for the men who followed him. "All new states are invested, more or less, by a class of noisy, second-rate men who are always in favor of rash and extreme measures," he wrote as newcomers followed the original colonists. "But Texas was absolutely overrun by such men." All of the delegates had migrated relatively recently to Texas from the American South, and fully 70 percent were slaveholders—wildly unrepresentative of the white population at large. Many were Knights of the Golden Circle, with fantasies of slave empires stretching toward South America. There were just eight unionists in the crowd, led by the respected James W. Throckmorton. But their voices were all drowned out.

Calling "the African race . . . an inferior and dependent race" for which slavery was beneficial, the convention voted at 11:00 A.M. the next day 166 to eight "to dissolve the union between the State of Texas and the other States, united under the compact styled, 'The Constitution of the United States of America.'" Houston himself was in grudging attendance. Texans ratified secession later that month by a margin of four to one even as North Texas threatened to secede and San Antonio seethed with pro-Union sentiment—as did the Germans, Poles, and Czechs.

In Austin, Houston was presented with a loyalty oath to the new Confederacy, which he steadfastly refused to sign. "In the name of the constitution of Texas, which has been trampled upon, I refuse to take this oath," he said. "I love Texas too well to bring civil strife and bloodshed upon her." For his refusal, the old general was summarily fired by the state legislature and he left Austin. Now, events in Texas helped to prolong the war that it helped to start with a struggle over the real strategic importance of the state, schemes of hubris, obsessive compulsion, and that which seems, now, to have verged on madness. In exchange for safe passage to the sea and the evacuation his 3,000 troops, U.S. Army General David Twiggs surrendered the federal arsenal in San Antonio to 700 Texans. Every single U.S. Army post in Texas was abandoned. Nearly all of Texas, save the coast, would be uncontested by the Union Army for the duration of the war as Twiggs practically ceded Texas single-handedly.

Cowboys began herding thousands of rangy longhorns eastward across Louisiana and the Mississippi River; the Confederate Army became dangerously dependent upon the beef supplied by Texas for its hungry, then starving, troops. A year before the Battle of Gettysburg, Confederate President Jefferson Davis foolishly launched a bloody and ill-fated attempt to invade the California gold fields and Pacific ports from West Texas. No army since Hannibal had survived so far from home and its supply lines and this one was no exception, never getting farther than neighboring New Mexico. Instead of encountering flag-waving Confederate sympathizers, the troops in gray met only local resistance, snow, and better-supplied

Union troops. Their wagon train captured, the survivors tried to avoid dying of thirst or starvation or being unmercifully killed by Apaches as they stumbled southward, in rags, back into Texas.

At home, some Texans turned on one another especially after forced conscription into the Confederate Army. Death threats arrived in the mailboxes of suspected Unionists; 25 of them were hanged outright in Cooke County, north of Dallas, followed by 40 more. In 1862, Confederate cavalry and a home guard of Partisan Rangers tracked 100 Germans on the move to Mexico, where they planned to enlist in the Union Army, and killed 32 men as they slept by the banks of the Nueces River. While it was called the Battle of the Nueces afterward, it was really a massacre. In fact, it was a war crime as the commanding officer exceeded his orders and his subordinate officer simply began murdering prisoners. Nine more Germans were summarily executed. Fifty other German Texans were caught in Gillespie and hanged.

With fevered dreams of a Confederate West now turned to desert dust, President Lincoln in Washington had his own obsession with Texas: Capturing it and severing it from the union. Urged on by New York merchants eager for Union Texas cotton, in short supply because of the blockade of Confederate ports, Lincoln commanded his admirals as part of Operation Anaconda to blockade, bombard, and land troops on the Texas coast repeatedly. Only once, at Galveston, did they briefly succeed before being driven back into the sea. Lincoln's Texas obsession was nearly as fantastical as Davis's. Nearly 400 miles of sparsely populated coastline would have left invading troops—unless they could successfully occupy Galveston—far from population centers, depending on supply lines that stretched unimaginably. By 1863, Houston, the hero of the revolution, president, senator, and governor, lay dying near Huntsville as his prophecy came true. Passing in and out of consciousness on July 26, 1863 his final words to his wife were: "Texas, Texas, Margaret."

In the very heart of the fighting in the eastern theatre, the Texas Brigade commanded by John Bell Hood was considered the finest in the Army of Northern Virginia and a favorite of none other than General Robert E. Lee. He called them "my Texans," for their valor in battle. They fought heroically and sometimes recklessly across Virginia to Sharpsburg, Gettysburg and back to Virginia in the desperate Battle of the Wilderness. Lee loved the Texans so much that he offered to lead them into the battle there; the Texans said they would charge but only if Lee, astride his horse, Traveler, remained at a safe distance.

When Lee surrendered amidst the burning bridges of Appomattox on April 9, 1865, his Texans were still there, though just 600 of the 3,500 original men still stood. Back in Texas, Lincoln's Emancipation Proclamation, issued over two full years earlier, had been kept a secret from slaves in Texas. They finally knew that they were free with the arrival of Union occupation forces under Major General Gordon Granger at Galveston over two months later, on June 19, 1865, known ever after as Juneteenth.

The true legacy of the Third Migration had been felt, now, not just in Texas but across America itself. The great American sin of slavery had been expanded by Texas, but only briefly, and as a result it had been violently expunged, if never completely erased. A Confederacy with a weak hand from the start had overplayed it, in part because of Texas and, as defender of the institution of slavery, the South now lay in righteously smoldering ruins. Following the public triumphs and disasters, the tragic consequences now came home to roost. But the matter was settled. Slowly, the country would pull itself back together. The industrializing North, not the agrarian South, would become the power center and economic engine of the country, propelling Americans into the West that Texas had been crucial in opening. Manifest Destiny could now gaze across the ocean at a new empire for America, a Pacific one. Because of Texas, the entire 19th century was recast amidst equal parts of hubris and madness, triumph and tragedy, sorrow and hope.

3

★ ★ ★

THE COWBOY

I n the ensuing defeat, Texas would endure Union occupation and Reconstruction and the ensuing whirlwind. For the time being, the great migrations to Texas ceased.

From 1870 until the dawn of the 20th century, farming and ranching reigned supreme and gave rise to the most mythical era in Texas: The era of the cowboy. Cattle were plenty. The head-scratching problem for cattle ranchers was the price they received for them: a steer was worth just $4.00 here in Texas while it was worth $40.00 in Kansas, where it could be shipped by rail to markets in the east. So, ranchers turned to the tough, rangy old longhorn, a descendant of feral Spanish cattle, whose beef was tougher than that of the short-horned English cattle but who could survive in the wild and had been so plentiful at times they were hunted from horseback. And if they could survive that, they could survive the 700 mile trek north to Kansas. Ranchers looked at longhorns as a way to fill their coffers in a place otherwise impoverished by war and occupation.

There was one important obstacle to success when a rancher surveyed the map of the landscape between, say, South Texas and Kansas: The Comanche. Skilled and ruthless raiders, some bands had amassed fortunes in stolen horses and cows. Fierce and pitiless warriors, they displaced the Kiowa and Jicarilla Apaches without a second glance. When they came into contact with Anglos the results were often horrific. Earlier, Texas had failed to ratify treaties with the Comanche and now attempts to move them to reservations in Oklahoma were failing. As S. C. Gwynne recounted in his masterful book, *Empire of the Summer Moon*: "No tribe in the history of the Spanish, French, Mexican, Texan, and American occupations of this land had ever caused so much havoc and death." In strategic terms, the Comanche threatened to roll back the western frontier in Texas and blunt the westward expansion of the United States. The Texas Rangers and the U.S. Fourth Cavalry moved out into the Hill Country and the flat plain of the Llano Estacado with a single mission: To deal harshly with the Comanche, even if it meant driving them to extinction. As Gwynne wrote: "It was the end of anything like tolerance and the beginning of the final solution."

With the cavalry and rangers screening westward, the now emptier route northward was safer than it had been. With their brands, saddles, spurs, lariats, and rodeos, one would be hard-pressed to know that the cowboy had inherited nearly everything he knew from the Mexican and Spanish *vaqueros*. There were lots of cowboys, too, looking for work. Some of the big, famous ranches like the King Ranch down on the coast could drive their own cattle all the way up the network of trails that constituted the Chisholm to Kansas, right through little towns like Panna Maria. But other ranchers relied on crews of hired hands. The first herd of just 2,400 steers moved out of San Antonio at the end of the Civil War; then 35,000 went north in 1868. The herds swelled, doubling every year until 1871. Trail bosses were paid about $100 per month to run a crew consisting of twelve cowboys, including themselves, the cook, and ten wranglers, also known as "thirty dollar men," because that's how much they fetched in a month of work.

Together, these men could handle as many as 3,000 head of cattle. The wranglers managed the cattle and a herd of spare horses, known as the *remuda*. Lightning was the most common cause of stampedes. Cowboy Don Lovell, whose father was quick to start moving cattle to Kansas, helped to herd 3,000 head of cattle once. He wrote that riders would nervously stand watch without sleep when the storms threatened. And when they bolted chaos ensued.

"Looking at a herd arising appears as if the earth is heaving up with an accompanying roar, a swish like sound, and the clashing of horns. While the cattle are running, the pounding to their feet on the earth sounds as a roll of many muffled drums. The clashing of the horns given off a sound similar [to] that of many muffled drums," Lovell wrote in a letter. "Most of the time we could accomplish our purpose in stopping a run, but occasionally we would fail. If we failed the cattle would be scattered hither and yon." After a single stampede, he recounted, half the herd was scattered and presumed lost.

Stopping stampedes and plucking newborn calves off the trail to plop them into a special wagon, the cowboys could go all the way from the Rio Grande, near Brownsville, through Montague County and across the Red River. Or, a little further to the east, they forded the Colorado River near Austin, Brushy Creek, the Brazos River, and the Trinity River, and headed north.

America fell in love with the cowboy, who—like Texas itself—quickly became romanticized, lionized, and mythologized before being lamentably caricatured. One of America's great short story authors, William Sydney Porter, better known as O. Henry, made a living as a cowboy before a later stint as a bank teller. He wrote of the fabled, dusty horseman: "He swayed on his horse; had he been on foot, the earth would have risen and conquered him; but in the saddle he was a master of equilibrium, and laughed at whisky, and despised the centre of gravity."

The cowboy may have come from Texas, with his deep Hispanic roots, but he became an American symbol as the 19th century closed. And because there was work, money, and land, some migration resumed—mostly American Southerners looking for a ranch or farm to work, either their own or someone else's, but also more Mexicans and Germans came. The population grew from 1870 to 1900, to a total of just over 3 million people. Fewer than 100,000 farms and ranches blossomed into over 350,000. Twelve million acres under cultivation became nearly 20 million. The great cattle drives ended with the arrival of the railroad and the barbed wire that fenced the Great Plains.

But the late 19th century proved unstable, too. All those longhorns glutted the market and prices plummeted. Disease-infected Texas cattle caused other states to impose quarantines and bar herds from Texas. National depression struck in the 1870s. Farm prices fluctuated wildly and then went into slow decline. Farmers and ranchers clamored for more dollars in circulation in order to get through another season or to pay off old debts with newer, cheaper dollars. Populist politics stirred in the heart of Texas for the very first time. Alliances of farmers and ranchers, known as the Grange, began as social gatherings but became political, too. Farmers and ranchers, now often thought of as lone individuals, worked together then to form cooperatives. They wanted to trade services for credits, at least, if they couldn't get cash.

Challenging the arch-conservative Democratic establishment which had taken root in Austin, they founded the People's Party, which included Socialists, Republicans, and Prohibitionists. It merged with the Populists made up of small farmers, sheep herders, menial workers, and African Americans. Women joined the work-force and rail workers struck. All demanded one thing: More money in the economy so they could make a living.

But by then, it was too late. Triggered by railroads overbuilt on unstable financing, stubborn bankers clinging to the gold standard as well as a series of bank failures, the national financial Panic of 1893 triggered the worst economic depression the country had known; the Gilded Age in America collapsed in a heap. Devastating drought had paid a visit in the 1880s and now returned to linger in the 1890s. Struggling under mortgages and other debt, ranchers and farmers watched helplessly as their herds of cattle and sheep fell in value. In 1890, 8 million cattle and 4 million sheep grazed across Texas. By the dawn of the 20th century, there were 1 million fewer cows and steers and nearly 3 million fewer sheep.

Just like that, the era of the cowboy was suddenly over.

★

It is difficult—nearly impossible—to understate the impact of mass migrations. Wherever and whenever they occur these migrations are spurred as much by need, even desperation, as ability. In many cases the people who most need to go cannot. Those with the most resources never need to leave. It is, instead, the people with just enough resources to make the journey—but not enough to stay—who find the motive to set out on a long trek toward a new and uncertain home.

The migrations that shaped Texas and reshaped America share some similarities to the other mass migrations of history. Some 95,000 years ago, the first mass migration from Africa, the very cradle of mankind, was spurred by drought, which brought with it its twin, starvation. These migrants brought with them the technology and the experience that enabled primitive Europeans to hunt mastodons. Subsequent tales of apparent hunting successes were depicted in the Paleolithic era cave paintings at Lascaux in France. The Germanic migrations southward from the Baltic into the expanding Roman Empire brought war from the fourth through the sixth centuries. The Great Atlantic Migration, from 1880 to 1919, brought 60 million Europeans to the New World and some 20 million of them to the United States. The forced migration of the slave trade sent 20 million Africans across the Atlantic, many of them dying during the passage. The mid-20th century forced migration of between 11 million to 20 million people by Nazi Germany included 6 million Jews sent to their deaths across Europe.

The economic consequences of mass migration have been vast. Consider the Great Atlantic Migration from Europe to the United States that ensued even as Texas withered at the close of the 19th century. Industrialization was proceeding rapidly in Great Britain and yet the raw resources needed for manufacturing were half an ocean away in the New World. That's where the largely unskilled labor was needed—in the United States and Canada in North America, as well as Argentina and Brazil, in South America. The demand for shipping was so high that transportation costs fell sharply for 70 straight years due to increased competition as wages fell in in Great Britain and Europe while rising in the United States, where the raw materials and the need for manufacturing resided. The poorest European countries sent the most immigrants to the richest New World nations. People uprooted themselves from homes, family, and nations and went—as they still do—at that moment when they absolutely had to, and while they had just enough time and resources to do so.

Mass migration fueled not just economic power but political power, too. New York was the most populous state in the Union in 1810 with a little less than 1 million inhabitants. Until the Civil War, some of the five largest states were Southern slaveholding states; these vanished from the top five after the 1860 census when New York still topped the list at 3.8 million people. After the war, New York received many of the immigrants coming from Europe and grew some 20 percent every decade. More growth begat still more growth. As New York swelled, it became the undisputed manufacturing and financial center of the nation and wielded ever more political power in Washington, both formally and informally. The larger the congressional delegation, the more favors its members had both to give and receive for their home state.

From 1860 through the turn of the century, Pennsylvania, Ohio, Illinois, and Missouri rounded out the top five population centers as they wielded economic power in agriculture, manufacturing, and shipping. And their power in Washington grew, as well, putting their men in the White House and sending more wealth back home. Then, as now, private interest groups turned to politicians to get access to public resources: Right of way for trains, mining rights, public land, and more.

Of the 22 presidents who served in the White House during the 19th century all but three—John Quincy Adams of Massachusetts, Franklin Pierce of New Hampshire, and Zachary Taylor of Virginia—came from one of the five most populous states. New York State alone boasted five presidents during this period. The first, Martin Van Buren, was elected just six years after New York became the most populous state. When a New Yorker wasn't in the White House, generally speaking, a man from Ohio, Inc. or Illinois was.

In the 20th century, there would be no greater example in the American experience, to date, of the effects of mass migration than that of the Great Depression. More than 1 million people uprooted to flee the Dust Bowl, their collapsing farms and ranches, and the very real prospect of starvation. Once a magnet for migrants, Texas was now exporting people westward. The combination of drought, poor agricultural practices, and erosion produced dust storms that spewed 300 miles eastward—off the Atlantic Coast. At one point, dust from Texas and Oklahoma blotted the sun from the sky over New York for five hours.

But if a family had ten dollars for gasoline and owned a vehicle they could make it from Texas, Oklahoma, or Arkansas all the way to California. Never before had California had so many poor migrant families; before they tended to be middle or upper income or, say, during the Gold Rush, single men. But these migrants brought entire households, were familiar with farm work, and they were unafraid of the harsh living conditions in the labor camps and shanty towns—their images memorialized in the photography of Dorothea Lange's *American Exodus: A Record of Human Erosion* and most famously in John Steinbeck's landmark novel, *The Grapes of Wrath*. But then something changed: War broke out and the federal government was spending $8.5 billion a year in California alone, compared to less than $200 million before the war.

Not only were there more jobs but higher-paying jobs at bases, airfields, depots, factories, and shipyards. The boom, coupled with the draft of eligible young men, spurred even more migration, dwarfing the Dust Bowl and the Gold Rush eras. Another 1.9 million new residents moved to California between 1940 and 1945 alone. In the latter part of the 20th century, California would come to dominate and define the American experience—economically, socially, and politically, just as New York had done before.

★

Heading east now, the Llano country gives way to the classic white limestone of the Hill Country, outside of Austin. About 14 miles out, a narrow two-lane road juts left off busy U.S. 290, turns into a caliche track, and drops through a mix of scrubby live oaks and mountain juniper toward a denser green of southern maples and Spanish oaks below.

Down in the draw is Barton Creek. It drains a vast stretch of Hill Country, at least as far away as some 50 miles. When the rain falls from the sky like cold bullets out here, the drops strike the flinty but porous limestone soil and then percolate through millions of tiny tunnels, which consolidate and grow as wide as pipes. The trickles become underground torrents. Then they tumble thousands of feet into the cold, dark expanse of the Edwards Aquifer, one of most prolific artesian lakes in the world.

Eventually, the water emerges—from this lightless world of blind catfish and salamanders—cool and clean, filtered by the rock itself, recharging clear, shallow rivers with cold water that burbles up out of the stone bottoms. Short rivers, like the San Marcos and the Comal, rise fully formed from hillsides. Long ones, like the Blanco and the Guadalupe, meander over dozens of miles to confluences with other rivers and then hundreds more, together, to the sea. The cool, clear water fills ancient *cenotes*, like Jacob's Well, just as it feeds the creeks that drain the countryside. From these openings in the earth tens of millions of gallons of crystalline water pour forth each day.

Barton Creek, 40 miles long, was guarded by the Tonkawa and Comanche in the 17th and 18th centuries. Now, its entire length is protected by dense thickets of southern maple, live oak, and mountain juniper; black-capped vireos and golden-cheeked warblers flit through the branches as the canyon walls grow higher and higher as the creek descends toward the Colorado River. The waters are filled with largemouth, barred Guadalupe bass, and red-eared slider turtles. Giant blue herons stalk the shallows, hunting, and coyotes sleep the day away in the canyon only to hunt in large and fearsome packs at night.

As the creek slides like glass, it passes a low stone house sitting on 250 acres of land known as the Paisano Ranch, where a man who loved Texas like he loved that house's porch once lived. From that porch, he collected and penned the folklore of Texas in the late 19th century and spun it, like gold, it into the dominant lore of the 20th. In many ways, Americans, and even Texans themselves, have come to know about Texas through his eyes, even though they fluttered shut for the last time a half-century ago. He was a man enamored of the land around him and the way he saw it shape Texas.

Born on a ranch in Live Oak, down in South Texas, in the fall of 1888, J. Frank Dobie's childhood home was on the sparsely populated plain of the Tamauliapan mesquital: Thorny mesquite trees, *huisache*, Mexican palmetto, tall grasses, and forests of yucca and prickly pear that easily concealed a man on horseback. This land is home to rattlesnakes of legendary proportions, bobcats, quail, giant deer, and tough, grazing longhorns as well as Brahma from India. I explored Dobie's old haunts with my friend Mark Seiler, near Alice, many years ago.

Despite the months of stifling heat and exposure to a relentless sun, this stretch of South Texas is harsh and surprisingly bountiful at the same time. We killed plenty of white-wing doves during evening shoots and took a few ducks off the cattle tanks in the morning. Dense and thorny thickets held coveys of quail and giant deer. For many years now, the largest bucks with the biggest racks have been taken in South Texas where they share an arid landscape with feral hogs and javelina.

★

One of six children, Dobie worked the ranch but his future would not be resigned to life as a callused and dusty old ranch hand. He had, after all, a writer's hands. So, he moved to the nearby town of Alice to finish high school, and from there he went to Southwestern University, a graceful campus near the San Gabriel River in Georgetown, north of Austin. It was there that he met Bertha McGee, whom he married, and there that he was encouraged in his writing by a professor, Albert Shipp. Earning his degree in 1910 he set out as a journeyman newspaper reporter, to San Antonio, Galveston, and Alpine, where he also taught for the first time. After earning a master's degree at Columbia University in New York, he taught at the University of Texas in Austin before leaving for World War I only to return quickly—the war was ending as his unit shipped out—and quit the university just as abruptly.

He was beckoned, once again, by the ranch; in this case his uncle Jim's ranch—thousands of acres in that rough mesquite country. His uncle was a stockman of some regard and he pieced together ranches covering tens of thousands of acres. He was also a storyteller and so the younger Dobie found his calling: To be the poet laureate of the land—and by extension of the people who lived on it. "In the university I am a wild man; in the wilds I am a scholar and a poet," he wrote to his wife. "It came to me that I would collect and tell the legendary tales of Texas as Lomax had collected the old-time songs and ballads of Texas and the frontier. I thought that the stories of the range were as interesting as the songs.

I considered that if they could be put down so as to show the background out of which they have come they might have high value."

The writing in the years that followed displayed a newspaper man's rather rough sensibility toward folklore, and included an onslaught of books, alternately raw and well-cultured, about the heyday of cattle ranching, about the Mexican *vaquero*, about Spanish mines, and even the longhorn itself. Noting that the longhorn had been a cultivated animal abandoned on the open range, then interbred with other cattle, it was Dobie in the 1920s who noticed them nearly passing into extinction. With a few others, notably oilman Sid W. Richardson, Dobie helped preserve a herd whose descendants are common today.

Dobie's vision of Texas and what it meant to be Texan was unabashedly romantic; he venerated Spaniards, the Mexican *vaqueros*, the Native Americans, the cowboys and their stock—mustang, cow and even the lowly goat—alike. This veneration, though, was rooted in their willingness to bend to the immutability of the land, to nature itself. Though he would go as far as Cambridge to teach in the 1940s, he wrote with a dusty simplicity that was elegantly paired with his beloved subject. He wrote:

"Here I am living on a soil that my people have been living and working and dying on for more than a hundred years—the soil, as it happens, of Texas. My roots go down into this soil as deep as mesquite roots go. This soil has nourished me as the banks of the lovely Guadalupe River nourish cypress trees, as the Brazos bottoms nourish the wild peach, as the gentle slopes of East Texas nourish the sweet-smelling pines, as the barren, rocky ridges along the Pecos nourish the daggered *lechuguilla*. I am at home here, and I want not only to know about my home land, I want to live intelligently on it. I want certain data that will enable me to accommodate myself to it. Knowledge helps sympathy to achieve harmony. I am made more resolute by Arthur Hugh Clough's picture of the dripping sailor on the reeling mast, 'On stormy nights when wild northwesters rave,' but the winds that have bit into me have been dry Texas northers; and fantastic yarns about them, along with a cowboy's story of a herd of Longhorns drifting to death in front of one of them, come home to me and illuminate those northers like forked lightning playing along the top of black clouds in the night."

And about those northers, like any folklorist, he simply could not resist when it came to the telling of a good tale—whether true or, preferably, not. After all, that's what folklore is all about. In his essay, "The Flavor of Texas," he meditated on everything from the land to what it meant to be a Texan. But he concluded with a yarn about the weather. Texans love to talk—and exaggerate—about the weather. If a cold norther blows through, Texans will crack that "the fence is down," an ironic, self-deprecating bit of humor as if a lowly a strand of barbed wire fence somewhere in the Panhandle could hold back the cruel determination of an Arctic storm.

Dobie, too, could not resist and so after his serious meditations about the existential nature of being a Texan he concluded with the story of a man on horseback racing to stay ahead of the chilling cold front which is moving so swiftly that as he rides through the open barn door his mare's forequarters are foamy from the effort—but her hindquarters are frozen solid. "She died," Dobie wrote, "of pneumonia right there and then."

Often seen wearing a floppy old Stetson and with a pipe dangling from one corner of his mouth, Dobie was a man with an easy grin—for which he had good reason. As the 1930s came he launched his syndicated newspaper column, "My Texas," as well as a radio program, *Longhorn Luke and the Cowboys*. Dobie came to be not merely the teller of Texas tales—but to embody them himself. He was as close as anybody would get to being the state's definitive chronicler—even though he was, in reality, just a newspaper man and folklorist.

His friend, Walter Prescott Webb, a PhD at the University of Texas was the real historian; though he wrote about the Texas Rangers, Webb's seminal work was on the Great Plains. Dobie, Webb, and another newspaperman-turned-folklorist and naturalist, Roy Bedichek, became fast friends and the trio was a frequent sight, swimming at Barton Springs. Subjected to the petty politics of academia, Dobie was criticized because he steadfastly refused to earn a PhD or engage in a topic more worthy of English department scholarship than the American Southwest.

In 1936, Dobie reached a professional apex. He was the top spokesman and leading literary light of Texas just in time for its centennial celebration, notably a celebration of 100 years of independence from Mexico—not 100 years of statehood. The Texas Centennial, in turn, would be the framework of the 1936 World's Fair in Dallas, the first time such an exposition had been held south of the Mason-Dixon Line. Until then, World's Fairs were the domain of places like New York and Chicago, where futuristic visions would validate the trajectory of already industrialized cities. With the centennial in Texas, Dobie arguably reached his pinnacle, regaling listeners and readers with his tales of cowboys.

But the men behind the World's Fair, its storytellers and artists, had a far larger ambition than merely to inform and entertain. The largest oil, banking, and industrial fortunes in Texas had gathered to reshape the narrative of Texas itself, once and for all, to enthrall and attract new migrants to Texas, in large part so that they could expand their already burgeoning wealth. Texas needed to grow. To grow it had to industrialize. And to industrialize it needed to occupy a new place of importance in the American imagination—all with the goal of turning more Americans into Texans.

4

★ ★ ★

A CENTURY OF OIL

Dobie was still in his infancy when all but the greatest Texas cattle empires went into decline and the frontier era in Texas closed for good.

The drought which reigned over much of the state from 1890s onward and its results were made that much more catastrophic by the rampant overgrazing of livestock. The entire landscape of the Texas Hill Country underwent a dramatic change as old-growth hardwood forests were cleared and grazed down to the soil, and hardy, drought-resistant species like the mountain juniper choked the hills and thirstily drained the creeks. The cattle drives from South Texas had literally spread the seeds of invasive mesquites far to the north into the Big Country. In the early years of the 20th century the last known bears and mountain lions to be seen for 100 years were shot. All but the scrawniest of white tail deer became scarce. Dobie's beloved longhorns were fast disappearing, bedeviled by disease and declining from interbreeding.

But in 1901, oil was struck at Spindletop and everything changed.

Texas was still culturally a southern state and it had remained one during Reconstruction and the early part of the 20th century. The Mexican-influenced cowboy culture that did arise, as Dobie knew, was a hard life—and a harder way to get to rich. Oil, however, was a different story altogether. Its discovery quickly flooded the state with cash and wealth on a scale never before seen in Texas. After Spindletop, oil was struck in North Texas and East Texas and, soon, most points on the compass.

And so it was with oil fortunes. While many who made their fortunes were in Houston, Tyler, and up in the Panhandle, more than a few called Fort Worth and Dallas home. One was H. L. Hunt, who gambled his last $100 in New Orleans, turned it into $1,000 and started buying oil wells, including the massive East Texas Oil Field. Before 1960 he was worth up to $700 million, which would be $4.5 billion in today's dollars. One of the eight richest people in the United States, he had 15 children with three different wives and once said, "I didn't go to high school, and I didn't go to grade school either. Education, I think, is for refinement and is probably a liability."

Another was the legendary Sid W. Richardson. On borrowed money, Richardson and his partner, Clint Murchison, struck it big in 1919, watched their fortunes decline and then made it all back—and then some—in 1933. And against the odds, that very year, Dallas won the right to host the 1936 World's Fair, just in time for the Texas Centennial.

So, these oil magnates and their business allies—such as newspaper publisher of the *Fort Worth Star-Telegram* Amon Carter and banker R. L. Thornton in Dallas—saw the opportunity to recast

Texas: No longer a broken-down Southern state of impoverished dirt farmers, but one with oil and industry—an inspiration if not a beacon to hungry Americans looking for opportunity in the midst of the Great Depression. A speech made in 1923 by a New York newspaper publisher, public relations man and unabashedly racist cotton broker, who traveled often to Texas, had attracted the attention of the rich and powerful new business class. Theodore H. Price had spoken to an advertising convention in the city of Corsicana about the "gloriously romantic history" of Texas. A centennial celebration, Price insisted, would be exactly the right time to capture the country's—make that the world's—attention. The money men did not think that 1924—the anniversary of Stephen F. Austin's first Anglo settlement in Texas—was the right year but they were willing to put their money on 1936. Copywriters, journalists, and artists were hired to tell tales of cowboys, oil, and industry in the years leading up to the World's Fair.

Price argued that the story of Texas was, on a defining and grand scale, the very story that Dobie was telling on a smaller, and as a result, somewhat more accurate scale. Whereas Dobie extrapolated opinions from folklore, certainly, Price simply whitewashed all of history with it. The Texas culture was the frontier cowboy culture. Gone was the Mexican *vaquero*, the African American, and the Native American, or at least they were relegated to the role of antagonist. Price was hardly alone, of course. The guide to the Texas exhibit at the St. Louis World's Fair in 1905 had already said this: "The progress of Texas is an object lesson of survival of the fittest, as shown by the final domination of the Anglo-Saxon over other racial elements." A centennial exposition, Price argued, would teach attendees that the cowboy story was really a story of racial triumph over the Mexicans, Native Americans, and African Americans. "Anglo American ancestry and democracy," he said, would go hand-in-hand from past to present to the future; his was not unlike other revisionist, racialist theories passed off as history far across the Atlantic.

It was expedient, too. Texas was still a poor state, despite the oil boom, and needed to jump start its agrarian economy by becoming a modern, industrial one. In Austin progressives were having a good run in the 1920s and, whatever their racial politics, they had no problem abandoning the Lost Cause of the Civil War for something that would be both popular and make money. As historian Greg Cantrell put it: "Certainly, the Texas public did not cease to be certain in many of its racial, political and cultural values. But by the second decade of the 20th century . . . the sentimentality of the Lost Cause with its reminders of slavery, defeat, military occupation and poverty held little appeal for the forward-looking leaders who wanted to build a progressive future in Texas."

The legislature promptly chipped in $3 million and the Roosevelt administration in Washington matched the funding. Newspaper headlines, stories, and radio were filled promotion and propaganda. Advertising was purchased not just in Texas but across the United States—and around the world. "A Century of Independence" in the *Houston Post* claimed that "a white population of only 30,000" had triumphed in war "over the Mexican nation of 8 million." Cullen Thomas, who ran the federal Centennial Commission, called the approaching anniversary nothing less than the opportunity to "Texanize Texans." Some 259 events were organized, the pinnacle of which would be in Dallas at the state fair grounds. Historian Kenneth Ragsdale later called it: "a thoroughly concentrated historical brainwashing."

Nevertheless, the gates to the Texas Centennial Exposition swung open to the public on June 6, 1936 to the eventual cost of $25 million and a crowd that would total nearly 6.4 million people over the coming six months. Inside was an array of sleek art deco buildings that alternately told stories of the past and held out visions of the future: Dinosaurs, dioramas of history, exhibits from General Electric, DuPont, Chrysler, Ford, Gulf Oil and other industrial giants, pretty girls in cowboy hats and boots, and none other than President Franklin Roosevelt welcoming the crowds. For the rest of 1936, the national media expounded upon the latest marvels from Dallas: A couple was even wed over television by a preacher. Everything was bigger and better in Texas. And Dallas, a hardscrabble town clinging to the South Plains during the Dustbowl, got a new name: Big D. The Texas that Americans would know in the 20th century—or thought they knew—had been born.

★

Dobie, the Texan, had never sought to definitively portray all of Texas in this singular and simplistic way; his was a collection of stories with his own occasional musings about what they might mean. In his essay, "A Flavor of Texas," Dobie seems to hold back from concluding what it means to be a Texan and when he does, he settles on a nuance about people, really—and less about the land and cowboys. Price, the New York public relations man, did precisely the opposite—conflating hundreds of years of complex human history into a single, simple and deeply racist story line: Man versus nature, followed by man versus man. The winner: The rough and tumble Anglo man who could lay claim to a brave cowboy past and a fearless industrial future. He need not be born in Texas, either. As long as he was an Anglo, he could come here and learn and adopt the ways. He, or she, could literally be "Texanized." This was a theme that would replay time and again in the coming decades.

Regardless, one man as folklorist and the other as propagandist had latched on to an idea of Texas that was powerful. It lent itself to the subtleties of humble storytelling, in Dobie's case, and to the power of propaganda in the case of Price and the organizers of the Texas Centennial, too. Inherent in this idea was the notion that the land itself was determinative. Its indifferent harshness sorted men and women into winners and losers; it was a profoundly Hobbesian vision, in which people were all on their own, bound only to the brutality of their largely solitary existences. Certainly, there is some truth: The original settlers, whether Athapascan, other Native American, Spanish, Mexican, African slaves, or Southerners from the United States did often face solitary and grueling conditions. And Texas was a violent place; the violence of the Comanche against Anglos and Mexicans alike, as well as the retribution of the Texas Rangers in the 19th century, is a clear example of that bloody history.

Of course, Texas in the 20th century was not a land of Indian wars anymore. The frontier had long since vanished. The idea that the modern heirs of Texas were inheriting—as they arrived in the swelling cities of Dallas, Houston and San Antonio—the violent struggle against land, predators, Mexicans, and Indians and thus could lay claim to supremacy because of their mere race was simply preposterous. It bore no relationship to reality other than as racist fantasy.

Yet it was convincing and powerful propaganda and it came ladled with just enough flavoring of history to taste convincing, even if it was, at best, caricature or, at worst, manipulation. The crux of this idea was not conservative in the sense of contemporary partisan politics. It was conservative in the sense that it implied a certain view of a natural order of things, stemming from the unchanging landscape. These things placed living things—animals and people alike—into an order that could not, as natural law would have it, be disturbed.

This implied version of natural law, simply put, was predicated on a single notion: That the human desire for self-preservation trumped all. So, if you were a Texan you were heir not just to a proud tradition of struggle and even violence. You were also something else: On your own. A simple man, even an Anglo rancher carving out a living in Marfa had too many other challenges—rustlers, rattlesnakes, and a distinct lack of rain—to worry about the big picture. That was best left to his betters, the educated politicians in Austin or the oil barons in Houston or the bankers in Dallas. They understood such complex things. And if you were a Mexican or an African American man or a woman? Forget it. Keep your head down and get back to work.

The reality was that a land as big as Texas in the 18th century was always going to be a place of lonely lives, carved out in small towns and isolated farms and ranches. But in the 20th century, as World War II approached and the cities swelled, all this was now more myth than history—and yet, portrayed as a sort of living history it served an interesting purpose. It kept people in their places—poor Whites, Mexicans, Negroes, and Indians alike, in the parlance of the period. They needed to mind to their own business and let the bigger men take care of the bigger things.

This cultural and political mindset could be transmitted, too. Newcomers could learn it quickly and easily. All they had to do was adopt the story and play their assigned role. Edna Ferber's novel *Giant*, published in 1952, was nothing but strong men and outsize characters in a harsh land. Many other literary and journalistic giants would follow, often into the blind alley of the mythology. Living in Austin at the end of his life, in the 1970s and 1980s, the prize-winning novelist James Michener embraced the myth with his huge work of historical fiction, *Texas*, and mired in it, published what was probably the worst work of his distinguished career.

Dallas, the television series of the 1980s, epitomized caricature: Its outrageous lead character, J.R. Ewing, was not so much based on oilman H. L. Hunt, a colorful enough character, as it was based on public perceptions of the man.

The great columnist Molly Ivins embraced the myth in the 1980s and 1990s in order to skewer it with sarcasm to the great delight mostly of non-Texans. Most of her newspaper readership resided elsewhere and her writing—however witty and provocative and brave in challenging the status quo in Texas—could fairly be described as that of a nearly self-hating Texan. Raised in an affluent Houston family, Ivins spoke French, was educated in the East, had worked for the *New York Times*—and wrote purposefully like a hick precisely to denigrate the myth. In recent years it has been easy for writers, both liberals or conservatives, to either skewer the caricature as everything wrong with conservatism or rather blindly embrace it and claim that it is some kind of vindication for modern, arch-conservative politics.

Overlooked was a long line of progressive figures, stretching back decades: Henry Gonzalez, Barbara Jordan, Maury Maverick, John Henry Faulk, Henry Cisneros, Dobie himself, and many more. More unfortunately overlooked was a far more complex list of real people who flouted the tired storyline about wilderness and violence inexplicably molding a kind of homogenous Texas personality. The history became myth which became satire, which ultimately just devolved into caricature.

★

Dobie eventually arrived at more subtle observations about the existential nature of Texas. In *The Flavor of Texas*, originally published in 1936 and issued again after his death, he struggled mightily to define his beloved Texas. He wrote of the unforgiving land, the brief republic, the Confederacy, violence, longhorns, and all the usual subjects. He became emphatic that Texas was far more western than southern.

Reading his words as I sat in the John Henry Faulk Central Library nearly seven decades later in downtown Austin, though, he seemed to circling around his point. Of course, I could not profess to know the mind of a man who died in the year I was born. But in my reading he then seemed to draw, in modern Texans, distinctions not along racial or ethnic lines but along the time lines of their arrival. In doing so he hinted at an alternate understanding of Texas—one based not on the immutability of the land but instead upon the dynamic waves of mass migration. The Texians had settled Texas after the Native Americans. They were Anglos, Mexicans, and even African Americans; three such men had died at the Alamo, after all, along with Hispanics who gave their allegiance to Texas, not Mexico, in the final, brutal moment. The Texans who came later in the Third Migration, as Houston had sneered, had no direct ties to the revolution but came and embraced what they were told anyway, exploiting it fully. The newest arrivals in Dobie's time were still trying to figure out what role in the myth they should play. Each, he wrote, changed the other and the very nature of Texas itself.

"If I had to divide the population into classes today, I should characterize a goodly number as Texians, a very large number as Texans," Dobie wrote. "And finally all too many people who just live in Texas. The Texians are the old rock itself; the Texans are out of the old rock—the others are wearing the rock away."

To be a Texan, in whatever epoch and of whatever race, was to be in the very throes of change. An old arrival, a newer one, or an altogether fresh one, all wearing away at the very rock itself—each other. It was the first time that a major, mainstream thinker about

Texas had at least shaken hands with—if not quite embraced—an alternative narrative, one that did not spring directly and fully formed from the limestone bedrock of nature. It was a narrative that hinted, instead, that the story of Texas might just be the story of a place that has been for millennia a magnet for mass human migration, not merely an unforgiving landscape of which, after all, there are many.

★

When Dobie wrote his essay, two of America's most powerful, larger-than-life political figures were vying for power. And the writer found himself caught between them. But the duel of these men was more than just political rivalry; it was a nearly-to-the-death kind of struggle between men who represented passing generations of Texans, not unlike what Dobie had written about.

The Democratic Party had held sway since the end of Reconstruction and quarreling over it were two outsized personalities—big men, each towering well over six feet tall—Coke Stevenson, a governor, and Lyndon Johnson, an ambitious congressman. The older man, Stevenson was a self-made, real cowboy from the farthest reaches of the Texas Hill Country who, even after becoming chief executive, refused to install a phone at his ranch and insisted on campaigning retail-style, town square to town square. He was also a reactionary and defender of racist laws. The younger man, Johnson, was an unabashed New Dealer, prone to flaunting his relationship with President Franklin Roosevelt while he was alive and flying by helicopter from campaign stop to campaign stop in the 1948 race for the U.S. Senate against Stevenson when he wasn't on that other newfangled contraption: The radio. His ruthless ambition was fueled by nagging insecurity. Their titanic clash was partly the Western versus Southern traditions but it was also the old, rural life against the increasingly electrified, motorized life of the 20th century.

In 1944, Dobie, the poet laureate of the long-gone open range, was a man with his own sense of power, too, and as power would have it he quickly got himself crosswise in the struggle between the old Texas and the new one taking shape. He wasn't just an English professor or a folklorist. He was also a liberal newspaper columnist who regularly chastised conservative politics and bad architecture and even academia itself. Stevenson, the governor, became the focus of his wrath when he fired the president of Dobie's chief employer, the University of Texas, a man named Homer P. Rainey.

A liberal Democrat, Dobie lit into the governor in his column, madder than a wet cat. The otherwise reserved Stevenson took notice and insisted that the most prominent chronicler of Texas be summarily dismissed from the state's flagship university. And so, he was; he had been on leave and was effectively exiled under a practice that would forever be known as the Dobie Rule. When he returned, Dobie lived out on in the Hill Country for a while but eventually retreated to the Paisano Ranch, on the cliff above the shimmering waters of Barton Creek, where he continued to write. After Johnson not only beat Stevenson in the race for the U.S. Senate—some, like writer Robert Caro suggest that he actually stole that election—he, of course went on to become president. Never one to leave a score unsettled, on September 14, 1964, Johnson awarded the old writer the Medal of Freedom, the nation's highest civilian award. Dobie died precisely four days later. His house still stands guard over the waters of Barton Creek, which slide on down to Austin.

★

The spigot of migration to Texas finally opened up again after oil was discovered in 1901. Myths, legends, and lies aside, the oil fostered jobs and the Fourth Migration was underway, again from the American South mostly. In short order, by 1910, Texas became the fifth most populous state in the nation. For the first time since the Civil War, congressmen from Texas grasped real power. Sam Rayburn, the legendary Texas politician, entered Congress in 1913 and served for 47 years, wielding the power of the Speaker of the U.S. House of Representative's gavel for 17 of those years.

When America entered World War II the government began to spend money on bases, bombing ranges, aircraft factories, and munitions depots, and the prospect of wealth expanded in Texas. By the 1950s more Texans were living in the cities—if just by a small margin—than in the wide-open rural counties of the Trans-Pecos, the Hill Country, the Piney Woods, or the Brazos River Valley. If water was the lifeblood of the Texas landscape, oil was the lifeblood of the burgeoning industrial economy that tied Texas to the rest of the country and much of the world. Manufacturing rose by the 1970s to take its place alongside oil. Then, in that notorious boom and bust cycle that plagued the economy in Texas, the price of oil plummeted.

By 1972, due to oversupply, a barrel of oil was worth as little as a hair-raising three dollars. In some fields, it was cheaper just to leave the oil in the ground. But Texas was lucky to be saved by Saudi princes, of all people. The OPEC oil embargo that resulted in the 1973 oil crisis caused hardship for most Americans: Soaring prices, limited supplies and lengthy lines. But it saved the Texas oil industry. Starting in 1973, the price of oil began to climb, soaring to $40 per barrel by the early 1980s. The country then tipped into a recession and the manufacturing heartland became the Rustbelt, collapsing in large part because of soaring energy prices as well as increased automation and the decline of the American steel industry. Once more, the people headed south toward the jobs and the oil: Texas.

The pumping of oil from Texas soil had peaked by this time but as the price of it rose and rose, the money flowed. The number of jobs increased 40 percent between the early 1970s and the early 1980s and migration to Texas soared accordingly. People abandoned Detroit and Cleveland and points in between and the population of Texas ballooned to 14.2 million people, trailing only New York and California. Houston was home to 1.6 million people, nearly overnight. Gushed *U.S. News & World Report*: "This is not a city. It is a phenomenon—an explosive, churning, roaring juggernaut that's shattering tradition as it expands outward and upward with an energy that stuns even its residents."

As the 1990s approached, Dallas and San Antonio had surpassed the threshold of metropolitan areas with more than a million denizens. A modernized version of that Texas myth propagated in the 1930s was now popular culture. Everybody wore a cowboy hat, many with feathered bands and everybody, it seemed, wore cowboy boots, not so much for any practical use but for the sake of fashion: Snake, alligator, and ostrich skin in every color of the rainbow. *Texas Monthly* touted itself as a guide on how to be a Texan. On television, *Dallas* seemed an updated version of *Giant* but it got people's attention nonetheless, not just in Texas but across the country. The Dallas Cowboys became "America's Team." On the big screen, *Urban Cowboy* told the story of a modern Texas cowboy—who rode a pickup to work in an oil refinery and never got closer to a corral than Gilley's nightclub, cold beers glistening on the bar and the only bull in sight a mechanical one. But as old-line Texans knew all too well, every boom carried the seeds of its own bust.

And bust it did. Oil prices plummeted to less than $10 a barrel in 1986. Jobs vanished and suddenly all that real estate was something that couldn't be unloaded. The state's savings and loans, which had lent furiously, were wiped out and over $5.1 billion went missing, nearly taking down the U.S. banking sector to boot.

The influx of new people from the industrial Midwest changed Texas politics, too, which went from conservative Democratic to increasingly conservative Republican. These newcomers were not the only factor, certainly, but their concentration in the suburbs of Houston and Dallas, both conservative citadels then, helped Republicans to win a seat in the Senate first, then the governorship and steadily larger shares in the legislature and Congress than any time since Reconstruction. Texas was sharply contested by both parties but became "Reagan Country" in the 1980s. Republican Governor Bill Clements became the first Republican in the governor's mansion since 1869, elected not once but twice, in 1979 and 1987. The father of Republican politics in modern Texas, John Tower, had already had a seat in the U.S. Senate. A Georgian by birth, Phil Gramm switched parties and won one himself as a Republican, too. The Democratic Party, which had ruled nearly uninterrupted since the end of Reconstruction, fought a furious rearguard action and in 1990 Texans sent Democrat Ann Richards to the antebellum governor's mansion.

In 1992, George H. W. Bush was running for reelection as president of the United States. Hailing from Connecticut but calling the Houstonian Hotel home, Bush had also served enthusiastically as Reagan's vice president—after opposing Reagan, of course in 1980. Recession, however, gripped the country—part of it structural and part of it a hangover of the go-go 1980s—in Texas and on Wall Street. So, in the spring of 1992, I returned to Texas for a rare visit to write about the state's new role in national politics. I was enthralled by the spring weather of March, so green and warm compared to the muddy, cold spring on the East Coast that was now home. However, as I walked the streets of downtown Austin, I was stunned at the ghost town-like feeling despite the new skyscrapers and storefronts on Congress Avenue. The buildings were empty and could be had for a song. The effects of the real estate bust, which followed the savings and loan bust and another drop in oil prices were on full display in the empty store windows and the "For Lease" signs on the vacant office buildings.

Austin had one of the lowest building occupancy rates in the nation and one of the highest unemployment rates in the country. The newcomers from the Rustbelt had clung to life in Texas even as others, like me, had fled the worsening and advancing economic storm. I was an early economic refugee and rode out the worst of it in Washington, D.C. With the other Texas expatriates of the Texas State Society, I had attended George H. W. Bush's inaugural ball and watched Lee Atwater play guitar. My wife and I marveled at being Texans in a faraway place, cowboy boots peeking out from under tuxedo pants. The only way you could otherwise tell I was a Texan was that I wore, when jogging, a t-shirt that was a favorite of the expats: Plain white, it had a big Texas flag on the front with the word "HOME" emblazoned above.

In Dallas, Houston, and points in between, people literally pitched their house keys in their front yards and just drove away. Yet the Rustbelt migrants of the Fifth Migration left an indelible imprint on their adopted home, one that is vastly underestimated even to the present day. The first mass migration of non-Southern Anglos to Texas ever, these Rustbelt refugees changed Texas at least as much—if not more—than it changed them. They had endured, admirably, the reward and risk of yet another ecstatic boom and bust.

Yet they were also crucial in realigning Texas from one-party Democratic rule to one-party Republican rule. George W. Bush's folksiness and Karl Rove's mad genius would eventually claim credit for this historic shift, which not only shaped Texas politics but cast a nearly indelible dye on American presidential politics. No Republican candidate since 1990 could ever hope to win the White House without winning Texas first. And that was because of them, the Fifth Migration.

In the early 1990s, one in every five Texans hailed from the Midwest. These migrants had brought not just their families and hopes to Texas but they had packed up their generally Republican politics with them during the boom years of the 1970s and 1980s and clung to them during the disastrous 1990s, now unfolding. They met up with disaffected Texans and other southerners in the state who had bolted from the Democratic Party, in no small measure because of racial prejudice. "Many had moved to Texas from the Midwest during the boom years," Rice University sociologist Chandler Davis observed in 1992, just as the process was beginning to unfold. "These immigrants seemed to be somewhat less conservative than natives but were unwilling to challenge the rightward drift of the Texas Republican Party." At the time, just how conservative these migrants were was unknown. Then again, Texas was a different place over 20 years ago: 75 percent of the state's population was Anglo and none other than Karl Rove told me at the time that the rural counties were Democratic strongholds, "blue-collar, hardscrabble, yellow dog, often-times labor-associated Democrats."

Like any newcomers, Midwestern newcomers sifted through the myths and symbols trying to learn how to be a Texan—to somewhat comical effect. I glanced at my watch and headed up the street to a lunch meeting with a pollster named Candace Windel at the Austin Club, a white-table cloth place that still smacked of its origins as an opera house built in 1878. We talked about the upcoming 1992 presidential elections, the odds on congressional races, and then she unveiled a surprise.

She explained that the arrival of a new Texan from the Rust-belt was a good predictor of his or her allegiance, as a voter, to the Republican Party; the more recent arrival was likelier to be a Republican than an old-line Texan. Then she smiled because her research had turned up something else, something that the two of us, raised in Texas, would find funny. She said that she had also asked about a few personal habits to see if they would correlate to more serious questions about geographic origin and party politics. I was intrigued. So she explained.

History, it turned out, was no stranger to humor as well as irony. These latest migrants were furiously trying to copy what they thought it meant to be Texan. They were more likely than old-line or native Texans to wear cowboy boots in public; we both stuck out a shoe and examined one high-heeled woman's shoe and one man's size 10 penny loafer. Newcomers were more likely to wash their barbecue down with beer than old-line or native Texans, who preferred iced tea. To boot, I had ordered the soup and sandwich and she had chosen the salad.

But here was the kicker. Newcomers were far more likely to eat chili *with* beans—an absolute abomination bordering on cardinal sin among old-line Texans, especially Anglo ones, for whom chili was meat only, in the Southern, not Mexican, tradition. I begged her to tell me more. So she did.

These Ohioans, Indianans, and Michiganders were trying to out-Texan the Texans. The more they were from the Midwest and wore cowboy hats and chowed down on chili with beans—well, the more likely they were to be, yes, Republicans. I chuckled and probed my memory for some kind of anecdotal confirmation. And yes, it turned out, the most Texan man I knew in Washington worked for a Texas Republican congressman, wore cowboy boots, drove a Chevy pickup truck, carried a can of Skoal in the back pocket of his jeans—and he was from Wisconsin.

The latest migrants to Texas had not just bought the myth lock, stock, and barrel but were living it. We finished our lunch and I walked her to her office and then strolled over to the lawn of the state capitol, so green and bright it almost hurt to look at it. I looked for a mailbox to mail a letter to my wife at the time, herself a Texan and a product of the University of Texas at Austin. Both of us yearned, increasingly, to find our way back to Texas. "Shoot the cats and burn the house, honey," I wrote, "We're moving to Texas."

It would take some years and we brought the cats. Later, Matthew Dowd, advisor to President George W. Bush, quietly downplayed Bush's folksiness and Rove's voodoo in turning Texas Republican. Of course, both men had talent in both areas. But the main factor in the realignment of Texas politics then was the convergence of migration and demographics, particularly in the suburbs of the big cities where the electoral swing really resided. The Rustbelt Republicans were, by then, proving themselves every bit as conservative as the natives—if not more so.

The national defection of conservative Democrats to the Republican Party, especially in the South, was a given in Texas, to be sure, Dowd told PBS later. Fueled by racism, the defection had begun with the Civil Rights Act in 1964 and was simply running its course among some white Democrats in the South.

But the other crucial factor was "the growth in Texas in the late '70s and early '80s, because of the influx [of] people from other states who had a tendency to be Republican, have a little bit of money, [be] more conservative. That in-migration changed the dynamics."

"It's when the suburbs around the major cities started to grow tremendously, around Austin, places like Williamson County,

around Houston, Fort Bendy County, Brazoria County, Montgomery County, places around Dallas, Plano and Fort Worth," he
continued. "So, these sort of big-growth suburbs that happened in
Texas began to push Texas more and more to a swing state, and
less and less of a Democratic state."

But in the late 1990s, Texas didn't feel all that different to most
people, particularly old-line Texans. Up in Granbury, south of Fort
Worth, Vanessa Parker (no relation) could trace her lineage back
to Cynthia Ann Parker, the mother of Comanche chief Quanah
Parker. But her upbringing was not unlike mine, 15 years earlier.
Life revolved around the predictable Texas rituals: pep rallies, bon-
fires, Friday night football, and the reservoir on the Brazos River.
Quirky individualism was not exactly celebrated. The sign entering
town read: "Granbury, Population 5,001."

"And I felt like I was that one" on that metal sign, she said. A
sandy brunette who tried everything but couldn't fit in with the
jocks, cheerleaders, and popular kids—all she could do was plot
her escape. There had to be something else going on, somewhere
else. Graduating on May 23, 1997 she headed for Colorado the very
next day: "I just couldn't wait to get out of here."

Though the culture of Texas may have seemed unchanged, the
Fifth Migration quietly cemented a big change in American history.

Now, Texas had become a recurring destination for American
mass migration. Other states had drawn more people, such New
York, the port of entry for over 20 million Europeans between 1892
and 1924. The great northern migration of African Americans in
the early 20th century emptied the South and forged an industrial
Midwest. California had been the final destination in the migration
westward, certainly, but those waves were now spent, as well. Yet
time and again—from prehistory to the turn of the 21st century—
Texas was the destination. And there was an important footnote:

No longer were these migrants overwhelmingly from the American South. The newcomers indeed wore away—ceaselessly—at that rock that Dobie had once described.

In purely political terms it was the Fifth Migration that also cemented Republican control of national politics in the final decade of the 20th and first years of the 21st century. But after nearly 20 years, the political balance of power was already beginning to swing in the other direction, for the same reason as before. The big cities turned Democratic and tended to stay that way. The surrounding counties started to become more competitive between the two parties. The rural counties were overwhelmingly Republican still, but their populations had nearly been emptied out and their votes were negligible compared to the big cities. It was the suburbs that Dowd described which held, still, the balance of power. But these, too, were already changing then. Nearly all the suburbs he listed in 2004 grew steadily more ethnically diverse, more densely populated, and more politically competitive between the two major parties in the ensuing ten years.

The flood tide that created Republican dominance over Texas ebbed and then quietly began to recede. Fully grasping the implications of the state's increasing diversity, the looming Hispanic majority, and the political value of the suburbs, Dowd opined on the potential political realignment of Texas toward the Democratic Party. "Will the growth of other populations, especially Hispanic and Latino populations [sic], begin to move Texas back to a swing state? It may," he mused. "I think it will, but it's probably going to take six to 10 years where Texas then becomes a state [which] becomes much more in play for the Democrats." That would make the date of Texas turning from reliably Republican red to at least competitively purple no later than 2015.

PART TWO

"I have said that Texas is a state of mind, but I think it is more than that. It is a mystique approximating a religion. And this is true to the extent that people either passionately love Texas or passionately hate it and, as in other religions, few people dare to inspect it for fear of losing their bearings in mystery or paradox . . . Rich, poor, Panhandle, Gulf, city, country, Texas is the obsession, the proper study, and the passionate possession of all Texans."

—*John Steinbeck, 1962*

5

★ ★ ★

AMERICAN COLOSSUS

T he calm of morning, before the sun is up and even the birds
stir, is shattered.

Clang. Clang. Clang.

Clang goes the diesel shovel inside the giant excavation on West
3rd Street. *Clang* goes the incessant hammering at the steady rate of
60 times per second, echoing off the new, shimmering towers surrounding the site: The 44-story Spring building, the 44-story 360
building and others, still under construction, still rising. Already,
the Gables Park Plaza Tower obscures the Colorado River from
view. On the banks of nearby Shoal Creek, one new building is
built so close to an older one that the residents of each can peer
through the windows at one another, just feet away.

By 8:00 A.M. in the autumn of 2013, not only is the steam shovel
hammering away with devastating acoustic effect, knocking a steel

and concrete piling deep into the alluvial soil, but the trucks have arrived. Eventually, a 30-story condo tower will rise next to the renovated Seaholm Power Plant, a landmark of Art Deco architecture built in 1951. Built nearly entirely of cast concrete, the plant had lain empty and dormant since 1990. By late 2014, apartments will soar over it and an upscale Trader Joe's supermarket will be appended, just steps from the global headquarters of Whole Foods.

So, now the dump trucks and 18-wheel dirt-haulers are queued up on Cesar Chavez Street, dipping into the construction site, roaring, struggling up the dirt track and then turning out on to 3rd Street, spewing clouds of dust. Blue and white concrete trucks stage on the same street, running their mixers and keeping their contents fresh, sounding for all the world like giant blenders; one, two, three, four, five, and counting. Encountering these giant vehicles facing the oncoming traffic in a no-parking zone, startled drivers dodge the trucks on a street that, until now, saw little traffic. After all, it's just three blocks long. Cyclists dodge the cars and the trucks. Dust and noise fill the air. Soon, more than 2,000 new apartment units and eight new hotels will soar into the sky over what was once the modest skyline of what was, only recently, a mid-sized American city.

Austin was once a laconic state capital, home to a part-time legislature, a quiet bureaucracy, a creative music scene, and one very loud state university: The University of Texas at Austin. While saying that life in Austin was once a simple life may be an oversimplification it is not a gross one. And the simple pleasures did abound. Swimming at Barton Springs in the cool, clear water that emerges from the Edwards Aquifer at the rate of over 30 million gallons a day. Watching the Longhorns play football on fall Saturdays. Music on South Congress if you are old enough and drinking on East 6th Street, "Dirty Six," if you are not. A Saturday spent on one of the lakes. The smell of marijuana drifting from Mount Bonnell. The relentless search for the best breakfast tacos, a subject of endless discussion, debate, and friendly suggestion, much like the discussion surrounding the quality of the margaritas at say, Guero's or, better, Fonda San Miguel. Or best of all, at home in the pool.

Still the smallest of the big cities in Texas, Austin is the most interesting city, for its culture, its easily accessible and sprawling natural greenbelts, creeks and impoundments on the Colorado River, as well its well-chronicled quirks. What other Texas city counts among its major events a parade in honor of a character in Winnie the Pooh? Not Dallas. But what also makes Austin interesting is its growth and whether that growth will sustain—or demolish—the city's fabled culture of acceptance, creativity, and playfulness.

Now, Austin is bigger than San Francisco, having grown 37 percent between 2000 and 2010, a rate of four times faster than the average American city. On average, there are more high school graduates in Austin than the nationwide average—and there are a lot more college graduates here than in the rest of the country, nearly 50 percent more. Many clutch freshly minted diplomas. One in 10 Austinites lived somewhere else only a year ago. Houston and Dallas receive more people but Austin receives, given its size, disproportionately more. If Houston was the heart of the Fifth Migration then Austin constitutes the very soul of this latest one.

★

Yet, have no doubt: the Sixth Migration was a Texas-sized phenomenon. Nearly 4 million people have arrived in Texas who did not live here at the beginning of the 21st century and more are still coming. Nearly one in three people who call Texas home have arrived from elsewhere in the United States in just the last year. Yes, the big natural gas developments of the Eagle Ford and Barnett Shales, as well in the Odessa-Permian Basin, drew drivers, roughnecks, sales people, and accountants out to rural Texas. Down in South Texas, front yards are rented out for trailers and mobile homes because there is nowhere to house the workers flocking in. The oil and gas boom created 116,000 jobs in twenty, mostly rural, counties, according to one study. The perpetually impoverished little town of Cotulla, where Lyndon Johnson once taught school before going into politics, was flooded with money. That little school house became one of the wealthiest school districts in Texas.

Back from her sojourn to Colorado after her graduation, Vanessa Parker tried her hand in the oil business where money in those parts of Texas almost littered the sidewalk. She sold fire retardant clothing to companies that didn't need them but were mandated to have them for workers. She hawked investment opportunities reopening old wells in Young County by cold calling 200 to 300 investors a day. "That was a tough gig," she said.

But it was the big cities in the Texas Triangle that were the main draw: 80 percent of the population growth was found in the Triangle, which constitutes less then one-quarter of the landmass of Texas but is home to its five biggest cities and 17 million out of the 26 million people who live in the state. A stroll through the downtown garage across from the Seaholm construction site displayed license plates from California, Florida, Illinois, Indiana, Louisiana, Ohio, Maine, Massachusetts, Mexico, and New York. Like every other mass migration, the people of the Sixth Migration were drawn to leave their homes because opportunity is better here. They came now not for land to work but for a modern-day equivalent: Better-paying jobs and bigger homes for less money.

But the boom in Texas was widely misunderstood outside its borders. The jobs and housing were not the direct result of government policy, especially the conservative government policy as has been claimed by politicians and observers alike. Governor Rick Perry did not single-handedly forge this roaring economy; his economic development initiative to bring companies to the state was ultimately just a well-publicized and well-heeled flop. Indeed, the fact that Texas had no income tax tended to be balanced out by the fact that it depends heavily upon property taxes and sales taxes, among the highest in the nation, to fill government coffers.

No, Texas was deleveraged—painfully so in the 1980s and 1990s. So, real estate, that bedrock investment or expense of businesses and individuals alike has been cheaper than elsewhere. Workers who struggled paycheck to paycheck on the East or West Coasts, as a result, could live comfortably here. The telecommunications, health care, and technology industries found pockets of highly-educated workers they could locate to Dallas, San Antonio, Houston and, most notably, Austin. Lastly, the simple dumb luck of timing and geography have placed Texas squarely in the path of the largest economic force of our time: Globalization.

These forces—deleveraging, diversification, and globalization and not the politician—were the real forces that transformed Texas in the 21st century into the role of economic giant. It's a role that's been played before by New York in the 19th century and California in the 20th century. Now, other advantages like youth, ethnic diversity, and population density recast not just the economy but the very society and politics of Texas—the new colossus.

★

Asked about the Great Recession one day in Houston in 2009, Texas Governor Rick Perry just grinned and quipped, "We're in one?"

It was a cocky and callous thing to say, as millions of Americans lost their jobs and homes and Perry prepared to run for president, taking the credit for the comparatively better economic conditions in Texas. Ever since then, two narratives purporting to explain the economic boom in Texas have taken shape. One narrative claimed that Perry was right to campaign on his role in the economic success of Texas, even in the face of a global economic meltdown unknown since the Great Depression. This narrative claimed that conservative Republican policies created an economic success story to be emulated by the country. But this tall, Texas tale—repeated by many since Perry—was entirely false. It contradicted the conservative notion that government doesn't create jobs and economic growth—people and companies do. All government, politicians, and policies can do are to help create conditions of confidence for that investment. That's all.

The countervailing narrative, by liberals, was just as predictable: That Texas was a low-wage, impoverished state with bottom-of-the-barrel jobs and that its economic boom was just another in the boom-and-bust cycles that have dominated much of its economic history. It was all just a flash-in-the pan, at best, built on the backs of the poor, thanks to the conservative politicians in Austin. Liberal critics of the Texas economy made precisely the same mistake as their conservative counterparts. They bought into Perry's story: That he and George W. Bush before him, made the Texas economy what it is today—all of which was not just economically impossible but historically illiterate, because it omittted the painful contractions of the late 1980s and 1990s, that set the stage for the boom in the 21st century.

The great real estate bubble of the first years of the 21st century grew in many parts of the country. But it did not arise in Texas, not nearly to the same extent, and that was the result of Texas deleveraging debt, particularly debt associated with real estate, long before the rest of the country—out of sheer unavoidability, not chin-stroking policy wisdom by Republicans in Austin in recent years. The savings and loan debacle of the late 1980s had arisen from a toxic mix of complex and misunderstood financial instruments, haphazard deregulation, and inadequate liquidity fueled by a lack of moral hazard. The American taxpayer, after all, was on the hook for deposits, with regulators looking the other way instead of closing down failing institutions, all of which invited more greed and ultimately fraud. If the story sounds eerily reminiscent of a later financial meltdown, it should. More than 1,000 savings and loan associations were finally closed or needed government help. More than half were in Texas, where oil prices had crashed, incomes had fallen, and fraudulent loans with exorbitant interest rates for inflated real estate could—quite suddenly—not be repaid.

Up in Colorado, Neil Bush, son of George H.W. Bush, was ensnared in an investigation and banned from working in the banking industry. In Arizona, Charles Keating dragged five members of the U.S. Senate perilously close to criminality with his requests for regulatory interventions; House Speaker Jim Wright of Texas was forced to resign over influence peddling charges on behalf of a savings and loan. In Texas, Empire Savings and Loan outright collapsed and was revealed as a nest of criminal conspiracies. It was the perfect financial storm, which cost some $150 billion to clean up afterward—about half spent in Texas alone—and led to jail time for 1,000 executives. The devastating net effect was to take all the oxygen out of the real estate bubble and nearly all the air out of the Texas economy.

Some 40 percent of offices stood quietly and eerily vacant in Austin in 1987. Dallas and Houston were hit hard, too. Construction of mutli-family housing practically ceased that same year. Markets were simply overbuilt and so home prices plummeted. Texas, like California, enacted modest restrictions on mortgage lending to try to prevent a similar debacle, under Democratic Governor Ann Richards. These measures included sharp restrictions on second mortgages and more rigorous appraisals. Construction perked up but only moderately in the 1990s, even as the Dallas Federal Reserve questioned whether Texas real estate was "a house of cards." Property values fell. Loans were written down or just off.

★

Every July for many years, I drove out of Austin with my former wife to drop off our daughters at summer camp in the Hill Country. My older one attended Camp Kickapoo, tucked in the narrow and beautiful Messina Valley near Kerrville. My younger one later attended Camp Champions where the winding Colorado River enters the shimmering waters of Lake LBJ, a reservoir created back in 1950. At the entrance to the camp, I was always struck by what appeared to be the remnants of an old ranch which had occupied this place before the camp opened, under the tutelage of legendary Longhorn football coach Darrell Royal and all-American swimmer Hondo Crouch, in 1967. There by the cattle guard was an abandoned and dilapidated old cabin, now surrounded by prickly pears. It was not hard to imagine how carving a homestead was hard out here in those previous Julys, before the dam, the lake, electricity, and air conditioning when hardly a breeze would blow for sweltering months on end. But there it was: Somebody's home.

Like food and water, shelter is a primordial need of people. It can be as a simple as a cave or as portable as a teepee. It might be made of adobe or hewn from rough cedar, like that broken down old cabin. It might be owned or rented. But a reliable place to shelter, undisturbed for the night, a safe place to protect and raise a family, is the first need of humans and the first desire of migrants and settlers on the move, even modern day ones.

The home was a compelling reason for me to move my own brood to Texas in 1999, providing a good example of the overall trends. An early arrival in the Sixth Migration, I sold our tiny Cape Cod in Arlington, Virginia and pocketed a healthy profit. On arriving in Austin, I bought a house that was twice as big with a pool in the nice, established neighborhood of Westlake which also had one of the nation's best public school systems—for nearly the same price. Housing in Texas was 20 to 30 percent cheaper than in the rest of the nation by 2000. Even then, Texas real estate would endure another price correction—downward, yet again.

The dot-com bubble had come to investors everywhere, certainly, but only to certain parts of the country in the late 1990s and it was highly concentrated in places like Northern California and Central Texas. In Austin, the convertible Porsche Boxter was the calling card of the new dot-com executive. New arrivals raced with realtors at breakneck speeds up the MoPac expressway to a house for sale, just to plunk down an offer—any offer—before it was snapped up. Each evening an American Airlines MD-80, dubbed "The Nerd Bird," connected the sparkling new airport in Austin with San Jose and Silicon Valley. As soon as the westbound traffic disembarked, the plane, crew, and fresh passengers pushed away from the gate for the eastbound red-eye flight back to Austin.

But when the NASDAQ crashed on March 20, 2000 the panic spread to the usually cocky technology business. The *San Francisco Examiner* announced the financial calamity the next morning in double-stacked headlines normally reserved for wars and earthquakes. In Austin, the reaction was, at first, more muted as if, no, this couldn't really be happening. But, yes, it was. The hot real estate market of the dot-com boom cooled with the bust. Companies started shedding jobs and foreclosures soared. The Super Shuttle now replaced the Boxter, collecting dozens of newly unemployed dot-com executives in the darkness of 4:00 A.M. to deposit them at the Austin airport on their way to all points on the map, not just to the valley, to eke out a living.

By 2005, the correction in Texas real estate prices was complete. The median price of a home in Texas was now below 60 percent of the national average even as much of the nation saw home prices rise in a spectacular bubble. In the following year, a house elsewhere in the United States cost nearly double that of one in Texas. Then the national bubble burst with devastating global effect.

Texas was not impervious to the recession which ensued, despite Perry's quip. In October 2011, as Perry stumbled through a series of gaffes on the presidential campaign trail, the unemployment rate in Texas rose to 8.5 percent—lower than the rest of the country, yes, but flirting dangerously with the high of November 1986, during the savings and loan bust. This was not something that Perry advertised, and the national press corps didn't even notice, let alone question it. Back in Austin, and now facing a $27 billion shortfall from projected revenues, the state legislature simply added to the unemployment rolls by slashing government spending, including spending on education. In rural Texas, a devastating drought cost another $7.62 billion that year in direct losses to farmers and ranchers alone; makers of farm equipment, fuel, fertilizer and other products took a $24 billion hit in indirect losses, too.

Yet in the cities, real estate prices did not collapse this time. Observers of the Texas economy often focus on the relative cheapness of things here: Land, homes, even gasoline, all of which is generally true. But the Texas economy by now more resembled an emerging economy—like the BRIC countries, Brazil, Russia, India and China—than much of the rest of the United States. Not only were workers younger and costs lower but there was also far less debt, both public and private. Despite the shortfall from projected taxes and other revenues, the state government was in the black. The greatest commodity of all—real estate—was burdened with less debt than elsewhere in the country. After all, cleaning up the savings and loan mess had meant cleaning up mountains of debt, too, through big taxpayer and smaller industry bailouts, and a wave of bankruptcies and debts restructured, written down, or just written off. The ledgers were simply cleaner in Texas because of previous hard experience.

So, real estate—crucial to homeowners but also businesses and investors—was not just spared the calamity that much of the rest of the country endured, it actually started to go up in value even as the Great Recession lingered. Prices sputtered a little in 2010 but then ticked back up in 2011. With a median price of about $135,000, the cost of a modest home in Texas was just 75 percent of the national average. In the end, the Great Recession dealt Texas only a glancing blow but the sole credit for it could no more be laid at the feet of Rick Perry than the man in the moon.

★

By the second decade of the 21st century, the Texas economy had become dramatically diversified from the one that existed just 20 years earlier. Where once the economy rested shakily on just one, or at most, two pillars at a time—agriculture and then oil and then, later, oil and real estate—today's economy was built on six major sectors, only one of which is energy, the smallest of the six. Financial services, trade and transportation, manufacturing, and government constitute larger portions of the $1.2 trillion economy than the energy sector which constituted only about 11 percent of economic activity in the state. Indeed, the professional and business services sector grew almost as large as the energy industry, even with its storied natural gas strikes down in the Eagle Ford Shale, up in the Barnett Shale, and over in the Permian Basin.

A technology economy, based first on hardware and then on software, matured in the Silicon Hills of Austin and dwarfed computer-maker Dell, based in suburban Round Rock. In the northern Dallas suburb of Richardson, the 25 million square foot Telecom Corridor served the banking, manufacturing, and transportation sectors. San Antonio's northwest suburbs became so dominated by the health care industry that it was common to ask for driving directions using the University of Texas Health Science Center as a landmark. The rise of the health care industry not only served an increasingly elderly Anglo population but exported products and services and invested, in its own right, all over the world.

A looming doctor shortage turned attention in the state capital to giving registered nurses greater responsibilities. Doing so, according to economist Ray Perryman, would increase economic output in Texas by $8 billion annually from the health care field alone and create nearly 100,000 jobs—not just for more nurses, but for the people upon whom they, in turn, rely upon for services. Perryman's forecast for job creation mirrored the population growth patterns. Jobs were being created along a nearly unbroken stretch of the Interstate 35 corridor from San Antonio to Waco, resuming again in the Dallas–Fort Worth area and reaching to the Oklahoma border, with other large clusters of new workers in the greater Houston area, as well as the Rio Grande Valley, and spots surrounding Abilene, Amarillo, and El Paso.

The big cities of the Texas Triangle now grew because of an ever-expanding diversification of the economy driven by sheer population growth, which demanded more goods and services for the fresh arrivals. Austin, according to Perryman, "will serve as the foundation for future strong performance." The city's highly-educated workforce—half the workforce has a college degree remember—was on course to create an economy growing at the clip of 3.6 percent per year, a rate seen only in the roaring emerging economies and increasingly in the frontier markets around the world—but nowhere among the world's established economies. Service jobs, ranging from lawyers to accountants to bartenders and everything in between, will make up 354,540 of the 558,100 jobs projected to be created in Austin in the coming decades.

Dallas is set to experience nearly as high a growth rate but far larger impacts in absolute terms: 1.3 million new jobs in the coming decades with 75% in services and the rest in retail and wholesale. Fort Worth will see similar growth rates, attracting service workers, information workers and, as it is on the edge of one of the natural gas fields, energy workers, too. The energy capital of the world, Houston, is opening more jobs in energy, to be sure, but requires still more service workers as it is now one of the fastest-growing cities in the United States. San Antonio is adding not just service jobs but, increasingly, jobs in finance, insurance, real estate and, as the gateway to Mexico, international trade.

Today, if Texas was its own nation—politically absurd but economically illustrative—its $1.2 trillion economy would rank 15th in the world, slightly ahead of Mexico and South Korea and just behind Australia and Canada. By 2050, the Texas economy is expected to exceed $3.6 trillion in gross product, accounting for fully one-sixth of the economic activity of the United States, still the world leader then.

The economic output of Texas will actually be the difference between America's primacy and China's number two ranking. But of course, by then, Texas will be the fourth-largest economy in the world, trailing only Japan, China—and the United States itself.

★

But there was a third secret to the growth of the modern economic giant that is Texas and that is dumb luck: Good timing and a great location. And though even a blind hog finds the acorn now and again, there is not a politician alive who could claim credit for either.

The Texas economy was cleaned up and diversified just in time for the first wave of globalization: Free trade with Mexico, beginning in the early 1990s. The approval of the North American Free Trade Act was certainly championed by Texas politicians of both parties but its passage and approval depended upon a national consensus in Congress and the support of not one, but two presidents: George H. W. Bush and Bill Clinton.

Much of the expanded trade, of course, passed through Texas and it boomed through the mid-1990s. Texas felt the results, not just in the roar of trains and trucks headed south and north but for every 10 percent increase in manufacturing in Mexico, employment in Texas border cities jumped 1 to 2 percent, too, creating newfound wealth in previously impoverished regions along the Rio Grande from the Lower Rio Grande Valley to far away El Paso. California benefited, too, but given its small border with isolated Baja California, that state was better suited to trans-Pacific trade with Japan and, later, China. For Texas, this was just the beginning in the fortuitous intersection of timing and geography. Even as investors moved some manufacturing from Mexico to China, Texas surpassed California back in 2002 as the top exporter in the country, accounting for fully 1 in 10 American exports and putting

700,000 Texans into jobs manufacturing goods for export—not just materials for Mexican factories but capital goods bound for the rest of Latin America, Asia, and Africa, the emerging and frontier markets of the rest of the world. And as Mexican manufacturing became attractive to investors again, as Chinese wages rose, Texas stood to gain in the very near future from America's relationship with its third-largest trading partner.

The single biggest driver in the role that Texas played in exports, though, was technology. Texas now outstripped even California in technology exports abroad. Nearly half of computer and electronic equipment jobs involved making equipment for export. And while Texas has done passably in exporting to the Brazilian, Russian, Indian, and Chinese economies it has outperformed most states in exporting in general to the established emerging economies like Mexico and Turkey as well as the dozens of nations that comprise the newest and fastest-growing entrants in the global economy—the frontier markets which span from the Philippines to Burma to the Baltics and West Africa. And more continues to beget more. A new free trade agreement between the United States and Europe would add about $10 to $30 billion in productivity to the Texas economy—not for any special reason but now, but just by virtue of its sheer size.

★

The Colorado River slips out of noisy, downtown Austin and meanders southward, toward the Gulf of Mexico, its final confluence, passing west of Houston before submerging itself in the warm, salty waters of the Gulf. Sixty miles eastward, a man-made waterway carves a route away from the sea and inland: The murky waters of the Houston Ship Channel, one of the world's busiest waterways, which presses its way well up into Buffalo Bayou. Some $3 billion is being spent here to accommodate a new class of ships and open a new chapter in global trade.

Down near the equator, Panama is widening its 48-mile long canal, which has connected the Atlantic and Pacific Oceans for a century. Workers are adding a third shipping lane in order to accommodate a new class of cargo vessels, three times larger than any which can pass through the waterway now, and that can carry up to 8,000 20-foot shipping containers that each hold 5,000 tons of goods from Asia. These vessels are so large that they account for just 16 percent of the world's cargo fleet but move nearly a third of the goods shipped by sea. In the United States, most Atlantic ports are too shallow for these behemoths which require draughts of 45 to 50 feet. Pacific ports are already at capacity and far from other major American markets, requiring long, expensive transcontinental shipments by rail and truck. Yet the Texas ports already handle the biggest cargo ships, with the deepest draughts, because of the energy industry. The ports have plenty of capacity. And Houston is a comparatively short train trip or truck ride to markets in the Midwest, the Deep South, the Southwest; it's nearly a half a continent closer to the big cities of the East Coast than Long Beach or Los Angeles.

The first of these behemoth vessels will likely slide through the jungles of Panama from the Pacific, ply northward across the Gulf of Mexico to sail up the 45-foot deep ship channel and, finally, dock in the Port of Houston next year, in 2015. There will be still more jobs, more people, and more money, of course, which will lure still more. Modern-day stevedores and their machines will unload exports from Asia and, once emptied, they will fill these vessels with American exports for the trip back across the ocean. Many more will follow and expand the global reach of Texas, the new American colossus.

6

★ ★ ★

THE FOUNTAIN OF YOUTH

O n a brisk winter day in early 2014, the sun bright and the wind howling, I take a walk across downtown Austin.

In search of a new office, preferably one where I could lay my head at night instead of driving back to the Hill Country, I walk north and east from the global headquarters and flagship store of Whole Foods. I cross West 6th Street and head for the John Henry Faulk Central Library, another good reason to visit downtown over the years. The neighborhood north of West 6th Street is a leafy place of law offices run out of historic homes, some more than a century old.

Yet it is impossible to escape one sensation: The relentless noise, the pounding and racket of construction. The back-up beeps of heavy equipment. The jack hammers and dirt-haulers. I count no fewer than four construction sites for high-rises in a walk of as many blocks and from the rooftop of a downtown garage I'd counted no fewer than nine construction cranes. And those were just the ones I could see. I really need to find a place to work, I conclude, without all this noise. Just short of the library is a two block-stretch of San Antonio Street with a few elegant homes that date back to the 1870s.

Many years ago, their ostensibly wealthy owners had partitioned some of them into offices and apartments for tenants. And the street itself was set a few blocks from the nearest construction project. Given the historic nature of the neighborhood it seems implausible that yet another construction site would break ground here. I realize I really crave the quiet, and downtown Austin had been strangely quiet, once. When I first moved to Austin 15 years earlier, downtown's western edge was populated by a few weedy car lots and it seemed to have as many yawning parking lots as buildings.

Now that emptiness is gone, swept away in a feverish building boom which has abducted the silence and calm, too. So, I make my way up the steep hill to a small sign, proclaiming: "For Lease." I wait out front for the realtor. He rounds the corner and unlocks the front door. Inside is the perfect office. Hardwood floors, high ceilings and the comfortable feeling of being old. A back room could easily hold a bed. There is a tiny bathroom and a galley kitchen to boot, all across the street from the library, itself adjacent Austin Historical Center. It is perfect. Though spotlessly clean, nothing has been updated. I stare out the back window, and remark that there is one of the last remaining and blissfully vacant lots downtown. The realtor pauses for a moment.

"I have to tell you," he offers, pointing at the window. "They're going to build a 22-story building on that lot."

I thank him for his time and leave.

★

For many Americans, their understanding of Texas has been roughly based on images of West Texas, a land of open skies, tumbleweeds, cattle, cowboys, oil, and football. After all, that is the Texas that has dominated legends and myths, books and movies from *Giant* to *Friday Night Lights*.

But to live in Texas in the second decade of the 21st century was to live very far from that Texas. Eight out of 10 of the people who arrived in Texas recently settled in the Texas Triangle, that swath of earth bounded by Dallas—Fort Worth, Houston, and San Antonio. Some 17 million people now called this area—just a quarter of all of Texas—home. There were as many people in the 68,000 square miles of the Triangle, an area the size of Georgia, as the entire population of Florida. This area wasn't just urban. It was densely so, swelling into a packed mega-region. And it was anchored by none other than Austin, a population of nearly 1 million people inside the city limits and some 2 million in the metropolitan area. Here, there were over 2,800 people per square mile here, 28 times the average for Texas—and a far cry from the wide open spaces of Judge Roy Bean or Hudspeth counties out in West Texas.

But why? Austin's perks have often been reduced to jobs, sunny weather, and lots and lots of music festivals. All these things are true but they overlook the fact that 25 years ago Austin was a place of no jobs, a hometown music scene, and a lot of those empty downtown lots. The secret reason for Austin's success is its youth. With universities in its midst, Austin has always attracted students. Yet a handful of visionary people, namely in the technology industry, saw this disproportionately young, highly educated population as the area's most abundant resource.

They had to start in entry level positions anyway so they were already willing to be paid a little less, particularly if they could stay in their beloved land of sunshine, breakfast tacos, water skiing, and music. At the bottom of all the buzz and the hype, the celebrities who increasingly called Austin home, and the tension over whether the city could somehow stay the same, was one thing: Youth. The youth that were educated here and now and the youth that were drawn here. The youthfulness of its culture; its mix of music, partying, and maniacal fitness is only one that the young can enjoy. The city looked and felt young and afforded the opportunity for people who are not young to act that way, even embarrassingly so. What other city would host an annual parade in honor of Eeyore, Winnie the Pooh's sad-sack sidekick—over 50 years running? And only youthful optimism would cause them to take on rents that soared like skyscrapers now; they will make more money next year, they tell themselves. In attracting and retaining a youthful population, Austin defied the downward gravity of American society, the aging of America. Few places in this nation could make a similar claim to such a large, young, highly-educated workforce, one that replenishes itself every fall. It is as if, along the banks of the Colorado River, there flowed not just clear artesian water but a fountain of youth itself.

★

Austin's first 150 years were admittedly inauspicious. As in the Texas of my own youth, not much happened in what became Austin. Then, in 1839 the leader of the fledgling Republic of Texas, President Mirabeau Lamar, considered the shooting of a buffalo on what is today Congress Avenue and 7th Street a sign of divine providence, or at least claimed it was to support his desire to move westward, away from the old Austin Colony and present-day Houston. He established the capital in a village until then known as Waterloo. By 1840, 856 people lived on the banks of the Colorado River. England, France, Sweden and the United States established diplomatic missions in the little town; the French Legation still stands as does a building on Congress Avenue that once housed the Swedish emissary.

Over the ensuing decades, political power amassed in Austin but not much else. In 1883, the University of Texas was established on 40 acres north of the river. Yet by the early 20th century, the bigger cities in Texas, such as Dallas and Houston, surpassed Austin in industry, wealth, population, and prominence. In 1961, novelist Billy Lee Brammer captured the intrigues and foibles of the city's political class as well as its relaxed, even lazy backdrop in his masterpiece, *The Gay Place*. Fiction could not be weirder than truth, though, in Austin. The powerful and rich publisher of the *Austin American-Statesman*, Charles E. Marsh took up with the shockingly beautiful Alice Glass—just after she emerged at six-feet tall, entirely nude from his swimming pool at the age of 20. Marsh left his wife, married Glass, and bought her an expensive estate in the Hunt Country of Northern Virginia—but not before she had taken up with Lyndon Johnson in 1940, then a lowly but ambitious congressman and one financed by none other than Marsh, according to the writer Robert Caro. Johnson became a senator and assembled his growing empire in downtown Austin. Not far from his office, the Brown & Root Company built its headquarters. Originally road builders, the company would benefit greatly from the largesse of government dams, highways, and military bases, all under Johnson's purview, especially as he ascended into the presidency in the 1960s. By the 1970s, Austin became a town full of hippies.

The Armadillo World Headquarters and other nightclubs became homes for the city's trademark sound in music. Janis Joplin's powerful voice gave way to Stevie Ray Vaughn's even more powerful guitar. Swimming nude at Hippie Hollow was not just legal, it was encouraged. So was topless sunbathing at Barton Springs. Austin's creative side extended beyond the bars and stages. Art cars—old vehicles painted in elaborate, multicolor schemes—appeared on the streets.

Austin was probably not more iconoclastic or creative than San Francisco, say, or even New Orleans. But it stood in stark contrast to the rest of Texas: The conformity of the oil industry in Houston and the stifling, cookie-cutter suburbs of the corporate executives up in Dallas. Amidst a largely conservative state, Austin was a liberal beacon, earning the nickname, "The People's Republic of Travis County." An environmental movement rose to fight and defeat the development of Barton Creek, now a greenbelt, to protect a tiny, endangered salamander. Nearly 15 years ago librarian Red Wassenich claims to have coined the phrase: "Keep Austin Weird" when calling into a community radio station to pledge a donation.

But some very smart people had set about transforming Austin by using its weirdness, not denying it. The city had little industry, beyond the university and state government, and Richard Linklater's independent cult classic film, *Slacker*, was set against the backdrop of recession and economic aimlessness of the late 1980s and 1990s. The nearly simultaneous collapse of oil prices and the savings and loan industry left much of downtown Austin nearly a ghost town.

Working with legendary technologist, businessman, and dean of the University of Texas College of Business Administration, the late George Kozmetsky, Laura Kilcrease was a royally-chartered accountant from Great Britain who helped size up a solution. The city's greatest natural resource was human: Legions of young, educated people. In any given year there was a permanent population of about 100,000 college students and those associated with getting them educated. Austin was home to 40,000 undergraduates at the

University of Texas alone. But there were still more, at private universities, community colleges, and what is now Texas State University in San Marcos.

"We needed to start our own companies," said Kilcrease. She, Kozmetsy, and others in higher education, as well as the private sector, and government began by fostering local technology companies that not only created jobs but also a lasting asset, intellectual property. "When you build one job at a time you build a very strong structure," she said. "In contrast, when you import 1000 jobs you can easily export 1000 jobs."

And for the tens of thousands of college graduates minted in the region, the sunshine, the lake, the music, and the freedom to not be in the rat race of, say, New York, Chicago, or Dallas climbing the corporate ladder, mattered, particularly in a period of economic downturn like the late 1980s and early 1990s. She added: "The culture mattered."

If job prospects looked just terrible, as they did, it made perfect sense for students to stay put if they could just pay the bills, and extend the languid lifestyle of college beyond the actual graduation date. As if to prove the point, Linklater captured the scene perfectly in his 1991 film, *Slacker*. The movie seemed documentary in nature as it catalogued characters with not much to do but a whole lot to say, some of it quite political, much of it a commentary on social drift, independence, and the repressive nature of the Regan era, all during a time of economic recession.

"I may live badly," one character said, summing up the film and the Austin it represented. "But I don't have to work hard to do it." Cast member Ron Marks was a high school friend from El Paso. He had been off at Columbia University in New York but on a lark, he visited Austin in the spring of 1983. "A topless girl at Barton Springs offered me a joint," he said. "And that was it. I was moving." After graduating from the University of Texas, Marks picked up odd jobs and when the call came he hung around the set of Linklater's bottom-dollar production doing odd jobs, like picking up giant bags of tostada chips that were about to be thrown out by restaurants to help feed the cast and crew. Though not as famous as, say, Teresa Taylor, drummer of the Butthole Surfers, who was also in the film, he was then cast in his role as the movie's chief political commentator. Punk was the music of the day; the Butthole Surfers had started down in San Antonio and Marks founded his own band. Linklater's film won the top prize at Sundance. In 1993, Linklater released *Dazed and Confused*, a film which chronicled the last day of high school, also set in Austin. Actor Matthew McConaughey led a cast of actors that would go on to be famous, unlike the largely amateur cast of *Slacker.*

In the film, they flew their freak flags, had a good time at any cost and disdained things like authority, status, and possessions. Linklater's Austin was an outpost in what the music critic Greil Marcus called the "old, weird America." Austin became home to equally weird artistic displays in front yards. Old junker cars were repainted and redecorated to become barely moveable pieces of art, usually providing some kind of social commentary or another. Halloween was marked by a fairly freaky parade down Congress Avenue that included not just giant biomechanical bats but an enormous rattlesnake float, powered by black-clad bicyclists from within its skeleton and stored the rest of the year over on Rainey Street. Austin was not so much weird, exactly, as permanently adolescent.

By the early part of this century, the energy was drawing people from all over Texas and, slowly, the rest of the country. By 2003, Vanessa Parker had returned from Colorado, gone to college and started a marketing career in Fort Worth. She left to go see what

Austin was all about, moving in with a pair of friends. She said. "It was the place to be."

The city remained perpetually young, educated, and ceaselessly curious. Nearly half the population was between the ages of 20 and 34, according to the most recent census; just 7 percent of people here were over 65 and 7 percent were children. Austin would likely remain young and educated for the foreseeable future. So far, all these relative newcomers seemed to invest, in their own way, in retaining what drew them in the first place.

"The culture is one of inclusiveness," said University of Texas professor Randolph Lewis, who has organized *The End of Austin*, a multi-media project documenting the city's startling change and debating its ability not to be subsumed by its own commercial and economic success. "And yet, underneath the 'Keep Austin Weird' cliché is a kind of traditionalism. People like the way Austin feels and there's an attempt to preserve that. There's a preservationist mentality underneath the eccentricity."

Joel Shuler came here to be a musician but wound up making Brazilian coffee. It turned out that the university had a center for Brazilian studies. He started importing 40,000 pounds of Brazilian coffee each year, saying: "Austin is the mecca of curiosity." Mark Seiler moved from the East Coast in the 1990s for the technology boom but left to start a soda company, Maine Root, which is still bottled in Maine, but the syrups are produced in Austin. He calculates that every Austinite buys $5.00 of his company's fair trade-certified, organic sugarcane juice soda—instead of mass-marketed, corn syrup sodas—each year. Austin ranks with New York, Los Angeles, and Washington, D.C. in the company's top markets. "I found Austin to be egalitarian," he said. And the people were "adventurous."

Leslie Cochrane, a homeless transvestite man was not just a fixture in front of the Starbucks at 6th and Congress, but a sharp critic of how the police treated the city's homeless and eventually a mayoral candidate. By then, Linklater was famous—and many famous people were finding their way to Austin. Marks eventually left music to devote himself more fully to his business. Kilcrease became a successful venture capitalist and expert on economic development in her own right.

The population within the city limits jumped from just shy of 500,000 in 1990 to almost 700,000 in 2000 and then soared. Wassenich and a local t-shirt maker got tangled in a copyright dispute over the phrase, "Keep Austin Weird." By then new bumper stickers appeared. My personal favorite: "Don't Dallas My Austin."

★

By then, just two words epitomized the star attraction that Austin, that sleepy college town and state capital, now lay claim to Lance Armstrong.

Beginning in 2000, the city and the cyclist shared a symbiotic relationship, born entirely of unrelenting ambition. Austin was swelling on the shoulders of the technology industry, which is second to none—with the possible exception of Wall Street—in its ruthlessness, despite the foosball machines and Hacky Sack. That year, I attended the South by Southwest Interactive Conference at the Four Seasons Hotel. The ballrooms were packed to the point of airlessness. Investors and entrepreneurs speed-dated lustily as they sorted out the B2B (business to business) from the B2C (business to consumer) from the hardware and software plays. Middle-aged angel investors honed in on start-ups, venture capitalists masked their greed with disinterest, and sweaty 20-something CEOs demanded stacks of stock options. I could barely breathe.

The relentless Armstrong, known to stop at nothing to win even before he was found to be a cheat, was a good match for the new era in Austin. No one embodied the rise of Austin out of its endearing aimlessness better than Armstrong, who went from a local cycling star to an international super-athlete in roughly the same years that Austin went from sleepy to sleek and hip. After winning his sixth Tour de France in 2004, he returned to a victory celebration and said of his adopted hometown: "This is the greatest hometown in the world. I think it's the best place to be a citizen. It's the best place to be a bike rider. It's the best place to raise your children." The city named a short bikeway after him and promised a grander one. His foundation, Livestrong, turned him into a global celebrity philanthropist. He opened a downtown bar named Six Lounge, before going on to win his seventh and final Tour de France.

His demise began slowly and then culminated all at once, in October 2012, when he finally admitted what was already being reported: He had used performance-enhancing drugs during his cycling career. His team had, in fact, operated more like an organized crime ring than a band of athletes, participating in threats, intimidations, and cover-ups. On the sun-dappled autumn weekend when Armstrong's world fell apart, Austin went on with the simple pleasures of Longhorn football, live music, festivals, and an amateur cyclist ride through the Hill Country. The city, it seemed, had had enough of the rumors and rumbling through the years.

Nevertheless, stunned and defiant Armstrong supporters arrived for his gala benefit sporting their Livestrong logos, even as the *Austin American Statesman* detailed the charges of doping and the subsequent cover-up, the flight of corporate sponsors, and the stripping of all seven of his Tour de France titles. With its success, Austin had developed a celebrity culture, built a sleek downtown, and even was even awarded a new sporting event, the United States Grand Prix, one usually reserved for the global elite. As Armstrong plummeted like a dark angel from grace, it was hard to overstate just how popular his adopted hometown had become in the American psyche. It consistently ranked near the top on lists of where to live, whether one was a college student, a recent graduate, single, or had a young family. With a nearly maniacal devotion to running, cycling, racing, and working out, Austin was among America's most fit cities. It seemed to constantly invent more fun things to do. Sperling's BestPlaces pronounced Austin number one in block parties, of all things. The local economist Angelos Angelou forecast that the city would see 18,000 new jobs in 2011. He was wrong: the city created 21,000 new jobs.

Of course, for all his athletic achievements, with or without doping, cheating, lying, and intimidation, Lance Armstrong was never a hero. Strangely, his confession—after a decade of being hounded for cheating his way to the top of his sport and the celebrity culture—provided an opportunity to rethink the very notion, and necessity, of heroes. It was absurd to create heroes of any sort from the worlds of politics and power, let alone from sports and entertainment. The very word hero is derived from the same Greek word of the first century—and it is almost entirely based upon myth. The hero, to cite Merriam-Webster, was either legendary or divine, or both. In not so many words it came down to this: The hero was never real. Over time, however, it became common for people with fame, money, and power to try to grab the mantle of demi-god, and for a very simple reason. Becoming one—or rather, convincing others that you are one—invokes more fame, money, and power. The notion that a professional athlete, who is hard-wired to do anything to win at any cost to anyone, could be a leadership figure is preposterous and has been all along. As for Lance Armstrong, he was obviously a very determined athlete and a highly-compensated entertainer—and that's all professional athletes are. But no, Armstrong was never a hero.

★

Yet, as nature abhors a vacuum, other celebrities began to call Austin home, or at least a second home. Residents could dine at one of Sandra Bullock's two restaurants or spot Dennis Quaid in a bar. McConaughey resided with his family near the Colorado River and often on the Longhorn sideline. The list of celebrities who called Austin home or who visited for a while grew long: Ryan Gosling, Christian Bale, Jack Nicholson, Billy Bob Thornton, Bill Murray, Elijah Wood, Owen, Andrew, and Luke Wilson, not to mention Willie Nelson—once the rebel of Nashville who now had a statue of himself in the slick, new 2nd Street corridor of upscale shops and restaurants.

In November of 2012, the city became the new home of the sport least likely to be associated with it: Grand Prix Formula One racing. This meant big-name sponsors, racecars going 180 miles an hour, $4,300 tickets to V.I.P. seating, champagne, and helicopters flying wealthy fans to the new $450 million race facility built by a bond trader and a billionaire. For three days, the global elite who follow Grand Prix racing would touch down in Austin from Abu Dhabi before taking off again just three days later, this time for São Paolo.

The major music festivals, South by Southwest as well as Austin City Limits, continued to draw hundreds of thousands of people—mostly from elsewhere—each year. In 2013, London-based Savages wowed the crowds and the critics alike, along with Jimmy Eat World and Shovels & Rope. Comedians Sandra Bernhard and Sarah Silverman appeared in time for yet another festival, Fun Fun Fun Fest, where Slayer, Snoop Dogg, and Ice-T appeared, among others. In November of 2013, German Formula One driver Sebastian Vettel burned a lap around the Circuit of the Americas in 1:36.338—a little more than a minute and a half and

.003 seconds faster than the next driver—and the fans drifted into a downtown party, featuring gold-infused champagne, each bottle worth thousands of dollars. Screens displayed the roaring history of F1 racing. By 10:00 P.M. the crowd was swelling. By 1:00 A.M. it was throbbing to the pulse of the DJ.

In the middle of the action was host Nicholas Frankl, a Briton living part of the time in Los Angeles who made a living throwing exclusive parties on yachts in places like Miami and Pebble Beach. Bereft of a yacht, he was nonetheless hosting his roving, high-end global party in downtown Austin for the F1 crowd. Along with soccer, F1 is one of the most widely watched sporting events in the world. "There are more people who know about Austin now because of two Grand Prix," he said. "If you are watching CCTV in Guangzhou you never heard of Austin. But you sure as hell have now."

In 2013, Linklater had his grand opening for *Before Midnight*, with Ethan Hawke, not in Hollywood but in Austin. He appeared on the red carpet and told a local television crew: "Is this the year of Austin film? Well, this is the *decade* of Austin film." Another Austin film giant arrived, Robert Rodriguez, the genius behind *El Mariachi*, its follow-on films, and the commercial giant *Spy Kids* franchise. Rodriguez would soon enough launch his own television channel, El Rey. "We didn't go to Hollywood," said Rodriguez flatly. "Hollywood came to us."

★

It used to be that no one ever honked in Austin.

When I moved here in 1999 from Washington, D.C. I was tempted to hit the horn one day in traffic until I realized that no one else was. Honking in the land of *Slacker* wasn't just rude. It was not cool. Now, honking has gone from rare social crime to offensively common. On any given day on Bee Cave Road, which connects downtown to the leafy and well-off suburbs of Westlake and Lake Travis, you can hear tires squealing, horns blaring and, yes, four-letter words streaming from pricey SUVS, worthy of any self-respecting Manhattan cabbie.

A half century ago, *Time* magazine published an unsigned essay entitled "What Makes a City Great?" The anonymous writer recalled Henry James' description of London in 1881, noting that the city was "not agreeable, cheerful, or easy, or exempt from reproach" before going on to list the great and up-and-coming cities of the 1960s: New York, Paris, Tokyo, Rome, and Mexico City. Nearly all were defined by the difficulty of existence there, as much as greatness, as much by the striving as the crowding. The writer sneered at Washington, Phoenix, and Cincinnati but allowed that Chicago, which the author termed a second-tier city, was nonetheless a great one, adding, "Whatever else it may possess or lack, a great city cannot be dull. It must have a sense of place and a feeling all its own, and its citizens must be different from and more vital than those who live elsewhere."

A place that was liveable while affording opportunity was increasingly more important than a place in which to strive and often struggle against the odds, particularly if the odds were against you. Just 15 years ago, another sun-dappled city, Los Angeles, was notable for having a terminal case of urban sprawl and no center, no real gravitas. The development of its downtown and cultural life, as well as the attitudes and values that birthed it increasingly turned it into a great American city.

Now, Austin was already a big American city. Whether it becomes a great one will rely, at least in part, on how it manages its most essential asset, its youth. Dell, famously founded in a dorm room at the University of Texas, went from public to private and Facebook, Google, Apple, IBM, Samsung, and others are all here now. Among those who can afford to indulge such debates after dinner or in a coffee house, there remained a tension as to whether some authentic Austin will survive the onslaught of growth, change and, invariably, transformation. What was authentic, of course, was up for grabs; hardly anybody who lived in Austin was actually from here. The closest you could get was someone who went to the University of Texas and stayed. Real natives were around but nearly as rare as the endangered salamanders. And every one was particularly suspicious of the Californians; they ruined Arizona, after all.

"It's clear that they're drawn to the same things everyone is drawn to in Austin, the quality of life aspect, the vibrant, funky, food truck culture and music scene. It's almost tribal that you have these like-minded people here and there," said Lewis, the University of Texas professor. "We're kind of the new California, California in the Sixties, a place where you could start over, where the weather was good, where social morays were inclusive. I feel like we've got that going on."

And the young, well, they just kept on coming: Individuals, couples and young families alike. They had all heard good things about Austin: plenty of fun, plenty of jobs and plenty of comparatively cheap housing. I met an ex-Marine who moved here sight unseen, a freshly-minted graduate of the University of Washington, even a couple who had left Hawaii to come to Texas. In 2009, Holly Regan announced to her friends in Seattle that she was leaving for Texas. They immediately jeered at the prospect of her living, as she put it, "among a bunch of cowboys and Republicans." Nevertheless, at the age of 25, she took an extended road trip across the American West and down into the Texas Panhandle. She gazed at the empty landscape, appalled, and wondered quite what she had done. Arriving in August, she endured a withering string of 110 degree days, she said. "It was miserable."

But quickly, the city grew on her. People were friendly. There was always a festival, a concert, a bar—and the omnipresent crowd of other young people who were "liberal, open-minded and approachable," she said. "It was Never Never Land."

★

Now, when I walk down 2nd Street downtown in the afternoon I feel like the oldest man on the planet.

Everyone seems young and sleek and beautiful. The men and the women alike look like they just handed their Porsches to the valet for the evening after yoga or jogging or both, showering, getting a fresh wax or deep-tissue massage or both, all before heading out for an expensive and invariably healthy dinner. At dusk, the running trail on the banks of the Colorado is filled with the fit and the young, kicking a cloud of dust into the cypress trees and the live oak.

Youth, after all, has the energy to do all this: Move to some faraway place, take some unimaginable chance, pack every spare moment stand-up paddling or going to work out—and then still have the energy to organize the whole group to go wakeboarding on the lake on a Saturday afternoon and then while away Sunday afternoon partying and playing ring-toss on Rainey Street. Once an isolated and hermitic corner of dilapidated iconoclasts, Rainey Street has now been converted into an industrial-strength, condensed theme-park of Austin, perfect for those Peter Pans who never want to grow up. Two blocks of food trucks and bars seem for all the world authentically funky, dating back to the era of *Slacker* itself, even though almost none of it was here five years ago.

So in this Peter Pan landscape and not yet weighed down by marriages, mortgages, children, and the slow but inexorable professional decline that comes with age, youth can be interested in everything because it is all brand new. And youth possesses an optimism that will fade only with the passage of time. It's hot and I head for a cold beer at Dogwood, a bar on West 6th Street. There behind the counter is a bartender I've befriended, Rebecca Fenby. Tall, angular, redheaded and all of 26, she epitomizes this youth. She arrived from Maryland by way of Florida and decided to stay. She complains that she is occasionally irked at the Austin that refuses to grow up but she is comforted by it, too. She's started writing songs and performing and when she bombs at an open mic nite, the crowd doesn't boo her offstage. They're supportive and encouraging.

She brings a cold beer and I ask her what's next for her. She replies with a smile and the utter audacity of youth. "Me?" she says. "I'm going straight to the top."

7

★ ★ ★

LEGACY AND PROMISE

Walking east, I cross a splintery wooden pedestrian bridge above Shoal Creek that connects the western edge of downtown with its center. A right at the Austin Ballet and a left at the sushi place, and shiny, luxurious 2nd Street unfolds, a district of expensive boutiques, Spanish tapas, very expensive tacos and wines, the statue of Willie Nelson, the black, gleaming W Hotel and the $1 million condominiums atop the soaring Austonian.

In the lingering evening sun, the sidewalks brim with crowds that grow particularly huge on the night of Austin City Limits Live show, the big night at the Moody Theater. Before the show, the bars at the W Hotel next door are standing room only. Women are chicly dressed in form-fitting dresses and tall heels, like they are on their way to pose on a red carpet somewhere. Men seem to wear the uniform: Some brand of expensive jeans, dress shoes, and untucked dress shirts—form-fitting for the fit, of course and mercifully blousy for the rest of us—or hipster attire. I am always struck by the scraggly looking guy holding hands with the stunning, Amazonian woman.

Back outside, black-clad police flit here and there on bicycles. There is one other thing that is hard to miss: Most of the faces in the crowd are white. Not all mind you. But overwhelmingly so. Despite priding itself on its inclusiveness, Austin remains the most homogenously Anglo among the big cities in Texas; almost half the population is Anglo. Austin is also the least Hispanic of the big cities in Texas. Only a little more than a third of the population is Latino while African Americans and Asians account for less than 10 percent.

Despite priding itself on being a liberal island in a politically conservative sea, Austin is something else, too: Arguably the most segregated city in Texas. It is a reminder that bias still exists, even if it's as subtle as a private grudge or just a historical hangover from an era long since passed. Texas, certainly, has changed. And its Hispanic population, like Austin, itself holds forth the promise of youth and continued economic growth, not just for Texas but for the country itself—but only if other barriers, just as real as the old ones if not as apparent, can be lifted.

★

Keep walking east from 2nd Street and you will cross Congress Avenue, pass by the convention center parallel to the light rail track, and you will cross under the perpetual traffic jam that is Interstate 35. Here you enter an entirely different world than the one you left behind. This is East Austin, a land of one-story wooden houses with palm trees in the yards, guarded by old chain-link fences. East Austin's southern area is predominantly Hispanic. The farther north you go the more it becomes an African American neighborhood. Here, Spanish is the language of convenience though everybody speaks English. A bottle of Topo Chico, the Mexican mineral water, costs 50 cents. Get to East 6th Street now and keep walking, past used tire shops and the gas stations and El Azteca, where real Mexican food—not a fancy interpretation of microscopic proportions—is served for a few bucks.

Hip, liberal Austin loves to peer down its nose at the rest of Texas and yet these very neighborhoods are living vestiges not of accidental segregation but racism enacted by government fiat. Nothing bothers the unexamined liberal conscience more than having one of its shining examples flipped over to reveal its underbelly. This is precisely what Cecilia Ballí did in 2013 when she wrote of her appointment to the University of Texas at Austin in *Texas Monthly*: "I was the envy of nearly everyone I knew. Wasn't it the coolest city in the state? The country? Quite possibly the earth?"

Yet she noticed she was often the only non–Anglo in, say a downtown restaurant, and that just 5.9 percent of the faculty was Hispanic. The student body, too, was not remotely reflective of the real social and ethnic makeup of Texas today. A conversation with an all-Hispanic construction crew where she lived revealed that the workmen all lived east of Interstate 35 but came to work here, west of the Interstate, each morning. She asked, "Was the state's most progressive city also its most segregated?"

She then went on to recount a shameful episode with results that linger to this day. For astonished Austin liberals, used to lauding the city's inclusiveness, it was like she had kicked over a beehive in a thunderstorm. African Americans had settled throughout Austin and, in particular, in Clarkesville, originally established as a neighborhood for freed slaves. But in 1928, the city proposed to concentrate its services for non-Whites on the east side, to avoid duplication and in accordance with the races being treated, as the Supreme Court had ruled in 1896, "separate but equal."

By the eve of World War II, African Americans were concentrated between 7th and 12th streets and the Mexican and Mexican American population lay to the south, precisely where it remains to this day. For decades, the apportionment of city council seats on a largely at-large basis kept African Americans and Hispanics from having a say in governing, Ballí noted. No African American sat on the city council until 1971 and no Hispanic did until 1975, by which time other cities were getting around to electing Hispanic mayors. The city council system in Austin was not substantially revised until 2012 and only in 2014 was it about to be tested by voters.

★

The institutional barriers that Texas erected against minorities through the mid-20th century were formidable.

Considered racially white but still ethnically distinct from the white majority, Hispanics from Texas could serve in non-segregated military units for example, but once home would have to send their children to segregated schools, face job and housing discrimination and could even be barred from jury duty. This had a political impact, too. In over 100 years of statehood, Texas never once sent a Hispanic to the U.S. House of Representatives in Washington— until the election of Democrat Henry B. Gonzalez in 1961. For his unabashed liberalism, he was called a number of things, including a communist.

About the same time, my own father chose not to attend the University of Texas because it forbade non-Anglos from living in married student housing, effectively banning my mother who was Mexican, and so he attended the University of New Mexico in Albuquerque. The passage of the Civil Rights Act in 1964 and its signature into law by the pen of none other than President Lyndon Johnson was followed in Austin by the repeal of state laws passed during the Jim Crow era. My parents eventually settled in El Paso where I was a comparatively rare product of a marriage between a Mexican and an Anglo.

El Paso, it turned out, was a living laboratory for the rest of Texas as the Hispanic population went from being a minority to a majority. In El Paso in 1975, a poor, mostly Hispanic company town in the shadow of the world's biggest copper smelting operations, was demolished. Smeltertown, beneath the towering red and white smoke stacks of the American Smelting and Refining Company was razed to the ground after a lengthy court battle. Smeltertown wasn't just a shanty town. Since its founding in the 1800s, it had been a place of immense, if silent, human suffering, too.

But now, the proof was in and a court had ruled. The smelter had pumped 1,000 tons of lead into the air in violation of Texas clean air laws and, worse, 75 residents of the 500 remaining residents of Smeltertown suffered from potentially deadly lead poisoning; 35 were children who had to be hospitalized. The company was forced to undertake a $120 million cleanup and everything but the abandoned church and school was demolished as the residents were forced to move, many against their wishes. A number of their children wound up living in what must have seemed a foreign housing project in the far wealthier Upper Valley. They became the new kids at Zach White School, my school, a big campus encompassing everyone from kindergartners to eighth graders. Some were a little edgier than others; *pachucos* was the term at the time. Some joined the football team; one I recall and befriended was a pretty good wide receiver by eighth grade. But still, every, once in a while, the differences emerged. The new kids huddled together during lunch. The most popular Anglo kids almost never sat with them. Years would pass and all would move on to high school before most of these differences were blurred, if not entirely erased.

Isolated in the farthest reach of West Texas, El Paso was actually a harbinger of things to come. Though they had lived in a deadly shantytown for a century, these kids were now out, after all having won their imperfect justice in a court room. The first Hispanic mayor in Texas, Raymond Telles, had been elected in El Paso back in 1957. By 1980 another, Ray Salazar, was elected at precisely the time that the population became majority Hispanic with six in ten residents being of Latino—namely Mexican American or Mexican—origin. Hispanics had higher birth rates and there was steady immigration, legal and otherwise, from Mexico; El Paso was at the very least an easy first stop. The demographic shift was then reflected in the city's politics: Two out of five mayors in the 20-year period between 1981 and 2001 were Hispanic men, two were Anglo men and one was a woman from the city's Lebanese-American community.

Down in San Antonio, the polished Henry Cisneros had become the consensus mayor not just of the Hispanic majority but the pro-business Anglo elite, too. Gonzalez, the crusading congressman, was called a communist again, this time in 1986 at Earl Abel's Restaurant on Broadway. In his seventies now, Gonzalez punched the man in the face. Charged with assault, he was quickly acquitted and served in Congress nearly to the turn of the century, a genuine hero in his city. Texas had most definitely changed.

★

Of course, prejudice and bias still existed. But these tended to be privately held grudges or the overlooked legacy of institutional discrimination, like the old line of racist demarcation that still ran unnoticed by most along I-35 in Austin. And make no mistake, the struggle over political power as a Hispanic majority arises—particularly by those who would make the democracy smaller, not bigger at the expense of Hispanic voters—has strong ethnic overtones, not merely undertones. But Texas had changed dramatically.

Twenty years ago, the population was 75 percent Anglo. Now, Mexican Americans and Mexicans were the majority in many walks of life in Texas. They made up more than half of the students who attend the sprawling Texas public school system, which educated 5 million students yearly. In Dallas, for example, Anglo kids comprised less than 5 percent of the student body. The same was true not just for big city schools but suburban schools, too, and schools in the smaller cities, even in East Texas. Down in Laredo, there were just 81 Anglo kids in a school system of 25,000 students, at last count.

A drive down the Rio Grande Valley from Laredo revealed an area that was still disproportionately poor, to be sure, but not medieval as it once was. Radio stations broadcast nearly entirely in Spanish, from both sides of the Rio Grande. Sleepy little McAllen had broad, paved streets punctuated by palm trees amidst gleaming office buildings with windows tinted against the harsh South Texas sun. There was a branch of the University of Texas system now, a burgeoning health care industry, and an entertainment district that rivaled that of Austin's 2nd Street. I'd say McAllen's was livelier, actually. Up in San Antonio, six in every 10 of the 1.7 million people who live in Bexar County were Hispanic. The top-rated evening news program was not broadcast by an ABC, NBC, or CBS affiliate but by Univision. Wealthy Mexicans had moved to the most expensive neighborhoods of San Antonio and Austin in droves. Mexicans and Mexican Americans now populated the once Anglo suburbs of Plano and Arlington around Dallas and Cy-Fair, Fort Bend, and the Woodlands around Houston.

And the greatest concentration of Mexicans and Mexican Americans in Texas? It wasn't found on the mesquite-studded coastal plain or the steaming fields of South Texas anymore. It wasn't even San Antonio. And the most diverse city in Texas? Well, it sure wasn't Austin. No, these distinctions belonged to the most densely populated area in Texas, none other than America's fourth-largest city: Houston.

★

She swept into the busy Starbucks and I could not help but to glance up at her because, simply put, she was the most beautiful woman in the place with her long, dark hair, big eyes and a jean jacket thrown over a flowing hippie dress and sandals. Then I recognized her: It was Carla.

Carla Ramos hadn't seen me yet as she stopped to talk to someone briefly before turning toward an older man, about my age, seated at the very next table. He was thickened a bit with age, just like me, and yet handsome with a full head of dark hair: Sergio, her father, was here to have coffee with his college kid. Having one, equally beautiful, myself, I silently mused about just how that conversation would go.

Sergio and I introduced ourselves—I knew Carla from a hamburger place where she worked part-time—and got to talking about Mexicans like himself who were changing Texas. He recounted the story of an acquaintance who had come on one of those millionaire visas to become a citizen. And he himself had, after all, raised Carla in the Woodlands, once a lily-white, Anglo enclave north of Houston used by wealthier Houstonians, frankly, to get away from the bustling—and Black—big city.

ABOVE: Austinites gather on the lawn of the Long Performing Center for an outdoor concert. The city loves bands, music festivals, and concerts. BELOW: As Texas becomes not just more Hispanic but diverse, so does the food: A *banh mi* taco that fuses Southwest, Tex-Mex, and Vietnamese cuisine. *Photos © Leslie Boorhem-Stephenson.*

ABOVE: A view from the hiking trail in the Barton Creek Greenbelt. The city has acquired tens of thousands of acres of greenbelt. BELOW: Austinites jump into the cold, clear waters of Barton Springs, which gushes millions of gallons of spring water each day. *Photos © Leslie Boorhem-Stephenson.*

Kira, a rescue husky mix, runs through the greenbelt in Austin, a favorite of people and dogs alike. *Photo © Leslie Boorhem-Stephenson.*

A college student from Houston, Carla Ramos embodies the new Texas majority, young, Hispanic, and striving for a college degree. *Photo © Leslie Boorhem-Stephenson.*

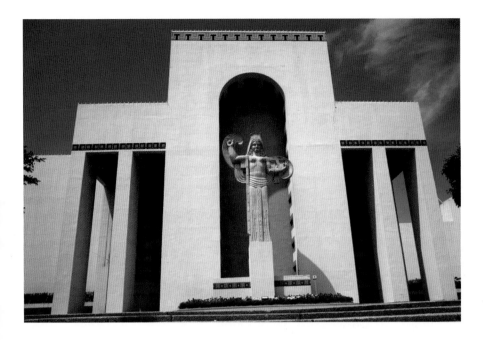

ABOVE: The Texas Centennial, celebrated here during the 1936 World's Fair, helped to fashion the myth of Texas that was later popularized in books and film and lives to this day. BELOW: The Colorado River below Mansfield Dam, which holds much of the water supply for the booming city of Austin. *Photos © Leslie Boorhem-Stephenson.*

Revelers at South by Southwest dance on 6th Street during the night. Millions attend the city's music festivals. *Photo © Leslie Boorhem-Stephenson.*

ABOVE: Drought brings brutal consequences to the land, people, and wildlife alike: the remains of a dead whitetail buck. BELOW: If Texas once boomed because of oil, scarce and precious water sustains today's soaring population. Here, the Devil's River flows to the Rio Grande. *Photos © Leslie Boorhem-Stephenson.*

The influential writer and folklorist J. Frank Dobie spent his final years on the Paisano Ranch southwest of Austin. *Photo © Leslie Boorhem-Stephenson.*

ABOVE: Political views in Texas are shifting. Democrats control the big cities and increasingly the suburbs are changing their views too. Here veterans march in a gay rights parade. BELOW: Holly Regan moved to Texas from Seattle; Marc Andonian came from Michigan. The couple, now owning a house and planning to marry, embody the movement of Millennials to Texas. *Photos © Leslie Boorhem-Stephenson.*

...know this in the premises are—by destiny rather than choice—the watchmen on the walls o[...]

[...]e must, these, like all they be worthy of our power and responsibility, that we may exercise our stre[...]

[...]To was within us an expe "that must heaven be our goal, and the righteousness of our cause must always underlie our[...]

EXCERPT FROM THE SPEECH THAT PRESIDENT KENNEDY WAS TO DELIVER AT THE DALLAS TRADE MART ON NOVEMBER 22, 19[...]

"except the Lord keep the city, the watchman waketh but in vain."

—JOHN FITZGERALD KENNEDY

Once known as "the city that killed JFK," Dallas has laid a new monument to the slain liberal president and will mourn his death each November. *Photo © Leslie Boorhem-Stephenson.*

Joel Schuler came to Austin to be a musician but has wound up an entrepreneur, importing coffee from Brazil to Texas. *Photo © Leslie Boorhem-Stephenson.*

Emily Silva hugs her little brother after graduating from Molina High School in Dallas. Hispanics are increasing high school graduation rates but in too many cases find college out of reach. *Photo © Leslie Boorhem-Stephenson.*

Leticia Van de Putte, a Democratic state senator running for lieutenant governor in 2014, at a campaign event. *Photo © Leslie Boorhem-Stephenson.*

The Ben Baxter Band, a local group, plays to a full house at Frank's in Austin's Warehouse District. *Photo © Leslie Boorhem-Stephenson.*

ABOVE: Mansfield Dam, which contains much of Austin's drinking water, was among the giant 20th-century engineering projects that created electricity, controlled floods, and now holds back water for thirsty downstream city dwellers and farmers alike. BELOW: Once Republican strongholds, the big cities of Texas are changing their politics. Dallas, depicted here, has had a string of Democratic mayors. Houston has a Democratic mayor, and the suburbs of both cities are increasingly competitive. *Photos © Leslie Boorhem-Stephenson.*

ABOVE: Ron Marks left Columbia University in the 1980s and has lived in Austin ever since, an actor, musician, and entrepreneur. Here he is depicted at the Highroad Lodge with the city in the background. BELOW: A little-known state senator until 2013, Wendy Davis became a Democratic superstar and launched a long-shot bid for governor in 2014. *Photos © Leslie Boorhem-Stephenson.*

Carla was only 18 but she'd skipped ahead in college and was now banking on transferring into the University of Texas at Austin as a sophomore. As American as Mexican, she represented the future; to her the idea that these two societies were separate nations seemed like a dumb assertion from an unhip parent. Youthfully optimistic, she planned on a PhD and she talked, as the young with opportunity do, about the big picture.

"My biggest thing has always been awareness, not being in denial but being aware of how our actions affect others, how you impact the bigger picture, not just on a country scale but on a global scale," she said, reminding me of what I must have sounded like when I lived I a dorm room. "I like being open to the fact that maybe what you're experiencing in terms of your reality is not the only reality that exists."

She was not a fan of the Woodlands, where she grew up, calling it "The Bubble." Yet she was part of a generation that was remaking Houston, once the home of the oil business, football, Enron, the late coach Bum Phillips, George H. W. Bush, and a thriving but small, historic African American community. Metropolitan Houston was now, in the second decade of the 21st century, one of the most diverse cities in the United States—African American, Asian and Hispanic—not merely one of the largest. Indeed, in one study, Houston was ranked the most racially diverse major city in the United States, surpassing New York and Los Angeles. Chinese, Cambodian, Laotian, and Vietnamese—the city's Asian population was its fastest growing group. Over 90 percent of the population growth of recent years has been of non-Anglos who comprised a declining 40 percent of the population.

Increasingly, Houston's endless broad streets and constellation of suburbs, like the Woodlands, were overwhelmingly Hispanic. The Hispanic population tripled in the 20 years between 1990 and 2010 to over 2 million people. As a result, Houston has become one of the three big coastal cities whose flavor is most decidedly Hispanic. The only metropolitan areas with larger Hispanic populations in the United States were New York and Los Angeles. In fact, certain Houston suburbs were even more diverse than the city itself. And Hispanics—like anybody else—were drawn by one magnet: Jobs. Houston arose every morning to its role as boom town, one of the fastest-growing cities in America.

"You are here to make your fortune; you are here to move ahead in the world. You are about making things happen," Mayor Annise Parker told National Public Radio's Elise Hsu. "There's no way that you could be a leader here in this community and not recognize that."

Despite the usual big city hassles, bad traffic, crime and, yes, oil refineries, Houston bustled with the energy of a global city on the rise. But this was not the energy of oil, as in times past. This was, instead, the energy—the raw power—of youth. And yet, there loomed on the horizon serious obstacles. Carla Ramos and her ability to go to college were not the rule but the exception. For many Hispanics, whether here for generations or recently arrived, college remained out of reach.

Almost as many Hispanics graduated from high school in 2013 as Anglos and African Americans and yet fewer went on to college. Much of that was driven by cost. In Austin, the state legislature has refused to pay for the expansion of college campuses busting at the seams. At the University of Texas at Austin, the state's premier university, the student body does not look like the new Texas; it looks overwhelmingly Anglo, and like the old Texas. Admissions policies to both the University of Texas and Texas A&M still gave a disproportional edge to kids from rural counties, as opposed to kids—of any ethnicity—from competitive, big urban and suburban schools. The future of the new growing majority and its shining youth was quite bright; it promised to rejuvenate the workforce and extend the boom and even reinvigorate the moribund American economy.

Yet the education of these very people and their ascent into the middle class was threatened by the politicians of the old Texas.

"If you want to see the Old Texas, come to the Texas Senate chamber or the House floor," said Gary Scharrer, a longtime journalist who gave up his press pass to be an aide in the Texas Senate. "If you want to see the New Texas, visit any elementary school classroom."

★

By the end of 2013 one thing was abundantly clear: The era of Anglo dominance in Texas was all but over.

And it will be soon in the rest of the United States. By around the middle of the century, Hispanics will be the majority population of this country. And never before has America undergone that kind of transformative experience, in which a minority became the majority. There are powerful and exciting prospects to this inversion—if it's carried out right. Not that long ago, demographers worried that the United States would go into a slow and irreversible economic decline as the Baby Boomers not just retired but became infirm. Who would care for them? And who would pay for their care? Who would pay the massive federal deficit that has built up over defense and entitlement spending on benefits like Social Security and Medicare? Only a young population could manage that. That youthfulness will not come so much from Anglo Americans as from Mexican Americans already here and Mexicans who are only recently arrived.

Esteban Dorantes was one such person and his young family exuded this powerful promise. Having arrived undocumented, he was raising his family on his earnings as a stone mason. At first, he made only enough money to send it home to his family. Later, he was able to bring them north to Texas. He worked seven days a week, despite being religious. He never drank. And by 2013, he had done well enough to run his own crews and buy a newer Chevy pickup. Barely into his thirties, short, taut and looking 10 years younger, Dorantes—not his real name—had a wife and three children. His obsession was their education and he wanted them first and foremost to become proficient in English, even though the schools tried to accommodate the children whose English still lacks by providing instruction in Spanish. It was a well-meant gesture to him but he wanted them to learn English in a way he hadn't.

"My biggest concern is for the children, their education," he explained. "The schools want to teach kids in Spanish if their English isn't ready. And I appreciate that. But I'm concerned—and many of us are—that our kids won't learn English fast enough. And they need to learn English."

Hispanics—like himself and his children—would keep Texas and, by extension America, young. Millenials, perhaps the last mostly Anglo American generation, are too few in number and their earning power is too small; there are only about 30 million of them in a nation more than 10 times that size. But the Hispanic population, which is overwhelmingly young, will crest at some 130 million nationwide around the middle of this century. And that youth—a kind of demographic rebirth—will be one that few major economies in the world can claim. Not Europe, not Russia, not Japan, South Korea and not even India or China, whose own populations are becoming relatively more affluent but will soon be reaching retirement ages of their own. Only the big Latin American economies—Mexico, Brazil, Chile—will be able to stake similar claims. And with them, so can the United States, which is poised—in an irony of history—to become an increasingly Hispanic superpower, entirely and merely because of the transformation of its population.

But first it would all play out in Texas. In Texas, the average Anglo woman was 42 years old; the average Hispanic woman was just 28 years old, according to Steve Murdock, who was the state demographer of Texas and head of the U.S. Census Bureau, appointed both times by George W. Bush. All the major Texas cities were on track to have Hispanic populations as the largest single ethnic group in the years to come if not outright majorities; in San Antonio, they already constituted an outright majority. And so, Texas was the giant, living laboratory of this grand and unprecedented societal transformation.

"If you are one of those people who think that Hispanic growth is confined to California or Texas, you are absolutely wrong," said Murdock. "How well they do is tied to how well Texas—and the United States—will do."

8

★ ★ ★

PROMISE AND PERIL

Driving just south of the Woodlands, I cross the Katy Freeway and make for the Sam Houston Tollway fumbling a map and keeping a hand on the steering wheel. Now, the strip malls and housing developments of Cinco Ranch—all kind of nondescript—whiz by outside the car window. The sky above is gray and brooding and the air is thick with the humidity of gulf air; inside, the windows fog a little.

Off to the left and far out of sight is downtown, big corporate headquarters, law offices, government buildings and a revitalized entertainment district in city center that was once empty of all but the homeless at quitting time. The old 50-story Enron building is now home to Chevron. But I turn left, instead, on to the Sam Houston Tollway and head south. I keep heading south.

Houston, after all, is big. At 10,062 square miles, the Houston metropolitan area is nearly as big as the entire state of Maryland, bigger than Vermont and New Hampshire and is home to 25 Fortune 500 companies. And it is a global city, too. There are over 90 foreign consulates and 22 foreign-owned banks here, at last count. The city is printing new street signs with translations in five foreign languages.

The concrete now becomes interspersed with open fields and rich forests, right about where the tollway meets U.S. 90. On display here is the new social reality of Texas—and the future of America—best showcased in these sprawling suburban counties. These suburbs are not the suburbs of the 1980s and 1990s, Anglo enclaves far from the big, bad city. The suburbs are now the places where migrants to Texas from around the world stream to make their new homes. This is where increasing numbers of Hispanics are settling, whether it is the Houston suburbs or the ones that surround Dallas to the north.

I jump off at the first exit. Welcome to Missouri City, Texas, the most diverse place in America.

★

Comprising just 30 of the Houston metropolitan area's more than 10,000 square miles, Missouri City straddles Fort Bend and Harris Counties and has been a commuter town for all of its history.

In 1853, the Buffalo Bayou, Brazos, and Colorado Railway ran out of here, the first railroad in Texas and one of the first west of the Mississippi River; eventually the rail lines that ran through here connected Los Angeles to New Orleans via the famous Sunset Limited train. But investors bought the land and advertised it in St. Louis, prompting it to be renamed Missouri City in order to encourage newcomers from the Midwest. The rail lines and later the roadways connected Missouri City with the behemoth of Houston as it arose to the northeast. In the 1950s, like people in a lot of Anglo suburbs, the people of Missouri City feared annexation by the big city and organized to incorporate a city of their own. In the 1970s, an influx of African Americans found inexpensive first-time homes. That event, and the racism of the time, triggered a wave of white flight. Property values fell. Then, the economic downturns of the 1980s depressed property values further.

But little by little Missouri City remade itself. Developer Larry Johnson set out to harness some of the lush natural landscape when he started the planned community of Sienna Plantation in the 1970s. The project stalled in the 1980s along with most real estate development. But in the late 1990s, Taiwanese billionaire Tan Yu finally finished it off. As the late Barbara Jordan put it slightly earlier: "How do we create a harmonious society out of so many kinds of people? The key is tolerance, the one value that is indispensable in creating community . . . One thing is clear to me. We as human beings must be willing to accept people who are different from ourselves."

Jordan's vision now unfolded in a seemingly unlikely place: The Houston suburbs. Now, mansions punctuated a manicured landscape of parks, trails, and lakes on the Brazos River, anchored by an 18-hole championship golf course, sports complex, and water park. The local lacrosse club trained over 100 kids from first grade through high school. But this wasn't your typical whitey-white suburb. Missouri City was a portrait of polyglot, according to the 2010 census. Of its 67,000 residents in 2010, African-Americans comprised the largest ethnic group, with nearly 42 percent of the population. Asians and Hispanics combined made up about 30 percent of the population. Only about 25 percent of the population was Anglo. Most residents were married. The median income was

$81,854 and nearly four in ten households had incomes in excess of $100,000 per year.

Athletes, like Hall of Famer Warren Moon, New York Giants quarterback David Carr, and Houston Texan cornerback Aaron Glenn all called muggy Missouri City home in recent years. Of course, there were more modest parts of town but Missouri City proved that being diverse didn't necessarily mean being poor.

Missouri City and neighboring Pearland were the most ethnically diverse places in America, according to researchers from Rice University. New York had a larger Anglo population than Houston and Los Angeles had a smaller African American and Anglo population. Most big American cities have a mix of the four different groups but two major cities, still, are decidedly Anglo enclaves: Philadelphia and Boston. Meanwhile, the Missouri City council included Americans whose heritage could be traced to Vietnam and India as well as the African American and Anglo communities. Drawn from all over the world by employment opportunities—and as the growth rate of the Anglo population falls dramatically—nearly 100 percent of the population growth in the Houston area in recent years was because of people who were not Anglos but instead Chinese, Vietnamese, Cambodian, Laotian, Guatemalan, Honduran, and Mexican. The food, too, was as good a reflection as the languges: From the Bangkok fries topped with crunchy, charbroiled pork to the kimchi tacos to the grilled fish masala and the seafood gumbo. But instead of concentrating in a handful of urban enclaves—like Chinatown in New York or Koreatown or East L.A. in Los Angeles—where cultures were preserved through isolation and segregation, these new Americans scattered across the vast coastal plain in search of the best deal on a house, the shortest commute time to work, and the best education for their children.

"This is where the future of America will be worked out," said Rice sociologist Stephen Klineberg, one of the study's authors. "This is what the world will be in 15 or 20 years. Houston is on the forefront of the global economy and civilization."

The transformation of Houston from the land of the Rustbelt Republican suburbanite took just 20 years, between 1990 and 2010, according to the Rice study. The Anglo population of Houston was now most decidedly a minority, falling to just 39.7 percent of the entire metropolitan area. The Hispanic population, now 35.5 percent of the population and rising, would soon rapidly eclipse the Anglo population. And yet, Houston had not torn itself apart in some sort of racial Armageddon or collapsed into ethnic and economic paralysis, as a lot of conservatives feared when it comes to people who don't look like them. Sure, Houston had all the problems of big cities and it had the particular problem of being a big city, practically on the coast during hurricane seasons and, now, climate change. Segregation—either by individual choice or economic reality—was still real: Anglos were less likely to live alongside African Americans than, say, Hispanics or Asians.

All that said, the mayor, Annise Parker, was the first openly-lesbian mayor of a big American city. Elected in 2010 and now entering her last term, she recently recapped her accomplishments in office. A lot of it was typical big city blocking and tackling. For decades, Houstonians put up with potholed streets but she claimed to have redeemed 450 miles of them, as well as cleaned out 550 miles of ditches and 150 miles of storm sewers. She counted 340,000 new jobs in the city, less crime, cleaner streets and a massive building boom encompassing 100 projects worth $7.5 billion. (She could certainly take credit for the cops and street sweepers. The jobs and building boom were the result of far larger forces.) She told the audience she planned to drive Silicon Valley's Uber car service out of the city and to build a botanical garden. Then she announced her big new initiative: a local civil rights ordinance that would extend equal rights opportunities in the workplace to gay and transgendered Texans. Houston, she argued, was the only big American city without a local law defining "how we treat each other."

All of this unfolded not in the distant future in some liberal metropolis like San Francisco or New York—but right now in the city that was the roughneck home of the mechanical bull, Big Oil, George H. W. Bush, all those Rustbelt refugees who turned Texas Republican in the 1990s, and the excesses of Enron—not all that long ago. Quite suddenly, Houston didn't just demonstrate the capacity for change and promise in Texas; it epitomized the speed with which it was arriving to shape the future. Texas, that immutable landscape once once thought impervious to change, was awash in it.

★

By the final months of 2013, Carla Ramos was living with her boyfriend in East Austin. Somehow, the ethnicity of the young gentry was lost on the locals. She laughed: "They call us 'the white people.' They point at our house and say, 'Look, that's where the white people live.'"

She still awaited an acceptance letter so she could transfer to the University of Texas at Austin, though. Her success in doing so—and the successes and failures of thousands upon thousands like her from Houston and elsewhere—would eventually help dictate whether the Texas boom survived and thrived into the future—or whether it would die. Whether they knew it or not—and most did not—the education of the new majority in Texas would affect the very people who, measured in sheer numbers, were passing from the scene: Anglos themselves. The fate of Texas, it turned out, was a shared one.

Not far away, on an autumn Saturday, a crowd started to mill around on the otherwise empty campus of the university. But they were not here for the football in what would turn out to be legendary coach Mack Brown's final season. The Longhorns were away this weekend. And the people milling around outside, as well as inside the AT&T Conference Center, were a little overdressed to be sport fans. Instead, the Texas Tribune, a non-profit news organization, had convened its annual Texas Tribune Festival. Less a festival, really, than a conference of public policy nerds, officials, college kids, concerned citizens, powerbrokers, and wannabe politicians it also drew the real politicians, many gearing up for elections in the coming year.

Waiting to be introduced by Tribune President Evan Smith to about 300 people was Steve Murdock, the demographer appointed by George W. Bush as state demographer and later director of the U.S. Census Bureau, now at Rice University in Houston. Up close in a hallway discussion, Murdock had a kind of quiet intensity. He was low-key, unassuming, and very patient but his eyes were animated, focused. Once on stage, he dove into a well-rehearsed death-by-Power Point on the changing demographics of Texas, punctuated by plenty of self-deprecating humor, mostly about demographers. As he flipped through slide after slide he demonstrated the loss of populations in the rural counties and the boom in population in the urban areas, the decline of the Anglo population and the boom of the Hispanic population.

"In San Antonio," he intoned, "some Hispanics have been there as long as any Anglos." The crowd chuckled. "Longer!" someone corrected from the darkness. He caught himself and smiled: "Longer."

But the big change that was sweeping Texas was not merely quantitative—the sheer ethnic makeup of the population. It was qualitative, too. "Education is the single best predictor of how someone does socio-economically. Education pays," said Murdock. "And education is the quintessential, American leg up."

But this was not a lecture about moral righteousness of providing the opportunity to go to college or to get into the middle class. Instead, this was a discourse on a shared economic fate. Murdock predicted a large increase in the number of college students in Texas who will need financial aid—just to keep up with runaway costs that are a result of 20 years of unconstrained conservative education and fiscal policies. Just as they have refused to help pay for the expansion of the state's public schools, even as the population doubles, the Republican-dominated Texas legislature has refused to use taxpayer funds to pay for the expansion of public universities.

At the beginning of this century, college tuition at a public college was about $4,000 per year. Then, legislators in Austin lifted the cap on public university tuition and fees and cut state money for Texas universities. And so, in the ensuing decade the cost of a college education at a public university rose a whopping 55 percent. By 2013, the University of Texas at Dallas, a branch of the UT system charged nearly $12,000 for tuition annually. That was more even than the flagship university in Austin and made the Dallas campus the most expensive public university in the entire state.

These short-term decisions have kept money in the state coffers, to be sure, and certainly avoided the need to increase taxes—an unpopular proposition in general but blasphemy to conservative Republicans. But these choices came at considerable, long-term cost. A college graduate, on average, would collect a paycheck 66 percent bigger than someone who did not have a degree. Because of the sheer number of people who will not be able to afford college, let alone attend, according to Murdock, the poverty rate in Texas could jump 172 percent by the middle of the century.

If more of the new majority in Texas don't go to college and increase their earning power, consumer spending will fall. The ability to sustain the tax base, particularly property taxes, will be in jeopardy. This will affect not just Hispanics; it will impact everyone, regardless of ethnicity or age, individuals, businesses and institutions—private and public—alike. The entire Texas boom, which could power the American economy through the rest of the century, would stutter and stall.

"We have to close the higher education gap to double income," warned Murdock, who did not mince his words, "to avoid a slide into the yawning jaws of mass poverty."

PART THREE

"Texas is a great state. It's the 'Old Man River' of states. No matter who runs it or what happens to it politically, it just keeps going."

—*Will Rogers, 1932*

9

★ ★ ★

DISASTER

As the summer of 2013 turned grudgingly toward autumn, the skies over Texas remained purely and cruelly blue. Texas was in its third year of drought.

It had begun two full years earlier, when the rainless days measured in the hundreds and there was no relief in sight. The parched earth split open. The Little Blanco River, upstream from my home, simply stopped running; the mainstem of the river grew warm and increasingly still. In the country, cattle died or were hastily sold at a loss at auction. In the city, limestone foundations cracked and thirsty and hungry coyotes increasingly turned up on manicured suburban lawns to drink from pools and snatch unwary cats and dogs.

The economic losses mounted into the millions and then hundreds of millions and then billions of dollars. Despite a relatively robust economy, when compared to the rest of the nation, the effects of the Great Recession were still being felt, too. Property values fell, though not nearly as much as in California and Florida. Work became increasingly scarce. Teachers and police were let go. That summer, everything that had felt so strong about Texas suddenly felt fragile—and very much in danger. Indeed, that summer underscored at least one, if not two, challenges that still confront Texas, even as drought has receded and the economy has become more certain.

Here was Texas, booming still with jobs, homes, and land. But Texas had seen many booms before and they all collapsed, inevitably, of their own weight into wrenching busts. Could the boom last? Was there something hidden beneath all the facts and figures that could threaten decades of growth and potentially a century of relatively unbroken prosperity? The tail winds of the recession and the head winds of the greatest drought in recorded history in Texas seemed strangely intertwined that summer.

Prosperity, survival, even life itself seemed to hang in the balance. And there was a reason. Sure, Texas was competitive in a global economy; but that economy was fickle. And the rising Hispanic population was running headlong into the limits of its expansion into the middle class. Texas, the very future of the American society and economy, was built upon a dangerously vulnerable foundation: The upward mobility of a people that had long been a nearly forgotten minority and a reliance on semi-arid land that was becoming ever more arid because of climate change. Those facts coiled like a rattle snake in the tall buffalo grass to threaten the very future of Texas.

At home, the dirt under my boots split from the lack of water. I noticed the old, dark-faced doe in the yard again. The fawn that had trailed her in the spring was gone. The doe's ribs now showed. The deer had become so hungry that they turned to eating things out of the garden that were bad for them: The yellow-flowered esperanza and the prickly pear; at least one had even sampled my outright poisonous oleander in apparent desperation. As the morning lengthened, the cicadas increased the pitch and fever of their song; all too soon they would sing in a maddening scream, sometime before noon today, I guessed. Their crazy song seemed to increase in unison and volume with the temperature. The heat was coming on again, having barely slackened with the dawn.

Most natural disasters are striking because of their fury. Hurricanes lash the land with increasing velocity as they come ashore, smashing homes and office windows with their screeching winds and rising barometric pressures, just as Hurricane Ike did to Galveston and Houston. When they pass, as I noticed from that largely empty city in 2008, the tempo declines to nearly nothing. I remember not just the empty streets and the flooding but the stillness as darkness began to envelop the vast and evacuated city. Fires gain in strength as they consume oxygen and fuel, until they are tamed or simply spent and exhausted.

Droughts, in contrast, are disasters in slow motion. Their very length is proportionate to their cruelty. The spring of Indian paint brushes and blue bonnets is the first visible sign. It is brief to the point of being stingy, a sign of the summer to come. The water holes and rivers are still low despite occasional rains. But the creeks give away the story. They shrink and dry long before spring is supposed to be over. The tall grasses turn to a dormant brown long before they should. Fire, born from a spark or just carelessness lurks. Life itself slows, falters, and begins to fade.

★

In 2011, all over Texas, the country's largest beef-producing state, ranchers sold off herds early, losing millions of dollars, or hung on just to watch the animals die for lack of water. Thirsty cows then died from too much water—dehydrated and moved to water, the cows gulped it down too greedily, bloated up, and keeled over, dead. Up in the Panhandle, farmers plowed under their dying wheat. Out in arid West Texas, fear of a second dustbowl was whispered about in small towns. Even the city of San Angelo announced that it would soon run entirely dry. On the Edwards Plateau, the numbers of quail were down by half in autumn. Local television crews cooked food on car dashboards to demonstrate just how hot it was. In Austin, they baked a batch of cookies. Not to be outdone, a news crew in Oklahoma grilled a steak. Strangers in line for coffee couldn't help but talk about the weather. Everyone seemed to ask the same question: God, how long will this go on?

Until relatively recently, droughts were the brief and seasonal problems of country people: Farmers, ranchers, cowboys, hunters, and Native Americans. Plus, the ancient technology of irrigation allowed large numbers of people to inhabit otherwise arid areas, usually by robbing country people to provide water for city people.

The growth of Los Angeles in the middle part of the last century was testimony to that. In 1900, the city was home to just 100,000 people, a crossroads for agriculture, oil, and shipping. Yet through a mix of power politics and stealthy greed, the city acquired the rights to much of the Owens Valley, far away in the Sierra. Over the protests of the ranchers and miners, the city—with the help of the federal government—built a concrete aqueduct over 233 miles long, the longest in the world then. Owens Lake was entirely drained and by 1927, Los Angeles owned 90 percent of the water rights to the valley. Ranching and farming there disappeared from the landscape as an increasingly arid environment set in.

Through the 20th century, the most populated parts of the previously sparsely inhabited Southwest followed suit. The Central Arizona Project cut an aqueduct 336 miles long to draw 1.5 million acre-feet of the Colorado River before it could reach its natural terminus in the Sea of Cortez; decades later the river's mouth is a delta of silt and reeds. The Salt River was diverted, too. Its population swelling into the millions, Phoenix tapped the groundwater beneath it; water levels plunged over 200 feet in some places and sink holes appeared.

Beginning in the late 1940s and stretching for a decade, even as it, too, was urbanizing, Texas entered into what was to be—until 2011—the greatest and longest-running drought in its recorded history. Known as the Drought of Record, it was an era of unprecedented devastation. Ranchers used flame throwers to torch needles off vast stands of prickly pear in an often futile effort to keep their cattle alive. The governor of Texas rallied governors from across the Southwest to demand more federal financial assistance for farmers and ranchers.

Finally, in the late 1950s, the drought began to break. The state government in Texas reacted by creating its first unified plan for water conservation—which meant building dams to hold back the water. It did not follow Los Angeles and Phoenix in building vast canals and aqueducts. Texas was, and remains, a land of nearly no natural lakes. At the time, the concern was really getting water to farmers and ranchers downstream. Water that fell on to the Edwards Plateau could be gathered in the reservoirs of the Highland Lakes and then sent down the Colorado River for use both by the city of Austin and rice farmers down on the coast alike. San Antonio could tap its aquifer. Dallas relied upon the Trinity River and Houston, with its bountiful rivers, bayous and marshlands, had plenty of water at the time.

On its face, the problem seemed solved. Of course, there were side effects. One was that water rights became concentrated in the hands of powerful, semi-public and semi-private institutions, like the Lower Colorado River Authority. Also, there was evidence that the salinity of the Gulf Coast rose; certain fish populations, like tarpon, practically disappeared.

Yet the understanding of drought in Texas was still predicated on a flawed and incomplete history. The entire recorded history of rainfall in Texas could only be traced, until very recently, back to 1895, when rain gauges were first employed across the state. The drought of the late 1940s and 1950s became the baseline for drought even though it was measured by a system just 50 or 60 years old at the time. Compounding the error, Texans continued to use that standard in the decades that ensued. But that water then nourished a population of just 9 million people, only about a third of the number that live in Texas today. Now, 26 million relied upon the exact same amount of water and more people were coming every single day.

★

Thousands of miles away, in the Pacific Ocean, a powerful current runs like a river through the sea itself.

If it stirs, particularly in the winter, it will start to move warm water from the equator northward. Some of that water will evaporate into the atmosphere to form rain clouds. The ensuing effects of the band of warm water temperatures, known as El Niño result in more rain for the Southwestern United States. But if the current stirs in the opposite direction, drawing cooler water from the upper reaches of the Pacific, the rain will never reach Texas and the desert southwest. La Niña, the opposite weather phenomenon, brings drought from the farthest reaches of this distant ocean. And how often La Niña has occurred, and the resultant effects in Texas, could never be accurately spelled out by several decades of rainfall gauges.

Instead, in the Texas Hill Country, the trees along the banks of the Blanco River and its nearby tributaries, such as Cypress Creek, tell the story that eludes the gauges and the record books. The bald cypress is a tall and graceful tree with thin needles and thick, thirsty roots that reach deep into the water, forming knots, or knees, as they drop further into the river bed. Unlike other cypress trees, the bald cypress loses its needles in the winter, presenting a stark silhouette of life waiting patiently for spring. Keen to grow only along the water, big cypress trees provide landing perches for blue herons and white wing doves. Over at Blue Hole, in the town of Wimberley, the cypress trees in summer are like a jungle gym in a park; clambered over by boys and girls alike, waiting their turn for rope swings with which to fly out over the water, letting go at just the last second, plunging into the cold, clear creek.

Many of these trees are old; some, however, are ancient. Down on the river near my home, there is one on the riverbank that is easily twice as thick as the rest. And one tree, still living, dates back to 1426. Some of these trees were saplings when Columbus arrived in the New World. So, in 2009, researchers from Texas and Arkansas carefully drilled into the trunks of 300 of these trees to extract a core sample of the tree rings which held a history of rainfall and drought going back centuries.

The bands between the tree rings told a startling story. The thicker the band was, the more the tree had grown that year, as there had been more water within the reach of its roots. The thinner the band was, the less the tree had grown. The more frequent the thick bands, the greater the periods of rainfall over the years. The thinner the bands, the more years went by in seasons of drought. And while people tend to think of drought in terms of a single year, generally speaking, these droughts were not measured in years. No. They were measured in decades.

The worst of these periods, known as megadroughts, gripped Texas and Mexico for nearly a half-century, from 1450 to 1489. Yet there were numerous droughts in the 1700s and early 1800s, before the Spanish, Mexicans, and Americans came and began recording the history of Texas. The driest 10-year drought stretched from 1716 through 1725 and the driest 20-year period took place from 1697 through 1716. Indeed, it appears that descriptions of Texas—particularly Central Texas—by early settlers were colored by their arrival during wet, El Niño years.

The Spanish, for instance, established their missionary trail from South through Central Texas in the late 1700s, arriving in San Marcos where the San Marcos River sprung from the hillsides, fully formed. The Spanish had missed the driest years of the century and so their descriptions home told of a lush, rich countryside. The arrival of Americans in the early 19th century and the push of German settlers westward on to the Edwards Plateau also generally matched the wet years. When the drought years came, these settlers undoubtedly found themselves not just in a hostile environment but a one that was so harsh as to be nearly unrecognizable from their very recent arrival.

I remember having the exact same impression the year I returned to Texas, in 1999. It was the first of several years of drought that would stretch for a decade and more. Driving west of Austin on Highway 70 in the early autumn, the land was parched to the point of desperation. I had told my wife at the time that I really wanted to live in the country, not in the city. But driving over the empty skeleton of Double Horn Creek, on the road to Llano, I had serious misgivings about my desire. And accustomed to the comparatively lush East Coast, which we had left behind, I remember wondering aloud: "What have I done?" The same question came to mind a decade later, in 2011, when I spent as much time as possible indoors. My daily walks had to be timed to avoid the heat of the day as the screaming of the cicadas threatened to drive me crazy, I thought. The effects of the drought were everywhere, a xerascaped garden struggling to stay alive even in its native environment, empty creeks, and the steadily warming water of the river which, if warmed too much, would be unfit to swim in because of rising bacterial counts.

Up on the nearby 6,000-acre Storm Ranch, the cruelty of the drought was evidenced in the victims it claimed first: The young. The malnourished whitetail does, unable to produce enough milk, left their fawns to die of starvation. The young maples and oaks died too, without the roots of the old trees to reach the falling water table, retreating ever further as the days passed without rain. Driving across the ranch, one of the largest still left intact in these parts, rancher Josh Storm, a big, ruddy-faced man, was alternately proud of his family's holdings and distraught at the effects of the drought. "I haven't seen it this bad," he said, wheeling his Jeep across the ranch, "in a long time."

Indeed, it was not yet clear if the first two decades of this century constituted a series of short droughts or one very long one. In 2005, the Dallas-Fort Worth Metroplex had endured its second-driest year on record. Lake Lavon, a prime water supply, dropped to less than 40 percent of capacity. Over $4 billion in agricultural losses set in and the drought endured into 2006. Dry years returned in the latter part of the decade culminating in the 2011 drought—which continued into 2012, 2013, and into early 2014.

The impact was nothing short of colossal. The year 2011 alone was the worst one-year drought in over 100 years of record-keeping, according to John Nielsen-Gammon, the state meteorologist in College Station. An area the size of Connecticut was blackened by fire. Ranchers not only lost money in auctioning off their herds before watching them die of thirst and starvation; they lost years, if not decades, of DNA for future herds, the cumulative value of years of breeding worth countless dollars.

Officially, direct agricultural losses amounted to $5 billion. But Ray Perryman, one of the most respected economists in Texas, told me that direct losses would amount to about $7 billion before year's end. Damage extended beyond fields and cow pens into cities and suburbs. In Austin, some $100 million worth of real estate was consumed by wildfires. Losses from the tourism industry went largely uncounted, even as lake levels fell. In coming years, water restrictions seemed likely to impact business, not just disgruntled suburbanites upset at their withering lawns.

Those direct losses would exceed the most recent estimates for Hurricane Irene which lashed the East Coast with August rains in 2011. Damages from Irene stood at $6.6 billion in direct losses, according to global reinsurer Aon Benfield. As a result, the Texas drought would stand in its first year as one of the 10 most expensive natural disasters in U.S. history, according to records kept by the National Oceanic and Atmospheric Administration.

But the damage by no means stopped there; ranchers and farmers were insured for some losses but are often highly leveraged. Perryman estimated that the multiplier effect—measured in farm equipment, seed, fuel, and consumer products not purchased as a result—would bring the indirect losses to a staggering $24.5 billion by 2012. "This," said Perryman, the state's most respected economist who sounded for all the world like a rancher with a furrowed brow, was "about as bad as it can get."

★

Perryman was right about the economy. Texas is a big, highly diversified and urbanized economy. The drought would do powerful damage but alone could not stop the economy's growth. But Perryman wasn't quite right when it came to the prospect of drought in the future. It can, indeed it likely will, get decidedly worse.

The drought's economic effect collided at the time with another largely overlooked problem: Increasing unemployment. Perry, campaigning for the presidency that year, liked to tell the story about how Texas created more jobs during the Great Recession than any other state; a fine and true story, in fact, though some smaller states saw employment rise at faster rates. But in late 2011, as the drought's vengeance was fully felt, unemployment in Texas approached the national average—fast. The unemployment rate stood at 8.5 percent, according to the Bureau of Labor Statistics. The last time that unemployment was higher in Texas was November, 1986, when a historic bust in oil prices collided with the aftershocks of the Savings and Loan Crisis to turn downtowns into ghost towns. It was pretty simple. The Texas economy was connected to the global economy, just as the landscape was connected to the global climate, and climate change.

Now, 20 years later, state and local governments were adding to unemployment in cities and towns alike, dampening the Texas boom. Facing a $27 billion shortfall—and being caught with just $9 billion in the bank, the state's so-called "rainy day" fund—the legislature and the governor in Austin simply slashed every facet of the budget. State agencies quickly dropped thousands of employees from the payroll—over 1,700 from the state prison systems alone.

The cuts then ripped through cities and school districts. Estimates from the state's school districts suggested that as many as 100,000 teachers could be laid off when it was all said and done. It was not exactly a prudent display of financial planning in Austin, especially given the foreknowledge of a national recession that had begun nearly two years earlier.

Of course, Texas escaped the worst of the Great Recession with fewer scars than most places. Texas was prone to the caprices of global forces, increasingly those that were manmade. As more than $2 trillion in mutual funds were wiped out, 4.5 million homes went into foreclosure and 6.8 million jobs were lost by late 2011, the effect could be felt even in my small town. A merchant in the town square confided that he couldn't take another year like the last two. A Mexican stonemason told me that a single project sustained his family through the winter. A realtor relayed that all over town, people who never took a mortgage they couldn't afford were looking to give up, sell out, and move on.

The alternative was grimly tallied and cataloged at the stately 102-year old, brick-and-limestone county courthouse over in San Marcos. Jack Hays, for whom this county was named, was a living legend for his exploits as a Texas Ranger, namely for fighting the Comanche. Now, people were losing their homes not to raiding parties but to banks. There were 157 properties up for auction in a single month. For 15 withering months there were 100 or more. George Roddy, whose company dutifully counted all of them: "This foreclosure storm is far from over."

The list carried the names of familiar ranches, springs, and creeks. Yet the tale of Hays County was, sadly, more emblematic than unique in the vast landscape that stretches westward beyond the Hudson and the Potomac. Up in Austin, $6.5 billion in real estate value was wiped out as if by a tornado. No less than the Federal Reserve Bank of Texas intoned: "Texas has been hit much harder by the 2008-09 recession than previous ones." One in five people struggled to feed themselves and one in five children lived in poverty. I took what I had and salted it away in a small Hill

Country bank. But I asked my oldest what she thought about possibly selling our little place high in the oaks and cedars over the Blanco. She looked at her little sister, reflected for a minute, and replied: "Dad, it's your house. You do with it what you like. But we've made a lot of good memories here."

I kept the house.

The lessons that emerged were simple.

Texas, where many a politician had denied climate change, was experiencing it harshly and before much of the United States because of its location in the semi-arid American Southwest. Global forces, too, shaped the Texas economy. Indeed, Texan's single greatest fear was not that the Texas economy would falter but that the American economy, linked to the global one, would fall into a second recession.

And both global systems—one made by God and the other made by man—could be made more volatile by the acts of man. As a result, when it comes to drought, the effects are going to be made worse because of manmade climate change—the increased heating and drying of the American Southwest. Said Dr. Malcolm Cleaveland, one of the tree ring researchers: "Texas is going to get hotter and drier."

Indeed, rainfall records showed consistently that rising temperatures in Texas and the rest of the Southwest were making it so hot that when rainfall came from the Pacific it was increasingly likely to evaporate before ever hitting the ground. These patterns could be seen in the rainfall and temperature data from the late 20th century and into this one. Climate change could no longer be reversed; that horse has long since left the barn. Perhaps the increase in carbon levels in the atmosphere could be slowed, and the effects, like the potential desertification of more of Texas, can be mitigated. But even that seemed daunting, according to a paper published in

Science in 2007: "Droughts will become the new climatology of the American Southwest within a time frame of years to decades."

★

On a warm September morning, in the hills west of Austin, a group of scientists led by Jay Banner, the University of Texas at Austin professor director of geosciences, descended into a cave near Hamilton Pool, a crystal clear swimming hole nestled partly in a giant cave.

Once underground, Banner and his team began to study not just whether the climate is changing—it most decidedly was—but precisely why. The rock formations, like the tree rings, contained the chemical clues to a question: Is Texas running out of water as the population soars and is it because of manmade climate change?

Along with the looming crisis over educating the emerging Hispanic majority, climate change in a semi-arid environment was one of two major public policy challenges simply left unaddressed by 20 years of arch-conservative politics and policies. This inattention, or worse, willful inability, to grapple with the important social, environmental, and economic issues of the 21st century indicate that something else was failing: Namely, conservative politics. It served its purpose in its first 20 years, putting the fiscal house in order, bringing a measure of accountability to a giant public school system, and building roads—though not enough and far too late.

But now, arch-conservative politicians and their policies ignored an existential threat even as it came sharply into relief as the population swelled. Today's 26 million Texans, concentrated in a fraction of its landmass, had only as much water—and quite possibly less—than Texas had in the 1950s when it held only a third as many people far more evenly distributed across the landscape.

Climate change was not a secret—certainly not to the ultra-rich Texas businessmen who wrote checks to the politicians. Some of Texas' most powerful businessmen knew that the Texas boom didn't run on oil. It ran on water. Water was crucial to the growth of Texas, indeed its survival, and so billionaires like T. Boone Pickens and Red McCombs were busy buying up water rights as fast as they could, envisioning a day when far away water reserves could be sold, at a fetching price, to the highest bidder. Already, the water was being pumped out of the ground faster than it fell from the sky, said Cleaveland, "Every year that you have a really bad drought, you're falling behind."

And the increasing water shortage was no surprise. In Austin, the governor and lawmakers alike had neglected for years to devise and fund a plan to conserve more groundwater—in a state that had nearly no natural lakes, and even as drought became steadily more common. Even before the awful nadir of the drought in 2011, drought had threatened the water supply of Dallas and wiped out crops and livestock to the tune of billions of dollars for years on end, as noted in author Alex Prud'homme's sweeping look at the future of freshwater, *The Ripple Effect*. Major drought had lingered from 2005 every single year through 2009. All Governor Perry did was declare an emergency and ask for financial help from the federal government.

In North Texas, the city of Wichita Falls turned to what had previously been an unthinkable source of drinkable water: Recycled waste water. There was the very real threat that the deserts of West Texas would begin to encroach eastward in the 21st century. When Prud'homme visited Austin on an absolutely sweltering Saturday at the end of October, 2011, I asked him if Texas was in danger of simply running out of water as supplies declined and demand soared with the population. "That's a very real concern," he said.

"I don't know the absolute answer to that question. But it seems to me that is a grave danger."

Down in the cave, Banner looked for additional proof of diminishing rainfall in the chemical composition of the limestone. But Banner has already published a peer-reviewed study on the subject, with a foreword written by none other than a Perry appointee. "Under essentially all climate model projections, Texas is susceptible to significant climate change in the future," said his study. "Most projections for the 21st century show that with increasing atmospheric greenhouse gas concentrations, there will be an increase in temperatures across Texas and a shift to a more arid average climate."

As the population is now set to double, the effects of drought—from prices of goods to restrictions on industrial, not just residential, water use—could be felt in the urbanized Texas Triangle, not just by the wheat farmers plowing under their crops on the Panhandle, the cattle ranchers watching their cows die, or the rice farmers near the coast. Some of them started digging wells as they could no longer rely on the Colorado River; the city of Austin was drinking most of that water before it ever slipped downstream.

10

★ ★ ★

ABDICATION OF POWER

So, Rick Perry prayed.

He asked Texans to pray. He called for seven days of prayer as the drought tightened its death grip in 2011: "I think it's time for us to just hand it to God, and say, 'God: You're going to have to fix this.'" He petitioned Washington for federal financial help, too. Then he made sure that prayers were not just private but conveniently public as he appeared and dutifully prayed before 30,000 evangelical Christians at Houston's Reliant Stadium—right before he announced his candidacy for president, of course. But those relentless blue skies, without a drop of rain in them, made one thing clear.

God wasn't listening to Rick Perry. Of course, the forces of nature are the work of God or fate or just mere coincidence, whichever you choose to believe. Drought in Texas and the rest of the Southwest was not merely an historic natural phenomenon, driven by events on the other side of the world and the equator; it was an entrenched prehistoric phenomenon. But man can make the impacts of natural events worse for himself. Increasing thirst, essentially, was a manmade event just like famine; crops may fail but rising populations, fuel prices, war and failure to plan—all the handiwork of man, not God—are what spawn the resultant human misery.

Perry seemed to have forgotten that his predecessor in the 1950s, Allan Shivers, a conservative Democratic governor took action. He rallied the Texas congressional delegation—as well as cattlemen across the Southwest and other Southwestern governors—to fight the Republican Eisenhower administration over its paltry drought relief during that historic drought. While Shivers was the leader in the fight, it was Senate Minority Leader Lyndon Johnson who put it best: The administration's offer "was just enough to liquidate the remaining assets and [buy] a coach-class ticket out of town."

At the time, Texas had responded in the manner befitting that era of massive engineering solutions to human problems by erecting a network of giant dams to store more freshwater, more reservoirs across a landscape that was home to no natural lakes, beyond a few ancient ones in East Texas. The public works projects of the Great Depression had strung the first dams across the big rivers, like the Colorado, mainly to halt flooding and bring electricity to the Hill Country for the first time. When the drought finally broke in 1957, after 10 merciless years, Texas proceeded to build more dams at nearly breakneck speed. Politicians practically threw money at engineers.

Between 1957 and 1960 alone crews built 69 more dams, including Longhorn Dam where the cattle used to ford the Colorado on the old Chisholm Trail. In 1960, the river backed up gracefully into what is now known as Lady Bird Lake in downtown Austin, joining the impoundments upriver that formed the Highland Lakes. Two lakes alone—Travis and Buchanan—held 2 million acre-feet of water, the drinking water of the whole region as well as water for farmers downstream, as much water as all of Southern California consumes annually now. But as the hot, dry years set in and the population exploded, the lakes held alarmingly less. Over 1.6 million acre-feet of water plummeted to less than 1 million in the first several months of 2011.

The drought was most certainly not Rick Perry's doing. He could no more make it rain water than create jobs, as it would turn out. But the blame for the failure to prepare for it after years of warnings from nature and data from scientists could be laid squarely on the doorstep of the governor's mansion, most certainly, along with a myopic Republican legislature better at pinching pennies and grandstanding than anticipating change and challenge. Public schools and universities busted at the seams. A new majority was emerging without a clear path to attaining and maintaining themselves in a productive middle class. Roads were being built but too few and too late.

It was becoming increasingly clear that 20 years of Republican rule was running its course in its ability to solve practical problems which, after all, is the very business of governing, if not politics. An iron-fisted Republican grip on power was now turning into a period of decadence in which politicians, like Perry, routinely brandished themes meant to stir up the arch-conservative base but that never became meaningful policy. Republican politics and policy was increasingly just for show, just a circus. But this showy inaction threatened real consequence. Failing to deal with climate change and social change could well forfeit the fruits of the promising boom years, all for short-term electoral gain. This all went unnoticed by the national political press, of course, which was more impressed with Perry's cowboy boots, his hair, his pistol, his rootin', tootin' dalliance with secession, and his nearly allergic aversion to the government actually doing anything.

So naturally, Rick Perry ran for president. It made perfect sense.

★

As he did, fire swept across Texas.

By the unofficial beginning of autumn—the opening of dove hunting season—some 4 million acres had burned to the ground, blackening an area larger than the state of Connecticut. Over 30,000 wild fires consumed woods, prairie, and 6,000 buildings including 3,000 homes. Firefighters from 43 states arrived to combat the waves of flames. Two were killed in Eastland and Moore Counties.

Then came Sunday, September 4, 2011.

I was driving to a dove lease, headed south on highway 360 in Austin, a beltway of sorts that encircles the city. In clear view and over 30 miles away, a giant mushroom cloud rose into the sky as tall as the skyscrapers of downtown Austin, looking for all the world like someone had set off a nuclear weapon. The town of Bastrop, a quant little town downstream on the banks of the Colorado was burning.

Its 7,000 inhabitants, their homes, and animals were caught in the hellish midst of the most destructive wildfire in the recorded history of Texas. Strong winds had toppled power lines in two places and then the wind fueled not just spreading fire, but conflagration. The tall loblolly pines, whose genes dated back to the Pleistocene era, burned like giant matches. Half of the state park was engulfed, adding more fuel as fire leapt from home to home and subdivision to subdivision. Two people quickly perished as the fire consumed 1,400 homes in the first few days. The ravenous fire refused to be broken, jumping the Colorado.

So big did it grow that its smoke plume that was photographed by a satellite in space, even as pumpers doused it from the ground and Chinook helicopters bombarded it from the air. A giant, converted DC-10, known as Tanker 910, swooped in, landing at Austin Bergstrom International Airport. It had risen to fame in California, fighting raging wildfires there. A single air drop from Tanker 910 would unleash 12,000 gallons of fire retardant on the flames in Bastrop. But the plane, instead, sat on the tarmac—Texas officials, it turned out, had the wrong tanks and pipes to load the giant tanker and so it never saw action in Bastrop.

Perry, of course, was in South Carolina announcing his plan for the country and his desire to live in the White House. Like the economy or the drought, the fire was certainly not his doing. But in a perfect demonstration of being penny wise and pound foolish his administration—that very spring—had cut the budget of the Texas Forest Service, the first line of defense against wildfire, to save $34 million. With the Bastrop Fire added to the growing toll, wildfires destroyed over $500 million in property and consumed over $1 billion in timber.

As search and rescue teams entered the charred remains of Bastrop, so much smoke billowed across Central Texas that the air quality in Austin was worse than anytime since the early 1990s. Perry arrived back in Texas two days into the fire, on September 6, 2011. Arriving in Bastrop, he appeared before the television cameras to meet with evacuees, look over maps, and tour the devastation by air. "To those who have been displaced by this fire, to those who have already lost homes—we're going to do everything we can," he said. "Whether it's putting them up, taking care of them, lovin' on them—there's a lot that Texans will do to take care of Texans over the next 72 hours."

Perry had his own plans for the next 72 hours or, more accurately, the next 24. The next day, he flew off to his next presidential campaign appearance—a debate in California.

★

It turned out that every time Perry left Texas, his presidential campaign fortunes dimmed because of stumbling public performances, a lack of preparation, and a very real policy gap with the Tea Party over immigration. To his credit, Perry had extended in-state tuition rates to college kids who were, through no design of their own, living in Texas as the result of parents who had arrived illegally. That was something the Tea Party could simply not forgive.

It also turned out, too, that every time Perry left the state he abdicated his executive authorities to the lieutenant governor, Republican David Dewhurst. A tall, patrician Houstonian who appeared impeccably dressed in public, Dewhurst looked for all the world like a smooth politician and he even had the resume, including a stint in the Central Intelligence Agency, to prove it. Worth an estimated $200 million, he bred Black Angus cattle for fun and invested money for a living. Every other year, when the legislature came to Austin, he presided over the Texas Senate, all for the gentlemanly annual salary of $7,500. Now, even though he was only number two to Perry, he was running the government, while eyeballing a seat in the U.S. Senate. In Austin's political circles a game of "What If?" broke out: Who would get Perry's job if Perry became president? Who would get Dewhurst's job if he became a senator?

But nobody was playing a different game of "What If?" What if governing Texas in a time of deepening trouble was a higher calling than, say, running for president? Up in New Jersey, for example, Republican Governor Chris Christie had promised to fulfill his term in office, despite the clamor among mainstream Republicans that he join the fray for the presidency. Christie was loud and clear: "I will not abandon my commitment to New Jersey."

On the stump, Perry liked to brag that 1 million jobs had been created under his tenure. They were actually created *during* his tenure. What he didn't talk about was how state government was actually adding to the unemployment rolls by slashing budgets for teachers and prison guards, while that unemployment edged dangerously close to the national average. Perry also touted the alleged success of his Texas Enterprise Fund, which frequently flew him to places like California and New York, where he would run radio advertisements and personally—and very publicly—woo businesses to relocate to the Lone Star State. The fund spent about $439 million and claimed to have created 59,000 jobs as he campaigned.

But in reality, the fund became an employment program for loyalists and a slush fund for allies. The net result in creating jobs for other people was just an exercise in crony capitalism, the exact opposite of bedrock conservative economics. The return on the taxpayer investment was abysmal. A subsequent audit, ordered by the legislature, compared official and actual results in 2013. The fund ultimately claimed to have created 66,000 jobs but had created not more than 47,000. One report said it was just 31,000 jobs.

As often as not, the fund was being used to keep corporations, like an aircraft company in Fort Worth, from leaving the state—not simply attracting companies to Texas. Too many of these companies, it turned out, were glad to take all of the taxpayer dollars without delivering all of the promised jobs. Despite the hefty travel tabs, the whole thing didn't amount to a hill of beans: .0047 percent, based on the official audit, of the over 10 million jobs in

Texas. The track record was so bad that Perry's anointed successor, Republican Attorney General Greg Abbott, would later suggest that he might abandon or disband the whole thing. One company that did get $1.8 million in taxpayer dollars was none other than CGI, the Canadian company that went on to greater fame, botching the rollout of Obamacare online in 2013. Despite his patronage of CGI, that was one scheme Perry refused to let Texas join, however, opting not to give Texas its own health care exchange.

Perry's governance was marked throughout by cronyism. He packed the regents of the state universities, namely the University of Texas at Austin, with political supporters. Some were political conservatives with deep suspicions about academic research versus the return on the tuition dollar, a valid enough concern. But they stressed metrics over academic independence. All promptly established themselves as self-proclaimed reformers. Some had radical notions about education. Perry himself attracted oil millionaire Jeff Sandefur as an informal education advisor; Sandefur entrenched himself in the graduate school of business at the University of Texas at Austin before departing in a public dustup over his choices for faculty. With his $500 million oil fortune, he took a dim view of professional academics. Later one, one regent was found trying to engineer the ouster of legendary football coach Mack Brown and the hiring of Alabama's nearly unbeatable Nick Saban, all without the university's consent. The same man and an ally of Sandefur's, Wallace Hall, was selected by a legislative committee for impeachment for engaging in what amounted to a witch hunt against Bill Powers—the university's president.

And when his tenure wasn't riven by cronyism, it was marked by delay. The state government had, in fact, drafted a plan to store more water across the state but it was essentially left in a desk drawer back in Austin. The legislature still had to approve it and then it needed to go on the ballot for voters to approve it because it was so massive it would require billions of dollars in bond financing as well as an amendment to the Texas Constitution. So that would just have to wait.

Perry's presidential campaign straggled on into early 2012, strangely resembling a game described by legendary Houston Oilers coach Bum Phillips: "The harder we played, the behinder we got." On January 19, 2012, 159 days into his quest for the White House, Perry mercifully withdrew from the race. His approval rating plummeted in Texas, even among conservatives. Texans hate losers, after all. *Texas Monthly* swiftly awarded its cover and its Bum Steer of the Year award to none other than Perry. The staff later claimed it had reached the decision in just 53 seconds—the time it took Perry not to recall that pesky third federal agency he would have closed had he made it to Washington.

★

In 2013, Perry was back in the governor's mansion in downtown Austin. The Greek Revival home, first built in 1855, was itself recently renovated after a mysterious fire and an extensive $10 million effort to rehabilitate it. Now, Perry set about rehabilitating his own reputation as he wound down his term as the longest-serving governor in Texas history. He had to decide, too, if he would run for yet another term in the mansion, the White House, or simply retire to the greener pastures of private life.

Across the street, though, the circus came to town: the 83rd Texas Legislature convened on January 8, 2013. Actually, as it got down to the business in earnest—after what seemed like weeks of ceremonies, lunches, glad-handing and just general milling around—it was less of a circus, it turned out, than a goat rope. (For the uninitiated, to quote Merriam-Webster: "A situation that is messy or disorganized, as in a goat roping or a goat rodeo" which is generally just performed for one thing: laughs.)

Exactly 22 days after the Newtown massacre left 27 defenseless people dead, most of them first graders, and a nation stunned in horror, the men and women of the 83rd Legislature decided that the public's most pressing business was this: More guns. More guns, particularly in schools. Proposals flooded the legislature. Guns for teachers and staff members. Gun classes in high school. Guns for college kids. Guns galore.

It got a lot of attention, for sure, even though it was a purely symbolic display for the arch-conservative Republican base and the party's benefactors at the National Rifle Association. It was strangely reminiscent of the flood of immigration legislation—and immigrant-bashing—aimed at tightening an already militarized border back during the 2011 session, it seemed to me. Along with talk of secession it was a good backdrop for Perry's run for president but the legislature passed hardly any meaningful legislation then, according to a Rice University study. Now, guns made for great political theater. So, this is what became of conservative Republican governance in Texas: Theater and symbols with nary a real outcome, let alone a practical solution to real problems and challenges. Forget droughts, schools, economic growth, the middle class, and a new Hispanic majority. Guns were the answer, whatever the question might be.

Perry got in on the action, advocating that school administrators and teachers be allowed to carry licensed, concealed weapons—at school. Not to be outdone, Dewhurst wanted special, state-funded weapons and tactics training for school employees; I couldn't help but imagine pudgy English teachers fast-roping from helicopters, armed to the teeth. State Rep. Jason Villalba, a Dallas Republican, proposed that schools just appoint armed employees as marshals.

Republican Rep. Debbie Riddle from Tomball proposed that college kids carry concealed weapons on campus—even as another shooting rampage wounded three people at Lone Star College nearby.

Texas law, after all, inconveniently prohibited guns in schools. A provision of the law allowed individual school boards to opt to allow selected employees with permits to carry concealed weapons on campus. This was an exception intended for small, rural districts that couldn't afford their own police forces, like the big city school systems. And precisely three, small rural districts—out of 1200 across the state—had quietly put the practice into place. The state teachers' association opposed more widespread arming of its ranks. Fifty-six percent of Texans opposed giving teachers guns; just 31 percent said it sounded like a good idea. A police chief pointed out the obvious: Even trained officers don't always wield deadly force with the precision of a scalpel.

But the line of politicians in Austin proposing more guns was growing longer and ever more distinguished. And the press, unfortunately, swallowed the bait—hook, line and sinker. It seemed that none of them could remember their own, ancient legislative history—back to say, 2008. That was when the legislature received the results of an investigation it had ordered into the criminal backgrounds of people working in the public school system. Over 1,000 people working in the Texas public schools had a rap sheet, ranging from serious complaints to criminal—even violent felony—convictions. One in six school districts simply had no idea if their employees had had a brush with the law. In the previous five years, more than 1,300 teachers—out of over 300,000 admittedly—lost or surrendered their teaching licenses for offenses that included homicide, assault, and sexual assault. "If a license is revoked or surrendered," said DeEtta Culbertson of the Texas Education Agency, "then they've committed a pretty senior offense." And there were hundreds of investigations still pending.

A lot of this was just common sense. Most teachers are fine people but there are a few rotten apples in every barrel. And I like guns; I have four of them. But even though Texans had 150,000 permits for concealed weapons, public opinion displayed a more nuanced view toward guns than a long, rural tradition would suggest. Instead, opinions reflected the reality of living in close quarters to other people in big cities and bustling suburbs. In the wake of the horror at Newtown, Texans actually favored a ban on assault weapons by a margin of 49 to 41 percent, a survey that simply went overlooked in a one-sided debate.

The line between reality and arch-conservative fantasy blurred. Attorney General Greg Abbott, the state's top lawyer, was widely known to be interested in replacing Perry in that posh governor's mansion and so he produced a commercial that ran on websites targeting people in Manhattan and Albany, inviting New Yorkers with guns to move to Texas. It got the attention it was designed to get, mainly from the news media, though it wasn't intended for actual Texans and it never aired anywhere other than the Internet. And left out of the discussion were troublesome items like facts and statistics, which painted a mixed portrait of gun laws. With almost 3 gun murders per 100,000 residents, Texas had a lower murder rate by firearm than New York, which had strict gun control laws. But the murder rate was inexplicably higher than California's. Largely unremarked upon was the simple and common-sense fact that most gun murders were the result of day-to-violence, not high-profile rampages and massacres.

The notion of arming teachers, frankly, was baffling—unless it was seen for what it was, pandering to the Republican base. Schools seemed like the last place to keep an armory. School teachers seemed like the last people qualified to defend dozens or hundreds of innocent children. Why wouldn't the legislature simply spend money on more police, so they could park a trained, armed officer and his or her cruiser in front of every single school? It seemed, to me, expensive but obvious—if this was really a public policy priority.

But it wasn't. Instead, the legislature got around to cutting taxes on businesses, ordering up more roads and highways—without a clear plan for paying for them—and finally passing that plan to conserve more water, though all the dam construction smacked of being very mid-20th century and funding all of it was a deed left undone, too. Not much was to be done, either, about schools and universities but abortion restrictions did rise famously to the top of the agenda as the spring turned to summer.

And what about all those guns? That was, indeed, all just for show. At the last minute, the legislature finally killed the last gun measure: A plan to automatically let elected state politicians, including legislators, carry concealed weapons. Clearly the lack of loaded weapons among state politicians was a pressing public policy problem. Strangely, the measure passed the House but the Senate changed it to allow members of Congress to pack weapons, too. The more the merrier, after all. But the House gave that the thumbs-down. That just went too far.

Like any self-respecting goat regarding a rope, the politicians were having none of that nonsense.

11

★ ★ ★

PINK, PURPLE, AND BLUE

A t precisely 10 minutes to midnight on Tuesday, June 26, 2013, tempers in the Texas Capitol building finally boiled over.

On the floor of the Senate, Democratic Sen. Kirk Watson of Austin stopped the debate to challenge the latest ruling from the tall, patrician Dewhurst, who presided. Another Democrat, a little known senator from Fort Worth, Wendy Davis was staging a marathon filibuster to stop new restrictions on abortion that would limit the number of clinics providing the procedure to just six, in a state the size of France. The proposal was one of several making their way toward law in a handful of states and, like guns, abortion was a favorite cause that rallied the most conservative, in this case evangelical, part of the Republican electoral base.

In pink sneakers, having talked and debated for 12 hours and unable, under the rules to sit, lean, go to the bathroom, or even sip water, a visibly fatigued Davis rocked back and forth in a pair of pink running shoes. But the gallery—filled with supporters of abortion rights—erupted in shouts and screams that nearly drowned out everything else, including the politicians down on the floor. The minutes ticked by and paralysis set upon the state Senate. The minute hand on the clock marched toward midnight and then past it. Clearly seeing the clock, Dewhurst tried to ram the bill through nonetheless. Slamming the gavel down, he took the roll and the bill was passed with a vote along party lines, but the constitutionally-mandated deadline of midnight had come and gone. The legislature's official website correctly showed the vote taking place after midnight. Then it was altered to show the vote taking place earlier.

Looks of disbelief and confusion danced across the faces of the politicians and the police cleared the gallery. But it was too late to just shoehorn the bill on to Perry's desk, across the street, for signature. Not only had there been onlookers in the gallery and reporters watching—now tweeting one another about what they had just seen—but hundreds of thousands of Americans had tuned in to watch the live video on the Internet. Screenshots passed back and forth on Twitter showing the before and after pictures of the altered website of the Texas Legislative Office.

Nearly three hours later, protesters still gathered outside. Would Dewhurst reverse himself? Would the bill still pass despite these oratorical heroics? Davis' filibuster was symbolic not just of the cultural divide abortion had come to symbolize, but of the entire Democratic party tasting something that they had not known in Texas for almost 20 years: Victory.

Suddenly, staunchly Republican women from leafy suburbs began to quietly grouse that the politicians, this time, had really gone too far in imposing these draconian restrictions. By imposing careful definitions of standards that clinics must meet—doctors with privileges at nearby hospitals and requirements of only the largest and most sophisticated centers for surgery—they had cleverly gotten around the messy business of Roe v. Wade, which had settled abortion as a constitutional matter decades earlier. Some of these Republican women plotted to throw fundraisers for Davis who, of course, would become a political superstar and a viable, well-funded candidate for governor.

Whether she was a good candidate or would be able to win was a matter left to the voters who wouldn't go to the polls until November 2014. What was unclear was whether Texas Democrats could get their act together after years of being used to losing. It certainly wasn't clear on that summer night if Democrats even had any answers, let alone good ones, to the pressing issues of change and challenge. But it was increasingly clear that Republicans were stuck playing an increasingly defensive game, not just fumbling strategy and tactics in the legislature; Dewhurst had slipped out for an expensive dinner as the whole filibuster started to get out of hand for the Republicans and then came back, literally too late.

Abbott, the presumptive nominee, was stuck parroting a lot of the ideological lines that were just for show and just for an increasingly, precariously, narrow Republican base. Indeed, he was the point man for trying to limit voting rights—disproportionately denying the vote to Hispanics, African Americans, and others. His role in doing so had landed him in a pitched battle with the Department of Justice and it put him on a collision course with that new Texas majority, Hispanics.

All these things had yet to resolve themselves as the warm night melted with sunrise, into another hot, summer day. But the tectonic plates of sweeping economic and social change had built up enough pressure that when daylight came it was clear. The hard earth of Texas politics had finally cracked, split like the summer soil itself: Wide open.

★

A lot of people have forgotten, but in one of those unusual ironies of history, like Lyndon Johnson being the father of civil rights law, a Texas woman is the reason for today's constitutionally protected reproductive rights and for the divisive controversy that continues to surround them.

It was a Texas woman, Norma McCorvey, known by the legal pseudonym of Jane Roe, who was the plaintiff against Dallas County Attorney Henry Wade in Roe v. Wade, decided by the Supreme Court in 1973. McCorvey would later become an anti-abortion activist and nearly 40 years later, the state's leading Republican politicians kept abortion at the top of the agenda. In 2011, they foreshadowed the fight to come by slashing state funding of family planning services and proposing invasive ultrasound procedures for those women who did get pregnant and considered terminating the pregnancy. "Of course it's a war on birth control, abortion, everything," Republican Rep. Wayne Christian said to the Texas Tribune. "That's what family planning is supposed to be about."

The regular session over, Perry called the legislators back for a special session, largely to pass the abortion restrictions which had percolated in the unruly House all year. Pro-choice Democrats comprised over a third of the Senate which, by tradition, gave them enough votes to even keep the measure from coming to the floor in that chamber. When the special session began, the Republicans scrapped the tradition. The Democrats had just one tool in the tool box—a traditional, no-holds barred filibuster that would prevent a vote. Davis was selected to conduct it with one specific goal in mind, run out the clock until midnight when the session would expire.

The Texas Tribune, alone among news organizations, had secured a live video feed of the legislature to its website under a brand new contract. Cameras and microphones furnished by the state recorded floor votes and selected committee hearings and absolutely nobody had watched it; it was usually informative and invariably lethally dull. It had been on the Tribune's site and You-Tube for months, largely unknown. That is, until Davis's filibuster stretched from the afternoon into the evening. The *Washington Post* posted a link to the video on its site.

The drama of the moment and the emotional power of the abortion topic—whatever side of the divide one occupies—drew people to the video feed in the night like moths to a flame. As day turned into night and night wore on, the usual trickle of viewers swelled into a river of 54,000 people watching. "Amazing," tweeted Evan Smith, the Tribune's CEO and editor-in-chief. Then there were 100,000 viewers—just on the Tribune site. Then the river became a torrent of about 200,000 viewers to the Tribune site alone. The video captured the way that politics could descend into silly pettiness. Republicans objected to Davis getting help putting on a back brace, and to her discussion of Roe v. Wade and a Texas law on sonograms as not germane to the bill at hand.

With three such objections reliably sustained by Dewhurst, she was in danger of being cut off, and Democrats turned to other strategies to run out the clock. More news outlets posted a link to the video stream and still more people watched. Minute-by-minute developments were now outstripping the ability of reporters to keep up in their online reports. The *Austin American-Statesman* flirted with its very own "Dewey Beats Truman" moment: Even as its reporters kept up with events on a liveblog, at 12:16 A.M. the headline on the paper's homepage still declared, "Challenge upheld; Davis' filibuster all but over."

By that point, midnight had passed and Twitter lit up even more as journalists, advocates, and citizens tried to suss out what had actually happened when Dewhurst incorrectly—or rather, wrongly—declared the bill approved along strict partisan lines and the session over. "Have seen nothing like this in #texaslege in 22 years. Not even close. Waiting for someone to yell 'Attica,'" tweeted Smith. "If Dewhurst can assert that it passed, I can assert that it didn't. I believe I was closer to the dais at the time," tweeted *Texas Monthly*'s Erica Grieder. One minute later, Grieder again: "From what I saw on the Senate floor, the last roll call vote was a motion to have a vote on #SB5, ie end discussion, not a vote on the bill". Around the same time, a pair of images began circulating on Twitter—screenshots from the Texas Legislature Online site showing a vote on the bill recorded on Wednesday and then, nine minutes later, altered to show the vote on Tuesday, before midnight. "TLO sheet has been edited!" Smith tweeted. The Tribune's Ross Ramsey had the screenshots, too, and passed them around on Twitter like favors. Soon, a tweet from the main Tribune account: "The Senate's revisionists are very fast. Nine minutes earlier, these showed the record votes on 6/26" (1,366 retweets).

Inside the Senate, the jig was just about up. "TexasSens say timestamp issue proved the end of #SB5," tweeted the *Statesman*'s Mike Ward. "No way around it." If the bill was passed after midnight, it would certainly be subject to a lawsuit as unconstitutional. Republican consultant Matt Mackowiak posted on Twitter: "Source inside TX Senate caucus tells me #SB5 will be ruled to have been voted late." Shortly after 2 A.M., the *Houston Chronicle*'s Peggy Fikac tweeted: "Re report that SB5 didn't pass: Sen West said, 'you're on the right road.'" Grieder, who had earlier posted a photo of printouts showing the altered time record, tweeted reports from the floor: "Vote happened at 12:03." To be even more precise, the official time stamp read 12:03:14 A.M., Ramsey would tell me the next day, after everyone finally got some sleep.

A little after 3:00 A.M. on what was now the 27th, senators filed back into the chamber, for all the world to see again. Looking more mortician than patrician now, Dewhurst gravely gaveled them back to order and announced that the abortion bill had, in fact, not passed before the midnight deadline. He turned to leave the dais, but then stooped back to the microphone one more time and grinned: "It's been fun but see ya soon."

He may have been smiling but he wasn't kidding. Dewhurst took a pummeling from conservatives the next day for botching the job. Indeed it was almost unthinkable that arch-conservative Republicans had actually lost a high-profile fight to a Democratic minority—and on the issue of abortion. But the Republicans devoted still more energy into turning this legislation into law, even though it was invariably headed for court and a constitutional challenge. Other matters might go unresolved, apparently, but not the business of grandstanding. Perry called the tired politicians back into a second special session—just to pass the abortion restrictions. But by then, the cleverest headline of the next day was already emblazoned across the *Houston Chronicle*: "About Last Night: How the Abortion Bill Failed."

★

But there was more afoot than just abortion politics in Texas.

The Democrats, as they had for nearly 20 years, had written off their chances of putting Texas in the win column in the 2012 presidential election. But on a sweltering July day during that election, Air Force One swooped out of the heavy clouds, landing first in San Antonio and then in Austin. President Barack Obama had arrived to pick up millions of dollars in campaign donations from rich Texas Democrats, just as national Democrats have shamelessly done for years—without bothering to come back to campaign.

Perhaps out of guilt or pressure, Obama let a cat out of the bag—almost unnoticed—for his rich friends. "You're not considered one of the battleground states," he said, "although that's going to be changing soon." Months after the fact, it would be revealed by *Politico* in Washington that the Obama team had what was, until then, a top-secret initiative to get Texas back into the Democratic column. "People are now looking at Texas and saying: 'That's where we need to make our next investment. That's where the next opportunity lies,'" one Democratic state senator told Politico. There was even optimistic chatter of Hillary Clinton's single handedly capturing the state's 32 electoral votes in 2016 if she was to run for president.

The broader forces were certainly indicating the potential for political realignment, just as it had happened in the 1990s—but this time moving power in the opposite direction, away from Republicans toward Democrats. Even Matthew Dowd had speculated that realignment could take place around 2015. "Will the growth of other populations, especially Hispanic and Latino populations [sic], begin to move Texas back to a swing state? It may," he had said years earlier in his PBS interview. "I think it will, but it's probably going to take six to 10 years where Texas then becomes a state [which] becomes much more in play for the Democrats." By 2014 some leading Republican consultants were starting to jump up and down, pointing at the maps of suburban Texas. More than demographics—the emerging Hispanic majority—was shifting. Population growth had turned into population density in the Texas Triangle. The very suburbs that had swung Texas Republican because of Anglo migrants from the Rustbelt were now turning into demographic polyglots.

But it would take more than money, fantastical thinking or a Clinton. Turning Texas immediately Democratic blue was unlikely, too. Political realignments are processes that take years, not events that happen overnight. Contested between the two major parties, a purple swing state seemed a more likely possibility. But the Democrats certainly had their work cut out for them and in declaring her bid for the governorship, Davis slung herself into a pretty big saddle. If she succeeded, she would be a hero to Democrats; if she failed, she would be a scapegoat for her failings as a candidate when there was lots of work for Democrats to do—from creating a political infrastructure in what had been a one-party state to fashioning a vision for Hispanic voters that transcended that reliable perennial, immigration reform. Hispanics weren't just immigrants, after all. They were people with clear aspirations, like making a living, owning a home, getting into the middle class—and getting their children into college.

The realignment of Texas into the Republican column perfectly illustrated the lengthy and sometimes tedious process of political change. Texas had been reliably Democratic for more than a century, from Reconstruction through the Lyndon B. Johnson years. Johnson ably—albeit cynically and sometimes illegally—harnessed the Hispanic vote to keep his more reactionary opponents off balance in primaries. But the liberal 1960s drove white conservatives into what was once a minuscule Republican Party. John Tower became the first Republican senator since Reconstruction in 1962. Republican Bill Clements was elected governor twice in the 1970s and 1980s, though not successively. George H. W. Bush won the presidency. And then there came the son, George W. Bush.

Much has been said and written about Ann Richards who was the last Democratic governor of Texas, 20 years ago, when the younger Bush appeared on the scene. She was lionized by

Democrats then and since her death, after a brave and difficult battle with cancer ending in 2006, she has passed into a halcyon of Democratic heroes, where the glare of the halos is so bright it's kind of hard to see the historical figures. Her daughter, Cecile, remains politically prominent in her own right and was at Davis's side that night of the famous filibuster.

All that said, a brief glance in the rearview mirror is instructive about Texas politics two decades after the fact. Like Davis, Richards overnight became a national Democratic darling because of a daring public performance. She opened her keynote address, as the state treasurer at the time, at nothing less than the 1988 Democratic National Convention in Atlanta with: "My name is Ann Richards. And I'm pro-choice. And I vote." She later, of course, delivered that devastating line about George H. W. Bush, who was seeking to ascend from the vice presidency to the presidency in Washington: "Poor George. He can't help it. He was born with a silver foot in his mouth."

Because she was a woman—like Davis more recently—she was treated to the worst misogynistic rumors, slurs, and insults. The primary race was a renewed blood feud between Texas progressives and the aristocratic conservative Democrats who had finally won control of the party. One of her Democratic rivals, Jim Maddox, accused her of being a cocaine addict—despite her painfully honest public confession to having been addicted to alcohol, and her years of sobriety.

Well into her general election battle against the Republican millionaire cowboy nominee, Clayton Williams, she was 17 points down, trying to forge an unlikely coalition of remaining Democrats, women, African Americans, and Hispanics into what she termed the New Texas. The smart money of the political insiders said there was no way she could win. Williams did what he could to help unintentionally, of course, by showcasing a bad case of misogyny, comparing rape to bad weather: "If it's inevitable, just relax and enjoy it." He compounded the matter by refusing to release his income taxes, then blurting out that well, there had been that one year, 1986, in which he'd paid no taxes, refusing to shake Richards' hand in front of television cameras, and later went before them without a single clue as to what the only constitutional amendment on the ballot was about, even though he had already voted.

Once in office, Richards spoke like a populist but governed as a more cautious pragmatist. She insisted on a new ethics law since legislators had made routine a practice of working for—and just generally taking money from—the industries they regulated. Chief among these was the insurance industry; she summarily fired the regulators for failing to stop collusion and price-fixing. And as Texas fought the vestiges of the crime wave that had engulfed the country in the 1970s and 1980s, she instituted mandatory drug treatment for prisoners with addiction before they could be released. In 1994, George W. Bush's campaign resorted to more smears because she was a woman, unofficially whispering—particularly to reporters and rural Texans—that there just might be a lot of lesbians on Richards' staff, given that a lot of them were women, after all. Reporters from the era pin it, to this day, on Karl Rove. Publicly, Bush's campaign preyed upon white voter's fear of crime, even though crime in Texas was actually falling, as it was nationally. Publicly, Richards made missteps in the struggle to win, unnecessarily belittling Bush as a "jerk," "shrub," and "that young Bush boy." But she also opposed one of the early proposals to allow concealed guns, at the urging of the police. And she was pummeled for it by the gun lobby and the Bush campaign.

But the biggest single factor was that the big city suburbs in Dallas, Houston, San Antonio, and even outside Austin had finished realigning squarely into the Republican column. That was almost a quarter of a century ago. And nothing, not even in Texas, lasts forever. Now, the big cities that voted Republican back then are voting Democratic, too. And the suburbs are realigning again—but this time in the opposite direction.

The Richards' story remains instructive two decades later not just because of the political realignments happening in the suburbs but also because the same sexism and disparagement surfaced again in the contest for the governorship, this time between Davis and Abbott. But this time, Davis, the Democrat, fought back. And Abbott, the Republican, was not himself a ham-handed sexist. He left that to Ted Nugent.

It was not so much a testament to some uniquely reactionary streak in Texas, *per se*, but a broader lesson about how the highest reaches of American politics was still a white, male game—no matter the makeup of the electorate. And that the club can go to extraordinary lengths to protect its power. Much was made, after 2012, of the 20 women in the U.S. Senate—even though women make up fully half of the American population.

Today, four sitting governors are divorced—in Colorado, Illinois, New York and Vermont—and there has been no outcry over the end of those marriages or the fates of those children. Then again, they are all men. Some 28 states, including Texas, do not have a woman governor or U.S. senator right now. And there was the real rub. Davis was vying to join a club of power politicians that was nearly universally male. This was not just a Texas phenomenon. It was an American one: Out of the 150 people occupying a major statewide office in 2014 in the United States—a governorship or a seat in the U.S. Senate—only 26, or 17 percent, were women, according to the *Almanac of American Politics*. Only one is currently divorced. If she wins, Davis would make that two.

The facts about the Davis's divorce, after the dust settled, were a pretty common tale: The final decree in 2005 provided for joint conservatorship of the one remaining minor, a 17-year old daughter with just a few months left at home as the other daughter was off at college. One parent, Wendy, moved out and agreed to pay child support while the other, Jeff, stayed in the 4,300 square-foot home. Regardless of when he wrote that last check for her Harvard Law degree, a full 10 years had gone by from her law school graduation until the couple split.

Nobody seemed to mind the male governors who were divorced. But Davis, divorced almost 15 years ago, was a different matter. So, Davis came in for her ritual whipping in early 2014. Conservative commentator Eric Erickson referred to her as "Abortion Barbie." The Sunday magazine of the *New York Times* published a long and interesting story about Davis—including how she seemed to fudge a few details in her early personal life, including the details of her divorce, while spinning the new public persona—but did so under the 1970s retro headline: "Can Wendy Davis Have It All?" I half expected to see a Kool's cigarette advertisement, replete with a beehive hairdo and a fresh black eye opposite a story on the whole new women's liberation movement. The *Dallas Morning News* pulled at the same thread of personal life and incorrectly characterized the custody arrangement that followed the divorce. KLBJ radio in Austin crackled with talk jocks and callers calling her everything from a home wrecker to just short of a whore. Actually, one woman caller did call her that.

About this time, I was walking down Sandra Muradia Drive in downtown Austin. A black SUV pulled up next to the sidewalk with official state senator license plates. Davis suddenly alighted, walking right in front of me. Dressed in a dark suit and heels she made a beeline for the door. She was awfully petite for a culture used to towering politicians. She was also an inexperienced candidate and it showed. What exactly she would do as governor was fuzzy. She fumbled badly in over-polishing her resume with regards to personality politics. She botched her response after, too, going into a near press blackout. And there was a lot of grousing about the campaign staff. But most of this was just tactics, the blocking and tackling of a political campaign. The election was a half-year away still.

Finally, Ted Nugent expounded on what a woman—20 full years after Ann Richards last ran for office—could expect for her audacious ambition, no different, of course, than all those men. Already, Nugent had called President Obama, who is of mixed race, "a mongrel"—a phrase not in favor since the Nazis ran Germany—and he had labeled women politicians "fat pigs." At a campaign stop in Denton, at Guapo's restaurant on February 18, 2014 Abbott unveiled the old rocker as his new trail partner as a result of his devotion to the 2nd Amendment. Together, Abbot and Nugent, the man best known for "Wango Tango," released almost a quarter of a century ago, would somehow "keep Texas free [and] keep Texas Texas." Whatever that meant.

Unspoken, of course, was the awkward fact that the cowboy hat-wearing ultra-Texan was really another one of those Rustbelt refugees from decades ago, namely from Detroit. His appearance was a prime example of a leading politician reaching into the grab bag of conservative symbolism as opposed to getting serious about the issues of contemporary Texas. But there was a rattle snake in this grab bag.

The Davis campaign had dug up Nugent's choicest nuggets and seeded them to the assembled reporters with a heavy helping of equally heavy-handed outrage. Among the nuggets was this one: Nugent had told MTV years ago that he had slept with underage girls on the concert circuit. This was sticky now, as Abbott had earned some of his political stripes by chasing child predators. Abbott came face to face with his own Clayton Williams moment, this time via a surrogate meant to bolster his credentials with the God, guns, and gays crowd. The reporters opened fire in the Mexican restaurant and started peppering Abbott with questions. The last anybody saw of him at Guapo's was his backside, as he headed out the door.

12

★ ★ ★

THE ANOINTED ONE

There remained a powerful and self-reinforcing conventional wisdom in Texas politics: Like the land itself, it just can't change.

Until, of course, it does. All the political professionals pooh-poohed the rise of the Republican Party as a practical impossibility for years—until there was a Republican governor in Austin. Now, a quarter of a century later, the conventional wisdom was precisely the same. It just ran in the opposite direction. Any seasoned political operative or journalist would gladly bend his elbow and your ear to tell you that Democrats couldn't win in Texas for years, if not decades, to come. And they should know: They just heard it from another seasoned political pro so it must be true.

Bringing up the subject of demographic change—namely the emerging Mexican and Mexican American majority—in Texas elicited the most interesting responses. They usually began with the words, "Yes, but . . ." Yes, there are some 10 million Hispanics but it wouldn't alter the political picture until around 2020; the date keeps slipping from Dowd's prediction of about 2015. Yes, Hispanics voted primarily Democratic but George W. Bush and Perry comfortably got 40 percent of the Hispanic vote; conveniently forgotten was that those figures were increasingly ancient history. Senator Ted Cruz barely netted any Hispanic voters at all in 2012, quietly denting this supposition. Rick Perry did used to get half the vote in South Texas—but there were more Hispanics in Harris County now than all of South Texas. Yes, but Hispanics haven't really turned out to vote—except for the half of the Hispanic voters that actually did cast a vote in 2012.

And low voter turnout was hardly confined to Hispanics. Texas actually has had one of the lowest levels of civic engagement in the nation, regardless of ethnicity, but it was still true that Hispanics tend to participate in civic institutions less, according to University of Texas professor Regina Lawrence. "If I just arrived here and I wanted to get plugged into the state," she said, "I wouldn't know how."

But here was my favorite: Yes, but there was no way Texas would turn Democratic soon. That was a very clever changing of the subject, of course, because that's not how political realignment has ever worked. First a place becomes politically competitive between the two major parties. Never does a state simply and permanently move from one column to the next. The progression is never from suddenly red to blue or vice versa. The first stop is always the color purple. The Republican realignment began in the 1960s with Republican John Tower's election to the Senate and seesaw battles between Republicans and Democrats over the governorship in the 1970s and 1980s, when Republican Bill Clements was elected twice. The election of Ann Richards to the governorship in 1990 was a rearguard action by the Democrats, or perhaps a last stand. Since then, Democrats have had themselves to blame, too, with years of losing and buying into the "yes, but" arguments. "If we start treating this as a purple state," said Democratic consultant Matt Glazer, "we would be one that much sooner."

In fact, the most recent election in 2012 held interesting and tantalizing clues, suggesting change was in the air. President Obama had lost Texas as predicted because he still lost most of those crucial suburbs. Obama swept all the big cities—Houston, Dallas, San Antonio, and Austin—and the smaller ones; unthinkable only a decade or so ago. And things were shifting in those suburbs, too, however subtly. In 2000, Vice President Al Gore lost Harris County by 11 percent and over 100,000 votes. He lost neighboring Fort Bend, also in the Houston area, by over 20 points. A dozen years later, Obama won a squeaker in Harris County and lost Fort Bend by less than 7 points. The gap was closing quietly but firmly and quickly.

There was more at work than demographics, though. Media mattered. Karl Rove, who rode that earlier demographic wave of suburban change in Texas, poured $300 million of other people's money into television advertising in 2012, flatly predicting that Republican nominee Mitt Romney would occupy the White House. Rove overlooked another change: The collision of demographic change and media consumption. These people didn't watch the evening news or even CNN. Hispanics, Asians, women, and young people were early and heavy adopters of smart phones instead. So, the Obama campaign outmuscled the Romney campaign in social media and collected mobile numbers so assiduously that it could text voters three times on election day and even remind them to stay in line to vote, even as Voting Day turned to evening and the lines grew frustratingly long.

At 10:25 P.M. on election night, November 6, 2012, Rove argued on the air of Fox News that the network's Decision Desk of pollsters should not be forecasting—as it was doing—that Ohio favored Obama. "If it's going to happen let the rest of the votes come in," Rove insisted, arguing with Megyn Kelly on air. Refer-ring to the political scientists she objected: "They know the sci-ence." The polls showed not only young people, Hispanics, Asians, and women voting—but turning out in larger numbers than Rove believed possible. The boy genius minted in Texas politics, now the guru of conservative politics, could not possibly be wrong. Politics couldn't change. Could it?

★

He was the chosen one. The front-runner. The presumptive nom-inee and even the likely next governor of the second most populous state in the country. Republican Attorney General Greg Abbott.

To political insiders and reporters in Texas, Abbott's story—after 10 years as the top lawyer for Texas—felt well-worn, like a comfortable old cowboy boot. He was the politician with a literal spine of steel, the result of an accident and remaining paraplegia. After serving on the Texas Supreme Court, he became the attorney general who had proudly made a living out of suing the Obama administration. He even had an equally well-worn line that he and the reporters apparently loved to recycle, again and again.

"I go into the office in the morning," he said. "I sue Barack Obama, and then I go home."

As far as bumper sticker politics went, it was a pretty good line. To the gaggle of insiders, the election—still a year away—seemed practically a foregone conclusion. A column in the *Austin American Statesman* declared: "No one has the cachet—or cash—to beat Abbott." Another in the same newspaper said: "Right now it looks like the best way to avoid having Republican Abbott as your next governor will be to move out of state." *Texas Monthly* placed a bold image of Abbott on its cover, shotgun slung over one shoulder as he sat in his wheelchair with the words: "The Gov." An asterisk led to a tiny overline saying, "Barring an Unlikely Occurrence." The conventional wisdom was affirmed as far away as the Washington press corps. A young writer at the *New Republic*—for whom I've worked—declared the race over: "A week after Perry withdrew his name from the race, it's already more or less obvious who his successor will be: Greg Abbott." The very day that Abbott announced in the merciless heat of San Antonio that he was running to succeed Rick Perry, *Texas Monthly* concluded that only two matters were unresolved: "Will a credible Democrat challenge Abbott now that the party appears to have reenergized itself around Fort Worth state senator Wendy Davis? And, given that a Democrat hasn't won statewide office since 1994, does it really matter?" Well, that settled that. That whole pesky business of voting could now be carefully laid aside even though the election was, then, 13 months away.

Some of the factors upon which these pronouncements were based were matters of tactics that would be easily erased and then changed yet again. Abbott's $20 million campaign fund, reportedly relying on many of Perry's boosters, was plenty of money but Davis quickly matched it with big money from both inside and outside Texas. The polls gave Abbott a big early advantage, but they narrowed, and widened, and narrowed slightly again by the middle of 2014.

But the big hitch was this: Nobody actually knew Greg Abbott. All those years being a down-ballot justice and lawyer, even in a statewide office, hadn't really left a huge impression on Texans, one way or another. One poll in 2013 showed that 43 percent of voters just were not sure—if they even had an opinion of him, actually, favorable or unfavorable. Another poll of by the University of Texas and the Texas Tribune found that 45 percent of Republicans definitely, most assuredly, had absolutely no opinion of the man. By the middle of 2014, 15 percent of voters said they still didn't know enough about him to form an opinion.

One reason was that most people didn't know or care who the down-ballot politicians are, Republicans or Democrats. Only they did, as they nursed feverish fantasies of making it to the top rung of the public ladder. Another reason was that as attorney general Abbott dealt with legal issues—many important, certainly—that were not issues that were usually part of the public debate. The attorney general's office, for instance, had a lawyer detailed to act as outside counsel to the University of Texas system on a range of legal matters, including those involving personnel. Vital to the workings of public institutions, certainly. But not quite as attention-grabbing as a showdown over, say, abortion. The attorney general's office didn't, say, set budgetary priorities involving billions of dollars, propose changes to the tax code, manage almost 300,000 state employees or wrangle unruly legislators who just dropped in from Odessa or Lubbock.

Two things were true about Abbott. His policy positions on a host of fronts were just as fuzzy as Davis's as the campaign got underway and Abbott went about the business of disposing of his primary opponent, Dallas businessman Tom Pauken. His original announcement speech was short on detail of what the main challenges were that faced Texas, let alone his proposed solutions. He did not seem to offer a single thought on the track record of the Perry administration. Abbott merely pledged a "level playing field that gets government out of the business of picking between winners and losers and by reducing taxes on employees."

Which sounded an awful lot like Perry. There was some specu-
lation that Abbott would somehow run to the right of Perry. But
how? Even after the summer brawl in the legislature over abortion, Abbott seemed to skirt abortion, a sort of hearty issue for the
Republican base. In purely tactical terms, abortion was kind of a
no-brainer issue for a conservative Republican politician in Texas
that was generally summed up in one word: No.

So, the *Houston Chronicle*'s Peggy Fikac, a very able columnist,
buttonholed Abbott as he began to appear around the state and was
unable to get Texas's top lawyer to provide a clear answer about
his position in just plain English, writing: "The language of abortion is usually clear-cut. Then you talk to someone like Attorney
General Greg Abbott." In Houston, KHOU's Doug Miller grabbed
Abbott at a campaign stop to try to get him to say where he stood
on the issue that had transfixed Texans and, briefly, Americans
that summer. Said Miller: "Abbott—a disciplined on-message
campaigner—dodges questions about just how far his opposition
to abortion goes. Questioned about whether he would support or
oppose legislation banning abortions for rape or incest victims,
Abbott avoids the question. When pressed again to directly answer
the question, he dodged it."

It would, of course, be interesting if a conservative Republican
politician had a nuanced opinion on abortion. But the Republican
Party, not just in Texas but across the country, has used the broad
paint brush of ideological rigidity on this—and other social issues—
to paint politicians like Abbott into a pretty narrow corner. The
only correct response would be to have enthusiastically condemned
the practice of abortion and embraced the most draconian curtail-
ment of women's reproductive rights by the government. But that
would make it tricky to reach out from that corner to suburban and
urban women who might vote Republican in the general election.

This was the effect of the steady narrowing of Republican politics into matters of social dogma, like abortion and gun rights. It wasn't just a narrowing of the electorate as the population grew more diverse and the party mined—over and over again—an older, dwindling Anglo population with pickaxes of ideology. The room in which to be a Republican had narrowed, too, so that it seemed as stifling as a broom closet. Abbott looked, in the television camera at least, a bit like a deer in the headlights.

Abbott is an intelligent and educated man. It would be impossible to believe that he doesn't have interesting and nuanced opinions on a whole host of subjects, whatever his politics. But because of the ideological and intellectual straight jacket Republicans have carefully stitched together over 25 years, Abbott had the same reaction to issues as voters had to him: He drew a complete blank.

★

There was a big difference between being attorney general and running for governor. It was one thing to, say, select and build a case for trial. It was another to declare a precise policy during a messy debate, and then later meet with these same adversaries and form a coalition. What was more interesting was this: Abbott had struck a very prominent stance on his work in the court room, fighting the Obama administration. This was, as he explained, his job. So, it could be more easily examined than his ideological fervor.

People who've worked with Abbott said that as he shifted from judge to attorney general he became a bit more of an operator, carefully calculating the politics. That's not surprising but interesting, the quid pro quo of trading the truth of the law for access to power. The *Dallas Morning News*'s Christy Hoppe also noted that with his first election in 2002 to being attorney general "he became much more conservative," too. Though he relied upon a wheelchair,

Abbott had opposed the Americans with Disabilities Act. Though a lawsuit and financial settlement had netted him a reported $11 million to compensate him for a severed spinal cord, he was the bane of trial attorneys. Yet for a man who made his living suing the federal government, his track record was, so far, underwhelming. He was prolific but not exactly productive. Out of 17 lawsuits, according to Hoppe, Abbott won just five. (Abbott says he's sued the Obama administration 27 times in other accounts.) The rest he lost or a judge just tossed the case out of court.

The list of cases that Abbott won was very long with the litany of conservative social ideology. He defended the Ten Commandments on display at the Texas State Capitol building. He threatened to sue San Antonio for prohibiting discrimination against people based upon sexual orientation. He had argued that Obamacare was unconstitutional, a matter later settled to the contrary by the U.S. Supreme Court. But even as he toured the state seeking the governorship, he was still in court on at least one important matter: Limiting the right of some Texans to vote.

★

Down in a federal appellate court in San Antonio was a case that, at first blush, only a lawyer could love.

In the wake of the U.S. Supreme Court's far-reaching curbing of a part of the 1965 Voting Rights Act in 2013, Abbott and the U.S. Justice Department squared off on how to interpret, in Texas, what the court said and whether Texas was imposing rules on voting that by their very design unfairly kept Hispanics, African American, old people and young people alike from getting to the ballot box. Even if they did there was another issue: The Texas Legislature was busy ensuring Republicans in Congress clung to power by drawing—the term used to be gerrymandering—districts that left entire cities without their own members of Congress. The tortured boundaries of congressional districts had parts of liberal Austin represented by arch-conservative Republicans in San Antonio and as far away as Fort Worth.

Abbott was squarely in the middle of the fight, with claims of ethnic and racial discrimination being made against his client, the State of Texas. Along with North Carolina, perhaps better known to the informed public, Texas was ground zero in whether the Voting Rights Act of 1965 signed into law by Lyndon Johnson almost a half-century ago would stand or fall. The challenges tended to get dressed up by political insiders in the language of camouflage. Abbott claimed that his efforts were invariably to stop the over-reach of the federal government into a state matter, except that was precisely what the Voting Rights Act was intended to do because voting was a fundamental democratic right and because in the era of Jim Crow some states had gotten quite clever in turning back African Americans and Mexican Americans, unless it suited the powers of the time. Claims of widespread voter fraud went unchecked and became the stuff of nearly urban legend in conservative circles, fueled in particular by the fact-free world of talk radio. The words "federal overreach" frequently appeared in the Texas press not as a quote by Abbott, or an assertion but as a plain and simple fact.

Dressed up in these uniforms, it was kind of hard to see what the fuss was really about. But when more direct and succinct terms were applied—gerrymandering, voter suppression, and political power—things became a little clearer. What was never pointed out was the fact that in fighting the federal government over these voting laws, Abbott was on a collision course with the new majority in Texas, the Hispanic population. Dancing around this particular problem and constrained by the three commandments of bedrock conservative politics—God, guns, and gays—he provided answers in court that only a lawyer could, indeed, love.

Was it gerrymandering or redistricting? After the 2014 Supreme Court ruling rolling back what was called preclearance from the federal government for changes to election laws in nine states, including Texas, Abbott immediately tried to reinstate congressional districts already dismissed by a three-judge federal panel. At that time, the judges ruled that there was already "more evidence of discriminatory intent than we have space, or need, to address here." It had been the first time since 1973 that a federal court found a state engaged in outright discrimination. But the new Supreme Court ruling gave Abbott his opening. Civil rights groups filed suit against Abbott. Then the U.S. Justice Department joined the fray in suing the state of Texas.

The legal merits aside, Abbott went far out on a slender political limb. He denied that the map of congressional districts was motivated by racism or ethnic discrimination. Instead, he argued, the politicians in Austin just wanted to make sure the people of Texas kept sending like-minded Republicans to Washington. It wasn't racist, essentially; it was just overtly partisan. If it had any effects on Hispanics and say, African Americans voting, well, that was just unintentional collateral damage. And that was something the Supreme Court now seemed to allow. To all the smart observers, the Texas case looked like it could well head back to the Supreme Court.

"The state thus is attempting to turn the new courthouse skirmish over a little-used section of the 1965 law," wrote Lyle Denniston, an influential observer of the Supreme Court, "into a constitutional battle with high stakes for the future of voting rights." The *San Antonio Express-News* ran an angry editorial focused on Abbott's brazen admissions of partisan gerrymandering all while denying that it was designed to keep the new Texas majority from voting, an argument it called "ethically corrupt."

Abbott's claim was one straight out of law school and one that had a hard time standing up to the absurdity of congressional representation in Texas where there are skinny lines connecting a diverse part of Houston, say, to a Republican congressman from Dallas. Austin, the nation's 11th largest city, had been chopped into six congressional districts represented by Republicans in San Antonio and Fort Worth.

Simultaneously, Abbott started to enforce another law, this one drawn up by the state legislature requiring voters to present a state-issued identification at the polls. That law would go into effect immediately, just hours after the Supreme Court issued the July ruling. Now, the Justice Department sued arguing that the law was clearly racially discriminatory—or in simple parlance, just plain racist in effect, regardless of design. Not to be outdone, the big cities started to react. Dallas County joined the suit—on the side of the Justice Department.

Although talk radio had for years fanned the flames of widespread voter fraud—thousands upon thousands of dead people casting ballots and the like—the facts belied the whole rationale for the law, other than one designed to disenfranchise certain Americans. Americans didn't carry a national ID card and never have. Over one in 10 Americans didn't carry a state-issued identification, the most common form of which is a driver's license, according to the Brennan Center for Justice at New York University's School of Law. About one in four African Americans in the country didn't carry one. Data from Texas, collected in 2011 and 2012, showed about 600,000 to 800,000 registered voters didn't have an ID card like a driver's license. Up to 40 percent of them were Hispanic. A lot of older people didn't drive anymore—so they didn't have driver's licenses. Some college kids carried college IDs but those did not qualify under the Texas law. So, how did the state go about making some other kind of ID available? By having the Department of Public Safety issue identity cards that were not driver's licenses for the very first time. The Texas Tribune reported that as Abbott campaigned, exactly six such ID cards had been issued in a state of 26 million people.

So, just how big was the wave of people trying to vote under the names of dead people or those filling up roles with fake names and addresses? Abbott had once claimed that he had personally nailed 50 election fraud convictions in the 10 years that spanned 2002 to 2012. "Only two cases [could be] described as 'voter imperson-ation'," according to Politifact. A database on alleged voter fraud nationwide, known as the News21 project, tallied 104 allegations by the state and precisely three involving voters masquerading as other people.

If the independent data was correct, Abbott nailed precisely two out of the three people charged in over 10 years, in a state with 13.6 million registered voters—who cast about 8 million ballots in the last national election.

★

Whether elected or defeated in his bid to become governor, Abbott was on a collision course with the new Texas majority, Hispanics.

And whether he personally endorsed the court fights he picked, it was clear that Abbott was constrained from tackling the big issues—education, upward mobility, drought, water, and climate change—because of the way that socially conservative politics had cornered him, like the Republican Party itself. Not only was there the losing mathematics of relying heavily on a suburban Anglo base even as the suburbs diversified, there was the logical impossibility of being able to tackle real problems. As *Texas Monthly*'s Paul Burka put it in late 2010: "To look back at the Bush years in Texas is to realize how much the Republican party has changed since 1995. In fact, he would not recognize it if he were running today . . . The transition from Bush to Perry was a turning point, the moment at which Texas completed its evolution into an indelibly red state and plunged into the politics of ideology, where it has remained mired ever since."

Even if he wanted to and believed in climate change, Abbott would have a hard time tackling it because he would have to admit to climate change. Even if he wanted to, he would have a hard time spending more money on schools and universities, essentially to get more Hispanics into the middle class so they could earn and spend more, because he would have to divert money from elsewhere or raise taxes. Instead, he was willing to make long-term trades for short-term advantage. He would go to court, even if many of the facts were against him and his arguments were tortured beyond common sense, to hold the line for an election cycle or two, against expanding the number of voters—who just might not vote Republican.

★

How a lawyer as smart as Abbott could get into this jam with Hispanics—over the long term and regardless of the election—said volumes about where the Republican priorities really laid. For years, Republican operatives loved to tout Bush and Perry's support among Hispanic voters—but not so much Cruz's, despite his Cuban surname. Now they pointed to the fact that Abbott's wife, Cecilia, was of Hispanic heritage. But so what? It didn't change what Abbott did in the court room. Or that Republican Sen. Dan Patrick, trying to unseat Dewhurst, called undocumented migration "an alien invasion" that spread leprosy of all things; Patrick had no compunction about hiring such undocumented workers, it turned out, for his bar business. Or that Abbott referred, in what he thought was a private speech, to the Rio Grande Valley as the "third world." Others said far worse, of course. Anne Coulter called Hispanics "roaches" who were "wrecking the country."

Whether in 2014, 2016, or at some later date, the Republican Party was on a collision course with the new Texas majority. Mexicans and Mexican Americans knew full well that Republicans, including the Texas delegation, had stalled immigration legislation in Congress. The mass deportations of people they knew under the Obama administration were grossly unpopular. And while Republicans cheered in February when one poll showed that 19 percent of Texas Hispanics called themselves Republicans, higher than the national average, the tide was turning. Even as Wendy Davis, the Democrat, could barely close the gap with Abbott overall, from 17 to 14 points in mid-April of 2014, she actually pulled way ahead among Hispanics, leading Abbott by a different double-digit margin, 43 to 33 percent.

"This year's election should not fall into that traditional zone of venomous nativist rhetoric that inflames the passion of white conservatives at the expense of the state's growing Hispanic population," the *McAllen Monitor* lashed out in an editorial at Abbott after his "third world" remarks. "Abbott has been guilty of such practices in the past and we need to declare as a region that we are tired of having Hispanics act as the bogeyman of Texas."

Yes, Republicans astutely controlled statewide politics for 20 years, built not only upon the collapse of the state Democratic Party but the shrewd vision of George W. Bush, Karl Rove, and Rick Perry. But nothing, not even in Texas, could last forever. That era seemed to be closing now, whether it ended now, next year, or the year after. Texas was not likely to turn stalwartly Democratic blue right away so much as increasingly competitive and purple between the two parties. The Democrats had their own problems after all. But the Republican position was simply untenable. Their position wasn't just cut off by demography and population density, then narrowed by its ever-smaller ideology; but now all these factors conspired to doom the ability to solve real problems, which was what governing was all about. In its frantic bid to stay alive, the party not so much resembled the elephant as the circus. And in this case, the circus had just one act: Spin as many plates as possible to keep the crowd looking even as the lights were about to go out.

PART FOUR

It is "the movement from country to subdivision, homeplace to metropolis, that gives life in present-day Texas its passion. Or if not its passion, its strong, peculiar mix of passions, part spurious and part genuine, part ridiculous and part tragic . . . the transition that is taking place is very difficult, and the situations it creates are intense. Living here consciously uses a great deal of one's blood; it involves one at once in a birth, a death and a bitter love affair."

—*Larry McMurtry, 1968*

13

★ ★ ★

TEXAS, 2014

Like a dandelion in the cool spring rain, Texas Governor Rick Perry appeared once more in the late spring of 2014. The presidency was still, quite apparently, on his mind.

His demeanor appeared to have changed. Instead of the 30,000–strong audience at Reliant Stadium in Houston, he took a private baptism, instead, at Little Rocky Creek, near Independence. His office did not make a big deal out of the event but confirmed it, noting: "Governor Perry has a deep and biding faith in God. Like many people of faith, the governor wished to reaffirm his commitment in a way that holds great meaning." Sam Houston, the father of the Republic of Texas, was baptized in the same creek and summed up the experience both more humbly and succinctly: "I feel sorry for the fish downstream."

But now, Perry was back on the prowl, it seemed, for more power. His handsome face featured cool Clark Kent glasses. The trademark cowboy boots had been shed for street shoes. Yet the leopard had a little trouble changing his spots. Appearing on *Meet the Press* on NBC in May, he professed his deep concern for the unemployed in America—all 91 million of them. The official number was a tenth of that but even assuming, just for the sake of argument, that the real number was double what the Obama administration claimed, Perry's newfound empathy for the unemployed suddenly ran deep, way deeper than say Little Rocky Creek. Then, in San Francisco, Perry compared being gay with being an alcoholic; he quickly apologized in Boston.

After all, he wasn't the only Texan with an eye on the presidency. Republican Sen. Ted Cruz, darling of the Tea Party, was exhibiting every sign of wanting to jump from a first term in the Senate to a bid for the White House. Now, not one but two men sought to export the politics of Texas' past—fashioned no fewer than 20 years ago and more—to the rest of America even as it careened uncertainly toward the third decade of the 21st century.

★

By mid-2014, contemporary Texas resembled a Western landscape painting: The foreground was bright, lush and bountiful. The cows were fat and the pastures tall. But the distant horizon suggested something else. The horizon bristled with thunderclouds, and behind them was darkness.

The economy could not be better and yet showed signs of only becoming exactly that: Better. Unemployment in Austin was less than half the national average, just 4.4 percent. Home values skyrocketed with all the new arrivals. With 4,000 new home-buyers arriving in Austin every few months real estate agents were gleefully making money on other people's investments hand over fist, selling as many hones now as before the Great Recession, over 27,000 per year at an average clip of about $224,000. Those commissions were stacking up.

But at the same time, the politicians in Austin hadn't done a whole lot about things like social and climate change. The bursting-at-the seam problems facing public schools and universities had remained unresolved. Perry and the legislators had approved a plan for more dams and canals but sent it to the voters to only fund part of it as the politicians, as public radio in Austin put it, nearly tore off their "rotator cuffs patting themselves on the back." Seizing the opportunity, private and global water corporations swooped in. One, Acqua Texas, bought water utilities in small towns southwest of Austin and immediately jacked up rates. The Lower Colorado River Authority, steward of the Colorado River which slaked the thirst of Central Texas, sold all of its water rights to a Canadian corporation. The notion of ensuring the growth of the middle class and battling the effects—forget the causes—of climate change had gone unmentioned. And they went on unabated. Drought was predicted for the rest of 2014, again and restrictions on the use of water were once more imposed.

But Texas continued to change, relentlessly. The traffic in Austin got steadily worse, to the point of becoming impenetrable at times. Everything got more expensive: A pair of fish tacos at The Tavern, a bar on Lamar Street so old that its signage still proclaimed the wonder of air conditioning, now cost more than $10. I even heard of a $15 burrito sold from a food truck not far away. As the high rises went up, they were just as swiftly populated with modern-day migrants to Texas. But this time they came not in covered wagons pulled by oxen but in U-Hauls, moving vans and luxury crossovers.

They came not to carve a place in the wilderness but to take jobs in technology or the service sector. They were not armed with a .50 caliber Hawken rifle; instead they came equipped to pay $2,200—far more than my mortgage—in rent for a one-bedroom apartment. And they were young. I groused to Katherine McCollough, a new arrival from Indiana who leased luxury apartments, about being the oldest man downtown some afternoons and she replied without a trace of irony or nastiness: "Yeah, it's really more for young adults."

I thought the phrase strange: Young adults, I thought, were 8th graders. Perhaps it was an unwitting commentary on the Peter Pan life of Austin.

And as day turned into night, they kept coming, as many as the stars, inevitably eclipsing those of us who had come before. The common lesson to be drawn from anecdotes like these normally was that paradise found was inevitably paradise lost. My arrival had invariably ruined someone else's memory, too. There was truth to that, of course; paradises get overrun. Yet that is all in the eye of the beholder. To today's newly arrived Texan, this is the halcyon era. To others it was 20 years ago, 40 years ago and so on. Who is ultimately right depends upon which Texan you were, the one just arrived or the one who has been here for years or decades, or all his or her life. There is really no settling that argument.

The most salient point is this one: Often portrayed as a conservative place that stubbornly refuses to change, Texas is anything but that. It is not the brittle and entrenched Old South. Neither is Texas the never-ending change of California; there are permanent characteristics shaped mostly by geography if not landscape. Decades have gone by and the pressures of change have built imperceptibly and slowly in Texas. But they built, nonetheless, and now—with a diverse, densely populated society—they have reached the point of creating inveitable, sweeping change. There is just one question: When?

★

On the morning of November 22, 2013 the skies over Dallas opened up and poured a spitting gray rain on to the city—just as it solemnly marked the 50th anniversary of the slaying of President John F. Kennedy on its streets.

The weather could be seen as just weather, or as the continued mourning of the heavens or, as I looked at it, the very bad luck that big, elaborately planned anniversaries of sudden and unforeseen historic events invariably endure. Certainly, there was no softening of the blow struck that very same day a half-century earlier: a president assassinated in plain view of the public in Dealey Plaza, as 100,000 people had gathered on the streets to greet the president, even as reactionaries seethed hatred toward the liberal JFK, including the leaflets that appeared with JFK's images resembling mugshots and the words: "WANTED FOR TREASON." In the backdrop was the city's deeply reactionary power structure of the time, which included billionaire oil men, a decorated military man ousted by Kennedy and Ted Dealey, the publisher of the *Dallas Morning News*. Dealey had dressed down Kennedy personally on what he saw as weak foreign policy and his paper had published an anti-Kennedy advertisement the very morning of the president's arrival. This was a community that Dallasite Bill Minutaglio dubbed, "The City of Hate" in his book, *Dallas: 1963*. That was probably a bit strong as a characterization. It didn't account for the crowds of cheering Dallasites, so many and so ecstatic that the White House staff and traveling press were pleasantly shocked—until the shots rang out, of course in Dealey Plaza, named for George B. Dealey, Ted's father, and founder of the newspaper.

As father and son, they could not have been more different: The elder had refused advertisements for hard liquor, speculative oil ventures seeking investors, and those that were just plain misleading. He had also campaigned against the Ku Klux Klan. The son, when he inherited the newspaper after his father's death in 1946, turned its editorial pages into screeds of anti-unionism and red-baiting. He advocated dropping nuclear weapons on Russia and was chastised by fellow Texas publishers as an embarrassment.

Nevertheless, once the deed was done and Kennedy lay dead and a stunned nation gazed at its television screens, traumatized, Dallas would always be known for that tragic day. Like the stains of a murder in an old motel room, the memory could never quite be scrubbed away even as the city could hardly be held responsible, whatever its backroom politics, for the killing. The people of the city did not kill JFK, after all. Either Lee Harvey Oswald or a cabal or both did. Oswald's link to the city was tenuous at best. Born in New Orleans, his mother had from there moved to Dallas and New York, back to New Orleans and finally to Fort Worth, before he enlisted in the Marine Corps. The label hung around the neck of the entire city of Dallas seemed unfair. After all, Memphis was not known as the city that killed Martin Luther King. And it was not as if Washington, D.C. ground to a halt each April 15th, to commemorate the equally tragic assassination of President Abraham Lincoln. For better and for worse, most Americans merely know that date as Tax Day.

The commemoration in Dallas now seemed, to me at least, an overly elaborate contrition for the city still known to resentful liberals as the "city that killed Kennedy." The small group of VIPs was enhanced with several thousand people who braved the weather for the tightly choreographed, high-security events. "A new era dawned and another waned a half century ago when hope and hatred collided right here in Dallas," Mayor Mike Rawlings told crowd. "He and our city will forever be linked in tragedy, yes. But out of that tragedy an opportunity was granted to us: The chance to learn how to face the future when it's darkest and most uncertain." Bagpipes played. A new monument to Kennedy was unveiled near the grassy knoll, in Dealey Plaza.

Dallas, to be sure, has changed a lot in 50 years; you would have to be past middle age to remember the assassination (I was not yet born.) Culturally, Deep Ellum became a boisterous and creative area for music and the arts. Oak Cliff, once a nearly solidly African American neighborhood that fell prey to crime and dilapidation now attracted the usual hip wave of urban gentrification. Politics in Dallas changed, too, in the early part of this century. In 2004, voters elected Lupe Valdez, a Democratic woman who was openly lesbian, to be their county sheriff. Republicans lost control of Dallas County in 2006, the last time a Republican won a county-wide election. Now Republican county commissioners come from the far suburbs. Elected in 2011, Rawlings was a pro-business Democrat, one of an increasingly long—and nearly unbroken—string of Democratic mayors stretching over nearly 20 years now. Democrat Ron Kirk governed from 1995 to 2002, succeeded by Democrat Laura Miller who ran the city until 2007. Republican Tom Leppert was mayor only from 2007 to 2011, stepping down to run unsuccessfully as a Republican for the U.S. Senate. That's when Rawlings, a former Pizza Hut executive and a Democrat, stepped in and won.

To some, the public act of contrition in Dallas now was too little or too late. Or both. Slate produced an interactive graphic in time for the commemoration mapping out the locations of Oswald, reactionary oil billionaires, and anti-Catholic church leaders at the time, based upon Minutaglio's book and entitled simply and unfortunately: "The City That Killed Kennedy." The *Dallas Morning*

News concluded an elaborate, year-long reporting project on the assassination, its aftermath and ramifications—a work so encyclopedic that it spawned a documentary and at least one e-book. All of it was published under the gaze of James M. Moroney III, the heir to the enterprise—and none other than the George B. Dealey's great grandson. Moroney, a thin, gray-haired patrician seemed easy-going, despite the pressures of legacy, a family fortune, and a news empire. But he was high-minded, too. He had come to Austin shortly before the commemoration for an event on the future of serious journalism.

"What, ultimately, are we really trying to do? We're trying to save democracy," he said. Turning to fellow news executives he added, "I don't care about the rest of you but we're trying to save democracy because without a vibrant, robust, free press, democracies don't work. There's not a country in the world with a real democracy that doesn't have rule of law, fair elections and a free press. All three of them. If you find two out of three? That's not a democracy."

Back in Dallas, overdone or not, the apologia to the nation and even to the world was finally done. Night fell. CNN's crews turned out their lights and headed for their hotels as the crowds went home. The local magazine, *D*, noted what the *Dallas Morning News* had done the previous year under the headline: "If Ted Dealey Could See His Newspaper Now . . ." And the city announced that it would observe his unfortunate death there—every November 22nd to come. In Dallas, grieving for the slain liberal president had now become a ritual.

★

Less than six months later, on the campus of the University of Texas, another reconciliation took place: That of the late Lyndon Baines Johnson with his place in history at the imposingly blunt,

1970s-style architecture of the Lyndon Baines Johnson Library and Museum.

From the outside, perhaps not unlike LBJ himself, it was not a pretty sight: Tall, square with an extended flat top, much of it windowless, surrounded by what seemed like acres and acres of concrete which turns hot as the day wears on. One of the 13 presidential libraries in the country, it was home to 45 million pages of documents.

Both LBJ and Lady Bird Johnson laid in repose here upon their deaths. On the top floor was a nearly full-scale replica of the Oval Office as it appeared during his tenure. And in this library, researchers famous and unknown, have come and gone to plumb LBJ's record. Most famous, of course, is the journalist Robert Caro, who has intricately, voluminously, and scathingly written on Johnson over the years. One researcher told me that it was clear that the library staff was glad when someone who was not Caro actually showed up. Of course, Caro's subject was yet another controversial, bigger-than-life Texan.

Liberals in the 1960s seemed to despise Johnson as much as conservatives had loathed Kennedy. And he was a complicated figure: A senator who may have stolen his first election; a reliably racist vote against early civil rights measures in the 1950s; and the man who expanded the Vietnam War. But he was also the one who created the Great Society, for better and for worse, and made voting rights and civil rights—equal protection under the law for everyone regardless of race—the law of the land, finally.

So, now 50 years after Johnson signed the Civil Rights Act into law, four presidents converged here in the library: President Obama as well as former presidents George W. Bush, Bill Clinton, and Jimmy Carter. Each man tended to sound his own personal theme in the context of civil rights—as politicians, even those out of office, apparently—are wont to do. Carter spoke of continued inequality and American apathy. Clinton warned that that very apathy would turn back the pages of history. George W. Bush reliably talked about the importance of education. Obama, equally reliably, intoned his personal experience. The doors of opportunity had swung open in 1964 for millions, he said, "They swung open for you and they swung open for me. That's why I'm standing here today."

The Johnson family, most notably daughter Lucy Johnson, were not only in attendance but had tirelessly worked toward the observation of this anniversary. The library underwent a $12 million renovation. Johnson herself met privately with the Obamas and publicly pleaded that her father's social achievement be weighed at least evenly with his tormented, wartime failure, a war that she said "was if as somebody was punching his gut, every night—the sleepless nights."

Outside the library and beyond the concrete plain that surrounded it, the city of Austin went largely about its business. Unlike the events in Dallas, fewer than 1,000 people could be accommodated after all, even with four presidents. But much like the event in Dallas, this high-security, carefully choreographed event was just as uncontroversial. Just as in Dallas—where there were no, say, anti-Kennedy haters protesting—no one protested the Voting Rights Act, even as it was challenged, piecemeal in the U.S. Supreme Court.

Fifty years ago, there had been controversy and struggle to be sure in Texas—and across the country. African Americans and Mexican Americans boycotted racist retailers. Nearly 1,000 marched on the state Capitol, within sight of the museum, in 1963 as the March on Washington was underway. Activists criticized the glacial pace of desegregation under Governor John Connally, who would be wounded in Dallas. But in 1964, the 24th amendment to the Constitution outlawed poll taxes and then came Johnson's Civil Rights Act, the death knell of Jim Crow. Under continued pressure, Texas actually followed the federal lead in 1969, repealing state segregationist laws.

Of course, racism and discrimination were not dead in America. But a walk west across the campus of the University of Texas revealed what now passes, even in Texas, for every day life. Students changed classes under the oaks, waited for a bus, unlocked a bike, or lingered in the sun: Mexican American, African American, Asians, Indians, Anglos, and countless more. Today, half of the university's 52,000 students are Anglo or white; 18 percent are Hispanic and 15 percent are Asian and, yet, just a staggering 6 percent are African Americans; the campus is not yet a reflection of the diversity of Texas. Then again, it is an increasingly elite university; this year's freshmen had an average SAT score of 1842. That said, this much progress was a far cry within my lifetime alone. It occurred to me that, jacked into their iPhones, most of these kids were blissfully unaware of the historic but stuffy goings on over at the library. To them it was all just part of the landscape, like the controversial Texas president who made it possible, buried now many decades west of here on his family's Hill Country ranch.

★

By the spring of 2014, Holly Regan, who had come from Seattle, had a whole new life. She had a job as an editor at a company recently acquired by the Gartner Group, the technology research firm. She was engaged to a freelance video editor, Marc Andonian, himself another member of the Sixth Migration, recently arrived from Michigan.

Though they had met in one of the most notorious bars of Austin's Peter Pan culture—Kung Fu—the two now had a house in South Austin, complete with three bedrooms and plans for both a wedding and a family. Her friends who had jeered her coming to Texas and dispersed to other parts of the country, like New York, struggled with expenses. In contrast, she and her fiancé had found a measure of prosperity. Now 29, she said: "We have our own little life out in the suburbs."

The journey in search of the answer to the question—When? When will politics in Texas realign?—invariably led to the suburbs. And there was no greater cluster of them than that megacity of the future: Houston and its surrounding counties. Just as time has always been a matter of math, so it has always been with politics, a game of either addition or subtraction.

And looking at the mathematics, if the Houston suburbs are any example, the political realignment of Texas will not happen in some distant future or a decade. It is happening right now and its results will be visible between now, the middle of 2014, and the end of 2016, the next presidential election. Matthew Dowd's prediction, made a decade ago, looked to be about spot on. Whether they won the governorship in 2014 or they lose, whether Democrats win Texas or lose in 2016 is not all that relevant. They are very likely to perform better and better, eroding the last stronghold of the Republican Party in Texas, other than sparsely populated rural areas: The suburbs.

None of this was to say who would be the next governor or what Congress or the legislature would look like; in the case of the former, how candidates perform really mattered. In the case of the latter, legal tricks could continue to skew the results by tampering with democracy unless, and until, the courts settle the matter. For example, one study in 2014, found that race was a reliable predictor of political party in the Texas Legislature. If a member was white or Anglo, there was a nearly 100 percent chance that he or she was a Republican. That was hardly a coincidence.

A few broad assertions that supported the conventional wisdom remained true and the truest of all was labeling. "There are simply more people in Texas who identify themselves as conservatives," said University of Texas political scientist and Fox News pollster Daron Shaw, "than people who identify themselves as liberals." Even a minority of Hispanics thought of themselves as conservative—and they did so even after they had chosen to support a Democratic candidate.

Another broad assertion—that Hispanics just don't vote—was becoming less and less true. It was true that Hispanic turnout in 2010 was small—just 34 percent of Texas Hispanics went to the polls. But that jumped to 50 percent in 2012, more closely mirroring voters in general in Texas. Political engagement has often been a function of income and education, too. But Census data was clearly showing a trend: The longer a Hispanic person was in this country, the more likely he or she was to gain, however modestly, in income. High school graduation rates closely tracked those of Anglos and African Americans now, too.

That said, by the arithmetic of deduction, statewide and national elections in Texas were not fought in all 254 counties. Nearly all are spoken for with rural ones going to Republicans and urban ones going to Democrats. Instead, 13 counties determine the outcome, delivering 60 percent of the vote. The biggest urban counties were reliably Democratic now: Bexar, Travis, Dallas, and Harris. They were also increasingly expensive. So, the Sixth Migration was moving out to the farther suburbs which, themselves, became steadily less Anglo, more diverse, more densely populated and more receptive to what Democrats have to say, even if they were not automatically convinced. Back in 2007, Wendy Davis herself defeated a Republican to become a state senator in a Fort Worth suburb by winning 95 percent of the African American vote, 80 percent of the Hispanic vote, and a helping of Anglo votes.

Beyond the broad swath of demographic change, there are what I call the four Ds at work in these suburbs of the Sixth Migration: demographics, diversity, density of population, and disposition to listening to what Democrats have to say. It could almost be expressed as a simple algebraic function: D to the power of four. When these factors converge, the loss of Republican strength in what had been their stronghold for 20 years is actually surprisingly easy to explain. The Sixth Migration is undoing, in the exact same suburbs, the political legacy of the Fifth Migration.

I compiled the four Ds for the five most populous counties in the Greater Houston area, pairing the most recent presidential election results with the most recent census data alongside Rice University diversity data, an index known as an entropy score. I then adjusted all the data to roughly mirror the Rice data, creating a rough index of the propensity to vote Republican. The closer the combined index got to zero, the increasing weakness of the Republican electoral results. Harris County went from 0.03 in 1992 to 0.00069 in 2012. Fort Bend—home to the most diverse city in America, Missouri City—went from 0.4, up to 0.7 at the beginning of the century and then plummeted to 0.2. The same was nearly true for Brazoria County. Galveston County was an outlier as it seemed to grow more competitive, after historically being an African American and Democratic stronghold. One county actually became more Republican and it was decidedly less diverse: Montgomery County.

So, to check my statistical skills, I disassembled my own index and then examined just the raw data. Simply put, the more diverse and the more densely populated these suburban counties became the less Republican they became, too. As far back as 1992, Harris, Galveston, and Fort Bend counties were within the 10 most densely populated counties in Texas. Republicans won handily in these counties as well as the other two but by smaller margins. 1992 was a strange year, because of Ross Perot. So I adjusted each party's relative strength—a surplus or a deficit—by dividing the Perot vote between the two. Population density in all three of these wavering counties was upwards of 400 people per square mile and in Harris County north of 3,000.

Their diversity was approaching or exceeding 0.8. In the more rock solid Republican counties, it was 0.5 or less. Bush's strength here was decidedly smaller with a surplus of 5, 8, and 13 percent. By the time of the 2000 census and election, not much had changed. The same three counties—Harris, Galveston and Fort Bend—were still in the top 10 in the state in population density. Their diversity, as measured by the entropy score, had barely changed. And the electoral results showed it. George W. Bush actually did a little better than his father, winning in double digits.

But right there, the story line changed. The census in 2010 showed an entirely different picture of the population. Recall that nearly 100 percent of the population growth in the Houston area was among non-Anglos. The diversity index went up dramatically, reaching and exceeding 0.8 and even 0.9 in Harris, Fort Bend and Brazoria now; a 1 would mean that the population perfectly mirrored the general numerical distribution of race and ethnicity. Only in Galveston did it fall along with population density, which may have been reflective of its dwindling population of now less than 50,000. People had moved out of the city, after all, in the disastrous wake of Hurricane Ike. The city was decidedly less African American, too.

Regardless, the Republican advantage was being erased in the most diverse, most densely populated counties—now beginning to vote increasingly for Democrats. The Democratic deficit in Harris was turned into a tiny advantage over Republicans. The margin for Republicans had fallen to just 15,000 votes out of over 217,000 in Fort Bend, a six percent lead. Indeed, the Republican advantage in Fort Bend had been cut in half in 10 years even as the population doubled, due entirely to the arrival of non-Anglos in the Texas suburbs.

And there is no question, even now: The Sixth Migration was far more diverse than any previous one. This is why conservative Republican politicians were artfully finding ways to make representative democracy both less representative and less democratic. Two trends in 2014 clearly demonstrated that realignment was well underway. First, political attitudes in greater Houston increasingly ran counter to the prevailing Tea Party-driven trends to make the Republican Party, and Texas by extension, even more conservative than it already was.

On the one hand, big majorities of people in the Houston metropolitan area favored increasing immigration or at least holding it steady, according to a study by Rice University's Kinder Institute. Fully 83 percent of Houston area residents favored creating a path to legal citizenship for those who had arrived undocumented. Six in 10 people believed that immigrants strengthened American culture. An identical number opposed making it harder for women to obtain abortions, though the same number said it was morally wrong in their opinion. Support for gay rights was growing though still a little tepid when compared to other parts of the country. And young Anglos were comfortable with the diversity of their megalopolis.

On the other hand, there was a politician named Dan Patrick, a figure so buffoonish as to have once been dismissed entirely, if he wasn't such a bigot: Dan Patrick. Texan by way of Maryland, Patrick defeated the patrician Dewhurst for the job of lieutenant governor in the 2014 Republican primary and runoff based in large part on promising to crack down on immigration and namely the

U.S.-Mexico border. A bar owner-turned-radio show host and now a state senator, Patrick had once hawked a book he wrote by saying it was second in importance only to the Bible. Vowing to govern as the "authentic, Christian conservative," he had said that God not only told him to pass anti-abortion legislation but when. Fellow senators called him a "narcissist," fellow Republicans branded him "pathological" and *Texas Monthly* pegged him to its list of "worst" legislators. In a bid to derail him during the runoff, it was Republicans, it appeared, who outed an eye-popping mental health history of Patrick's from the 1980s.

And yet—all that not withstanding—he still won the Republican nomination, defeating the incumbent Dewhurst 41.5 percent to 28.3 percent in March, triggering a runoff, where he won again, this time by about two to one. Upon closer inspection, though, his victory displayed just how narrowly his candidacy was. He garnered just 488,150 votes out of a state with 13.6 million, or 3.5 percent—in a state where most voters describe themselves as conservatives. He performed very poorly in the 13 competitive suburban counties.

The realignment of Texas was already underway, Republicans were on the wrong side of it, and it would continue to gain strength, too, as long as the population does what it is expected to do: Boom.

14

★ ★ ★

TEXAS AND AMERICA, 2050

Ultimately, Texas is at an important crossroads, a place on the high plains where two dusty tracks meet. There are no landmarks. But there are signs.

Down one path lies the choice of exclusivity, essentially—and let's be blunt—to deny the totality of the American experience in the 21st century to people whose faces are not necessarily lily-white. These people, including many new arrivals and migrants to the cities and the suburbs, would be barred from good educations, college, the middle class, and even the most basic act of citizenry, voting. Instead, these people would be consigned—unlike any previous majority in Texas and American history—to life in the underclass, while a tiny and aging majority controls the wealth and reserves all the political power solely for itself.

It is quite possible for Texans to go down this path. The current conservative Republican power structure is trying to fashion this very future through its actions, or lack of action, on education, which is the key to the middle class. In failing to confront the results of climate change vigorously, the same Republican power structure risks the demise of the economy in the coming years—forget the morality the issue. And in jiggering the democracy, the same conservative Republican power structure is simply trying to limit it. Keeping nearly 1 million people from voting over the lack of an ID card, or denying big cities their own members of Congress is not democracy. It is oligarchy.

Down the other path lies the choice of inclusion, of expanding the teaching of the human mind, not narrowing it, of ensuring that the land-grant colleges educate all the young people—rural, urban, suburban, Anglo, Hispanic, African American, Asian American, women and men alike—who desire such an education. This is not a radical notion; it was hatched, along with the concept of land-grant universities in Texas in the 19th century as the very heritage of the landscape. The universities were apportioned land as assets of the people in order to create revenues, fees, and royalties to educate all Texans who came. And making sure that the land has water to sustain itself, and the people living on it, is hardly a flight of socialist fantasy. From Indian to cowboy to roughneck to suburbanite, doing so is merely the stewardship of a semi-arid land.

Down this path is the expansion of the right to vote, not to some new and unqualified class, but simply to all citizens who have never relinquished their right to vote by becoming felons. That's all. And down this path is the provision of duly-elected representation in government. These two rights are among the most simple, respected, and core tenets of a representative democracy.

On the face of it, the choice doesn't seem complicated. All of the signs leading down that first road, however, do list temptation and short-term gain as a destination. But those places are just waypoints of human avarice that will benefit those whose lot is favorable already. And when night falls in those places, instability and purgatory arise for them and everyone. The signs on the other road point to destinations that are more fruitful, though they are a little further away. These destinations will heal the afflicted and even harbor the comfortable when night falls. These destinations will prove more permanent for more people. All of them, after all, are migrants on the move across the plains of time.

★

The year is 2050.

All of the major cities of the Texas Triangle—Houston, Dallas-Fort Worth, Austin, and San Antonio—are dilapidated shells of their formerly booming selves. Unemployment is twice the national average. The city of San Antonio has declared bankruptcy. In each major city and even the smaller ones, like Corpus Christi and El Paso, specially appointed federal officials, known as masters, are making decisions on which schools to close.

In Austin, the state government flirted briefly with massive deficits but elected to keep taxes low and simply chose not to fund, beginning in 2015, the growth of enrollment in the state's sprawling public school system. Now there are too many students and not enough money. Of the state's 9 million students, two in three of these students are Hispanic. Half will never graduate from high school. Without taxpayer dollars approved by the legislature, the once-thriving public university system has continued to raise tuition and fees. Now, a public education in Texas costs at least $50,000 per year. But only 4.5 million public school children here will finish high school anyway. And only one-tenth of them can afford college at any public university in the state. Those who can will simply leave; a new Texas diaspora is underway. Those who stay will struggle to find work.

Already the prospects for staying are quite clear: one in five people in San Antonio, 20 percent, are unemployed. The city government has sold off as many assets as it can: Public buildings, art museums and collections alike, even the old limestone football stadium that had hosted decades of Friday night games just off U.S. 281. The once world-renowned San Antonio Zoo was purchased by a private collector and though people can still occasionally hear the lions or bears roar at night, the zoo is closed to the public. Brackenridge Park, a vast urban park running through the center of the city, was sold years ago to developers. The municipal hospital system was auctioned off to a private company. Much of the health care industry which flourished in San Antonio in the late 20th century, focused on research, has become devoted to prolonging the lives of aging people with private insurance who can pay hefty fees for long-term care.

But the jobs in this sector are very low-paying service jobs, helping with menial tasks like cooking and cleaning for the wealthy, elderly remnants of the Anglo Baby Boom and Generation X. Bexar County, which surrounds metropolitan San Antonio, is not just the poorest county in the nation. It is the hungriest, too, with more people on food stamps than any other place in America, leading to its own set of health problems that range from malnourishment to obesity, diabetes, and heart and kidney failure. The average life span, for the first time in American history, is actually falling.

The people who do find work in San Antonio cannot afford the usual steps up the ladder of upward mobility. They cannot afford college for their children because they could not even afford to have bought a home in the first place. So, real estate values fall. With fewer property tax dollars there are fewer police and little work, the city is plagued with crime: From robberies to drug-trafficking to murder. San Antonio, in fact, has become the murder capital of the United States.

So, the tourists have largely stopped coming. The River Walk still is home to a dilapidated Hyatt and a Hard Rock, open only on weekends. But much of its length is abandoned and boarded up. Even the boats that once hauled tourists up and down the iconic little river are gone. The Alamo is closed to the public, behind a tall chain link fence topped by razor wire. There is talk of selling it and moving it, stone by stone, to Mexico City. On the north side of the city, Sea World and Six Flags have been torn down and sold, their once festive and packed playgrounds plowed under to make way for a scrap yard that is a sea of used electronics. Scrapped computers, mobile phones, and tablets arrive daily from all over North America for safe disposal of their hard metals which, improperly treated, would otherwise leach into the soil. That would have been a problem but rain is infrequent. The scrap yard is San Antonio's largest employer now and is so large that it can be seen by satellites in space. City leaders strangely boast that it is the largest such site anywhere in the world in the nearly futile quest to attract more industry.

Throughout Texas, a deep and distrustful two-class system has been firmly established. A handful of legislators in Austin are elected every two years. But not a single governor in over two centuries, now, of statehood has ever had a Hispanic surname. Restrictions on voting and successful court defenses of gerrymandering, enacted 35 years earlier, have generally worked to drive down Hispanic voting even as the Hispanic population swelled into an outright majority. Only two members of Congress from

Texas have Hispanic surnames, one from Houston and one from San Antonio. No U.S. senator since Ted Cruz has even had a Hispanic surname. No woman has occupied a U.S. Senate seat from Texas since Republican Kay Bailey Hutchison retired in the first decade of the century. Nor has a woman has ever sat in the governor's mansion in Austin in the 21st century—even though two did in the 20th. The leaders of most important corporations and all important financial institutions are Anglos who have lived in Texas for years or are freshly imported. Tiny and affluent Anglo enclaves are surrounded by razor wire, private security, and golf courses. In Dallas, Highland Park has become the model for such communities throughout Texas.

At its heart is a wealthy, Anglo, and Christian university originally Methodist and now Baptist, with a much smaller enrollment. The university is ringed by fairly large homes, many of Georgian design and sturdy red brick. Leafy streets are patrolled by a municipal police as well as Statewide, a hired security force largely made up of ex-military whose cars and weapons are easily mistaken for those of police. A complex barrier, modeled on the fence along the U.S.-Mexican border, has been erected around the entire city of Highland Park. Twenty feet tall, it is topped with the same kind of razor wire that is employed by the military as well as over 3,000 motion-activated sensors and 1,000 digital video cameras. Small drones with cameras, infra-red, and listening devices fly the perimeter day and night and flit across town, recording everything.

There are precisely three checkpoints into and out of Highland Park. All the rest of the streets connecting to Dallas were closed off years ago, at first by hastily-imposed, concrete jersey barriers and later by the new fence. Police check the driver's licenses of all who enter, to verify either that addresses check out or that the driver is on a list of people invited by a resident or employer into the city.

The peak times for traffic at the checkpoints are 8:00 A.M. and 6:00 P.M. because that is when landscape crews, house cleaners, and repairmen start their day in Highland Park—and later, when curfew is imposed. Violating it, or simply not having a state-issued ID card is grounds for immediate arrest. The jail is operated by a private contractor.

The urban cores of the big cities, however, are now where the super-rich live. During the boom times of the early 21st century, largely neglected downtowns were redeveloped with an eye toward older, affluent people downsizing from big homes as their children grew into adulthood. Many of these people remained in, say, downtown Austin even as the economy soured. Some were young couples; some were single. The couples were nearly uniformly childless. For the older ones, that period in life had come and gone. For the younger ones it was a simple matter of economics, particularly given the complications and costs of education. Nearly all are Anglo.

The 2nd Street corridor of downtown Austin is fairly emblematic. Steel and glass towers soar over what had been modest, old retail buildings and parking lots. A one-bedroom condominium can easily cost $1 million and rent is now the equivalent to the cost of living in Manhattan. Stylish retail shops, salons, gymnasiums, personal trainers, and expensive restaurants await on the streets below, patrolled heavily by the city's police force. The black-uniformed police in their black cars seem particularly zealous in their dedication to this zip code and its tax base—even if the Department of Justice has opened an investigation into the record number of shootings by the police of largely young, Hispanic males found in the area.

The city of Houston has had a Hispanic mayor, generally, for decades now. But the tax base has crumbled and the once thriving consumer economy—that built houses and bought the durable and non-durable goods that went inside them—has simply imploded. Services by the city and surrounding Harris County are on a shoestring. Roads and highways are still congested but they have long since buckled and filled with potholes so that drivers must now slowly navigate around them during the steaming commute. The waiting time for an ambulance or some kind of first responder in the event of an emergency is now longer in Houston than anywhere in the United States. And it has been that way for nearly 20 years. A popular bumper sticker reads: "If you're going to need an ambulance you'd better not need one in Houston."

So many people are now trying to leave Texas for parts elsewhere that it is impossible to rent a U-Haul trailer anywhere inside of the state's border. In each of the major cities a line stretches each day in front of the Mexican consulate. People—mostly Hispanic but African American and Anglo, too—are patiently seeking permission to immigrate to Mexico, where a middle class has now thrived for over 30 years. The American economy, after all, long ago slipped into second place as the Texas economy foundered. China is now the richest nation on earth.

★

The account above, of course, is a starkly dystopian scenario of the way that Texas could evolve if it goes down that first road, blazing a trail for the rest of the United States in its footsteps. Many of the examples, however, are quite real possibilities. Americans have witnessed in their own time the once unthinkable decay and collapse of Detroit, once one of the country's biggest and greatest cities, but now a shell of its former self and home to just a few hundred thousand residents. The drain of workers and students from Texas already happened in the 1980s when talent left the state in droves. The lack of municipal services, namely ambulances, was a reality in New Orleans during the same period when it was the murder capital of the United States. The examples of poverty and hunger are drawn from Hidalgo County in what is now metropolitan South Texas, not rural South Texas, in 2012. And the lynchpins that connect this fictional account of the future to the decisions of the present? Upward mobility. A college education. Prudent policy in a period of climate change. The right to vote. A functioning democracy. All of them mean the difference between continued and expanding prosperity or a descent into hopelessness, despair, and poverty.

★

The year is 2050.

The Texas economy now accounts for one in six dollars in the gross domestic product of the United States. One in 10 Americans calls Texas by a more familiar name: Home. And there are now 50 million Texans, vastly outstripping the projections. One, issued in 2009, forecast that 24 million Texans would live in the Lone Star state in 2025, a number surpassed more than a decade earlier.

More populous than California, Texas seats the largest delegation in the U.S. Congress in Washington. In just two years, another Texan will be president. She is the fourth Texan to occupy the White House, the second Hispanic, and the third woman, in fact. But by now, these are mere historical footnotes. Long a society divided by race, nationality, and ethnicity, Congress has decided that with the new census, the government will no longer track people's racial and ethnic identity. Intermarriage has made it ridiculously irrelevant anyway.

By now, Texas is the red hot super charger in the economic engine of the United States. Long feared that America would fall behind China in economic power, Texas has been the difference. The economy in Texas alone has eclipsed that of Germany, an inventive but aging society. The youthfulness of Texas, in fact, has provided a powerful edge over other economic rivals. Only Japan, China, and the United States itself boast a bigger economy than that of Texas. The successful rise of a Hispanic majority into the middle and upper classes in large numbers is replicated across America, which in 2050 becomes majority minority itself.

And while America remains the greatest global power in the world, with interests and relationships that span the earth and a military capable of securing them, it is also an increasingly Hispanic super-power. Indeed, after centuries of eyeing Europe, the Middle East, and then Asia, Washington has fixed its gaze more firmly on the Americas. From the wealth of Canada and the United States to the booming economies of Mexico, Venezuela, Brazil, Argentina, and Chile, the Americas have become the most educated, wealthy and powerful societies in the world. Europe never really recovered from the global financial meltdown of 2008. China's giant workforce has aged and is retiring. The nation that was once the workshop of the world became a comfortable consumer society, its economic growth slowed by debt, certainly, but cushioned by the comfort of its earlier success.

The world now belongs to the youngest, brightest, most energetic and unlikeliest of generations strung around the unlikeliest places in the world, the Philippines, Indonesia, Bangladesh, Nigeria, much of the Americas and—oddest of all—that relentless behemoth, the United States of America.

★

This account above is the other scenario.

Its facts and figures are drawn from the U.S. Census Bureau, a range of population projections, economic projections of major banks, the U.S. Federal Reserve in Dallas, and the work of inter-disciplinary experts involved in a project called America 2050, which has tried to address everything from population growth to economic change to the infrastructure needs of the American economy in the 21st century.

The account above is best described as a projection, based upon a variety of current trends. But those trends cannot continue without investment in education to create a viable middle class forged out of the new Texas majority, as well as maintaining a representative democracy capable of making these choices—choices that address the economic effects of climate change, namely the availability of water.

Only these choices will lead to this future, this destination on that signpost out there on the crossroads. The opposite will lead to that other place: Perdition.

★

Back in the present, mid-2014 in Austin, the near future seems bright, on the one hand, and threatening on the other.

The economy continues to swell. Unemployment in Austin is well below 5 percent, and the city will likely add nearly 30,000 jobs, according to economist Angelos Angelous. On the other, another year of drought has come to visit or, rather, to stay. The politicians are crisscrossing the state, many with the usual agenda of God, guns, and gays but they're also calling once more for a crackdown on the border with Mexico, already one of the most militarized international boundaries on earth.

It is not clear that the Democratic Party offers Texas a brighter future, frankly. Based upon the performance of the Democratic Party nationally, that might be a dubious proposition. The Republicans may refuse to pass a comprehensive immigration reform bill. But the Democrats have a hard time thinking of Hispanics as anything but immigrants and that is an insufficient vision. Neither party seems to have grasped that Hispanic Texas wants what everyone else always wanted, a leg up into the middle class. According to Shaw, the University of Texas pollster, Hispanics have a strong interest in the economy—jobs and possibly entrepreneurship. "Any politician who doesn't address that," Shaw said, "is just another politician."

All that said, a return to genuinely competitive politics—in Texas and across America—would be a healthy development for the democracy, forget about one party or another. The emergence of a more competitive Democratic Party in Texas will likely not mean, however, the emergence of a terribly liberal strand of politics both in Texas and, as a result, nationally. Progressives hoping that somehow Texas will become a hotbed of left-wing politics are likely to be sorely surprised.

Instead, a successful brand of Democratic politics is likely to be more centrist than liberal in nature. Certainly, it would be free of the ideological straight-jacket of Republican politics—particularly on social issues—but Texas voters are likely to still want politicians dedicated to at the very least the platitudes of strong national security, a capitalist economy and, yes, the Second Amendment.

Already, the handful of successful Texas Democrats that exist readily pronounce themselves "pro-business Democrats." They seem to nearly stumble over their words trying to get that "pro-business" part out before that dirty, dreaded word, "Democrat." Nevertheless, the emergence of a competitive Democratic Party in Texas will not only push the state into the territory of purple, competitive politics—it will have the added effect of pushing American politics towards a place it sorely needs: The pragmatic center. The governor's mansion would no longer go to a candidate who can be elected with a minority of the electorate, further fractionalized by then peeling off the disproportionate number of conservative voters. It would instead go to the candidate who can forge coalitions of pragmatic conservatives and practical liberals into a strong center. The same would be true in presidential elections to a very powerful effect, given the state's 38 votes in the electoral college. And, on balance, this would be true of the House of Representatives and the Senate though House members have—and will always have—more license to buckle to petty special interests and powerful donors.

Politics aside, policy must confront the impacts of climate change ahead on, acknowledging that human activity is responsible for less rainfall and more evaporation in a hotter and drier Southwest. The plan for water resources approved in Austin is long on plans and very short on financing. It is also very heavy on 1950s and 1960s-era engineering solutions like more dams to hold back more freshwater in the rivers. But a hotter, drier climate will only evaporate more of that water. And the next generation of dams will only compound problems downstream, withholding water from farmers and ranchers and likely increasing the salinity of the Gulf of Mexico. The dam-building of the early 1960s may have already done that, damaging the ecosystem and nearly wiping out fish populations like those of the tarpon.

And nothing in Austin suggests that Texas will curtail its continued addiction to the problem of carbon emissions. Texas is the epicenter of the renaissance in American oil and gas. It is also leads the nation in carbon emissions. No place, other than an increasingly arid Texas, has a greater responsibility—just for its own sake—in curbing the vicious cycle between the earth's heating and the pumping of carbon into an increasingly dry atmosphere.

At the University of Texas at Austin, Richard W. Fisher has come to talk about the economy. With his slicked-back salt and pepper hair and steel glasses, Fisher walks to the podium, looking like a taller and more youthful version of Donald Rumsfeld. The son of an Australian father and a South African mother, he is about as global a figure as any. A Californian raised in Mexico, product of Annapolis, Harvard, Oxford, and Stanford, a banker, diplomat and a Democrat, he was appointed to run the Dallas Federal Reserve by George W. Bush. Before the financial crisis of 2008, Fisher told other members of the Fed that he worried that a serious recession was in the offing and he opposed the cheap money policy of former Federal Reserve Chairman Ben Bernanke, who dumped billions of dollars into the big banks, but pumped comparatively little into the economy.

Fisher's talks are prone to colorful titles, nearly always illustrated by facts and figures showing how the Texas economy is performing better than the rest of America, reciting the state's status as the leading exporter, sending $280 billion in goods abroad even as it handles about half the nation's imports. He forecasts continued growth. He is bullish about Texas and down on his old home, California. Increasingly, though, he wonders aloud about public policy choices including those about water and climate change that can damage a flowering economy. His urging is simple.

"If the fiscal and regulatory authorities that you elect and put into office to craft taxes, spending, and regulations do not focus their efforts on providing incentives for businesses to expand job-creating capital investment rather than bicker with each other for partisan purposes, our economy will continue to fall short and the middle-income worker will continue being victimized," he says. "In addition to being Longhorns and prosperous Texans, be bold Americans."

15

★ ★ ★

TEXAS, RECONSIDERED

The land in Texas is often just as David Crockett once described, back in 1836.

A drive between Dripping Springs and Lake Travis in spring is a tour de force of green woods, sparkling creeks, and wide open space, more reminiscent, say, of the African savanna than the deep woods of the Old South. When the ferry departs for Port Aransas down on the coast, the thick salt air feels good to breathe in, the sand trout flit through the water, and you feel like you are suddenly someplace else. Down in the Big Bend, the Window is literally a high-altitude view into Mexico but on the lip of Santa Elena Canyon the two nations are indistinguishable—just purple mountains fading into purple mountains. Some things don't change.

And yet on the pitch-black night of Halloween, 2013 the skies over the Texas Hill Country brooded and knit themselves into clouds that were a deep and foreboding gray as the sun went down. For weeks, after another dry year, the skies had threatened rain but only rarely delivered. I ventured into town after dusk. The streets were quiet and nearly deserted, as always in this small town. I bought milk and coffee for the morning and drove back up the hill toward home. A spotty drizzle turned into a steady one.

And around midnight all hell broke loose. The steady drizzle erupted into a gusher falling from the night sky. Lightning bolts exploded past the window and thunder rattled the dishes in the pine armoire. The valley was lit for seconds like it was broad daylight. I stumbled around in the dark putting an extra tarp on my otherwise exposed car, fearing a shower of hail if all this rain crossed into cold air, high above. The lightning was so close and the thunder shook the house so hard it became impossible to sleep.

When dawn came, 14 of inches of water had filled the rain gauges. After that the water just spilled out. Hillsides were washed into roadways. The wet-weather creek behind my house jumped its banks and came up six feet. Down below, the normally placid, clear Blanco had transformed itself into a roiling, angry brown flood, coming up 25 feet and tossing cypress trees and debris just as high. Worried homeowners waited for the water to seep in. Closer to Austin, it did: Onion Creek, a pretty, winding, lime-stone stream came up more, forcing 4,000 people to flee their flooded homes. Back in my small town Cypress Creek roared dozens of feet higher washing across Ranch Road 12, one of only two roads in and out of town. The storm was the talk of Texas; we do love to talk about the weather, after all. Friends in Dallas and El Paso texted me to see if I was okay as my little town had gotten clobbered nearly as hard as Onion Creek. I replied that I was high and dry on my hill, looking out across the valley. Several days later, as the river simmered down and cleared, I went for a walk along its banks, the fly rod in hand, again. And I noticed something: It had changed.

★

If I have learned anything from living in Texas since 1999, it is that things change. The world has changed since that year. A global economy has become a fact of life. Life lived in that fourth dimension—online, in social media and mobile—has become a simple and expected convenience, not just in America but for much of society. Life changes. One day you are in the throes of love. Life is new and shiny and limitless. The next, it seems, you are middle-aged, and a little worn down. There is a beauty in that, though. It's like an old, broken-in pair of boots or the smell and taste of a cup of coffee, as my mother recently related, on a bone-chilling autumn morning in the high desert of West Texas. I write this only to reflect on that relentless change in a personal way, because, after all, that is the thesis of this book. Texas remained largely the same for thousands of years of human history. But right now, in front of our very eyes, it is changing. It is changing, too, the very nature of America itself. And it will continue doing so while being paradoxically more like America, too—and yet, particular and distinct.

As I wrote this book, I thought often of an existential question: What does it mean to be Texan? What has it meant and what does it now mean? While as a Texan I admit I'm biased, I found the notion that Texas would eventually lose its quirks, cultures, and traditions—all laced with good and bad, admittedly—somewhat disheartening. Would the cowboy and cowgirl, already an endangered species, vanish forever as the cities grew and life there became the dominant experience for the coming generations of Texans? Would centuries of stoic cultures—whether Anglo, Mexican American,

Mexican, or African American—be replaced by gentrifying, ironic hipsters who can really be found anywhere? What would happen to the rodeo, the gun rack, the pickup truck, and church? Seriously, what would happen to that one or two finger wave—the fingers barely lifted from the steering wheel—that rural Texans use to say "hi" on a lonely road? Will it just disappear? What about the perfect strangers who look you in the eye and say hello on the sidewalk or in a grocery store line—who often scare people from Los Angeles who are not used to strangers saying hello? Would the generations of Texans to come just pass each other on the concrete sidewalks of Congress Avenue, eyes down, hands shoved in their pockets like awkward commuters on a cold Manhattan morning?

"It's just the whole story. The reality is that life in Texas is urban and suburban even if the image of a Texan is rural," Jake Silverstein told me during a conversation one day in his office. At the time, he was editor-in-chief of *Texas Monthly* before departing to run the *Sunday Magazine* at the *New York Times*. We got to talking about a cover story by S. C. Gwynne, whose daughter had grown up with mine, called "The Last Ranchers," a bit of a tear-jerker about the demise of the family ranch. It seems writers, since Larry McMurtry, have been bidding so long to cowboys for decades now. "But we can't ignore the fact that there is a myth," Silverstein said. "Those stories still mean a lot to people."

To non-Texans, these may seem like small questions, after all the evidence of the sweeping, even revolutionary change that is taking place. But they are not. First of all, Texans can sit around all day talking about this stuff if they ever get done talking about the weather. These ideas challenge—even threaten—the idea that there is something special about Texas, an article of absolute faith certainly over most of the last two centuries, even if it was often backed by myth. And if Texas is not unique, at best, or distinct, at worst, then it will wash away, like a hillside after a rain storm. And beyond the sentimentality, it would mean that the ability of Texas to change the nation will eventually spend itself, not unlike a flash flood that rises in the night—only to disappear the next morning. So, intellectually, as well emotionally, it's worthy to explore what it is to be Texan. After all, tens of millions more Americans will find themselves not just living here—but living with that very question. In the end, after all, the story of people on the move—whether in the thousands 7,000 years ago or in the millions today—is an intimate and personal tale.

They will find themselves, yes, living in the broad sweep of history—within the context of social, economic, and political change, true. But they will experience this history individually or in the company of a handful of loved ones. That is how the human experience works. History itself is like looking at the Hill Country sky on a moonless, winter night: It is millions and millions of points of light that collectively tell a story. Millions and millions of human lives will find themselves unexpectedly part of the history unfolding now in Texas. There will be many differences in those stories, certainly. But understanding their stories—yes, imperfectly—in their totality is what will make the history of the future, so to speak.

Driving back and forth to Austin in the spring of 2014, I begin to notice the return of roadside merchants that I'd not seen in great numbers, at least not noticed, since around the turn of the century when I came here at the beginning of the Sixth Migration. They sold bits of Texas: A set of horns to hang on a wall, metal forged into shapes of lone stars and the outline of Texas. It made me smile because I was one of those people, 15 years ago, who pulled over to buy a trinket as if to prove that I really was a Texan now that I was back.

The culture of Texas seems a hard thing to stamp out of existence, even as it changes. Rodeos come every spring and on holiday weekends, regardless of the changing suburbs, the changing face of society, and globalization. In 2013, Vanessa Parker, the wandering, small-town, fifth generation Texan from Granbury, became—of all things—the queen of the Fort Worth Livestock Competition and Rodeo. Though the position is normally reserved for 18 year olds, the 35-year old brunette galloped out into the arena each night in her cowgirl duds, a giant American flag at her side, to the accompanying strains of Lee Greenwood's, "God Bless the U.S.A." Afterwards, rodeo fans of all nationalities and ethnicities came up for photographs, some of them with their newly-purchased cowboy hats on precisely backwards. She said, "It brought a tear to my eye every night."

In 2014, she completed her journey and wound up right where she had started out: Right down the road, in Granbury, Texas. Indulging her love of horses and animals she left the latest boom in oil and gas and settled into her mother's empty home. She started buying and selling furnishings from the mid-20th century, all the rage for people with money who are moving to Texas.

"I swore I'd never be back here, ever, ever, ever, ever," she laughed. The town has changed. It's bigger. It has a bigger Walmart. She has neighbors where once there were none, she said, and yet "a lot of things are the same in a lot of ways."

I ponder the Texanness of my own small town. The Texas one-finger salute has for decades been a staple of the back roads: One stranger saying hello to another on an isolated two-lane road by lifting just the index finger off the steering wheel, with the gesture modestly returned. Now, I noticed that some people just don't say "hi" back.

But then something else sealed this issue, at least for me. A poll in 2014 asked Texans to identify which they were first: Texans or

Americans? Most people said they were Americans, of course. But the largest number of people who said they were Texans first? They were the newest arrivals of the Sixth Migration, in particular the Mexicans. I expect we'll be flying those barn door-sized Texas flags for many years to come.

★

The river is cool and clear, clearer even than it was before the storm. Peering into it is like looking into my aquarium at home. The flood waters have left debris high above my head, strung in the boughs of the bald cypress trees. Many of these trees, I am reminded, are centuries old. Some were saplings, even, when Columbus landed in America and still young when Cabeza de Vaca stumbled across Texas.

I fish less than I used to and on some days—like this one—I'm largely content to walk the river and count the fish. There is the spot where we used to plunk our chairs in the water on a hot summer day. There is the spot in the deep water where I took the occasional girlfriend, much to the amusement, it turned out, of my neighbors on the river. As I walk up to the Ranch Road 12 bridge, there is the spot where my friend Mark caught a monster smallmouth in just inches of water, the fishing staring at him, nearly begging him, to toss a fly.

The sky is growing dark again. I release a small bass I caught in spite of myself, and walk back, headed home. The clouds are thick but they do not threaten any more rain, at least not this evening. And I realize two things, nearly at once. Everything changes, of course, but in this case, even the land does. The Halloween storm has not just left trees, uprooted and snapped like matchsticks where they didn't belong. It didn't just leave flotsam and jetsam stranded in the cypress branches. It didn't even just scour the river. It altered its very course, depositing giant beaches arched in graceful half-moon curves along the banks. Where there were no beaches I now count four, at least, that kiss the river current and numerous ones on the banks that once held none.

If a river that has run for millions of years can change and, yet, retain its essential nature it seems to me that Texas will, too. Though we were all city dwellers, I took my girls horseback riding out in Bandera; we climbed Enchanted Rock and attended the small-town rodeos on sweltering summer nights in Wimberley. Their mother, Laurie, has passed on many of her family's Texas traditions, most notably the black-eyed peas at New Year's, an ancient southern custom intended for good luck in the coming year. Isabel and I greeted her birthday, and spring itself, for many years at the livestock show in Austin. Every once in a while, on a Saturday in the autumn, I would still get a text message from Olivia, her older sister, who has become a Longhorn fan. Did we and the millions of others begin to change Texas? Of course. If you must think about the political and the personal, just consider how the politics of the big cities have changed.

Often my friends on the East Coast have wondered what the hell I'm doing out here. And I wonder, too: Was it worth it? Was it worth it for us? Is it worth it for the 1,000 fresh faces that arrive in Texas every single day? Will it be worth it for the 26 million more people who are coming here to Texas? The answer is: It's hard to know. To be perfectly honest, living here, just like living anywhere, has booms and busts, personal and public. But when I think about the girls the answer becomes quite clear: Yes. Olivia and Isabel have had the chance to grow up in a unique place framed by a unique time.

Like lucky kids everywhere, one won a lacrosse championship and the other fought her way to qualifying for the national championship of softball. They smiled and laughed and fought injury, sweating in that unrelenting Texas sun. Unlike kids anywhere else, they knew the simple joy of Barton Springs, caught red-eared sliders out of a canoe, watched the foxes from the back porch, had the good fortune to go to great public schools—where they both learned to sing "The Lord Bless You and Keep You"—and got the opportunity to attend fine universities, all close to home.

As they grew up and grew away, they learned about healthy food and independent music without ever having to travel. Children of the sun, they've never known a harsh winter, though they have witnessed violent thunderstorms, the occasional snake, and nearly perfect daily sunsets. With a modest upbringing in both the city and in the country, they've known the tastes and sounds of downtown and the simple pleasure of an afternoon on the river.

So, anyone who gets to my age, to this stage in life, and says they have no regrets is, in my book, a liar. I have plenty. So will the other 26 million people who are coming to Texas. (Secretly, I hope they all move to Dallas.) There will be highs and there will be lows. And those will likely be as much the result of their personal stories of migration, regardless of scale and destination. Migration is, of course, the most dangerous time in the life of any creature, any family, any flock. A few will succeed. Most of them will make it, somehow. Some of them will not. Some will pack up and go back, bewildered by the place, their hopes and dreams and families shattered either by their choice or their fear. But in the end, those who make it will not likely live long enough to see it enrich them; they will, with any luck, see it enrich their children, though. And that is the ultimate hope of any Texan, any American, and any human being.

★

I have not seen the black-faced doe in a long while.

By December, the deer are deep into the rut. Testosterone-fueled bucks charge through the woods, nearly day and night, chasing does and chasing away younger suitors. I put away the fly rod, leaning it up against the wood-paneled wall with the others, stacked together beneath the few fish that wound up unreleased and uneaten and instead, hung on the wall for all eternity.

I switch on a lamp by the books and the one in the gun case and walk out to the porch to see what emerges from the dusk. There are frogs and toads, a gray fox that roams around some evenings and that I feed and, very rarely, a pair of coyotes I have only spied twice. The rain storms, I notice, have filled up all the ponds and cattle tanks. In my yard, the water features and the butterfly garden have prospered, too, though rather late in the year. There is enough forage that the deer have quit—for now—raiding the esperanza and the prickly pears, even. A small buck emerges from the tree line across the street and comes close. Then he picks up the pace and runs downhill; I expect he is being spooked by a larger one.

Sure enough a big, thick buck—probably weighing in about 160 pounds, big for around here—emerges. He neither sees me nor smells me as there is no wind, not even a breeze. Instead, he noses around the edge of the garden—not 10 feet away. He goes into a crouch to mark his territory. I say, suddenly, "Hey, big boy." And he startles off into the gathering darkness.

The next morning I decide to make the very long drive to El Paso to see my parents. I am remiss. It has been years, I admit. Regardless, I choose not to fly, nor to take the interstate at its nearest junction but instead to take the back road for about half the distance, up through the Hill Country and towns like Llano, Mason, and Menard, cutting northwest for Iraan where the Hill Country gives way to the Edwards Plateau and finally the vast

Trans-Pecos desert, where the back roads meet the big, broad interstate.

The streets and roads are nearly deserted. Eventually, the highway flattens out. I can tell I am now out of the rolling Hill Country and crossing the Edwards Plateau. A few crews are working new gas wells. Suddenly, outside Iraan the road drops steeply, hundreds of feet—right off the edge of the plateau—plunging like a roller coaster toward the creosote flats. Interstate 10 is not far and when I reach it I can look back and see the plateau is now guarded by hundreds of wind turbines, each churning its propellers into the wind and making electricity bound for someplace hundreds of miles away. These didn't used to be here.

It is then that I realize it has been 15 years or perhaps more since I drove this stretch of highway, which opens up to the Western United States. I am closer now to the Pacific than the Gulf of Mexico. I used to drive this highway all the time. It was the road between home and college and then between home and the East Coast.

Despite the passage of not just years but decades, I know this open and empty land defined by its army of big rig trucks and punctuated by its Flying J truck stops. The drive to see my parents, now in their late seventies, becomes a race against the sun. The air is cooling as the sun falls to the west. But I've had the convertible top down so far and I see no reason to put it up as I pass through Fort Hancock; I'll reach the outskirts of El Paso, precisely at sunset. So I drive as fast as I can.

I know this road: It goes home.

ACKNOWLEDGMENTS

I certainly wish to thank all the people who spent their time with me; they are merely too numerous to mention here but they appear within the pages and the sources of this book. I am thankful for the time of the insightful and expert as well as that of the rest of us, too, who experience real-time history with perhaps less sweep but, perhaps, more personally. I'm also intellectually in debt to some very fine writers, some of whom I've met and others whom I never have, including the great T. R. Fehrenbach, author of *Lone Star*, and historian Randolph B. Campbell, author of *Gone to Texas*. Each so thoroughly explained centuries of history that I was afforded the luxury of focusing on the present and future.

Certainly, I must thank Claiborne Hancock of Pegasus Books for enthusiastically embracing this project by a writer entirely unknown to him at the time, introduced through the good and tireless offices of Nathaniel Jacks at Inkwell Management. Nat was careful in helping me not just find Claiborne and Pegasus but tireless in selecting just the right topic, Texas, and shaping the concept. Jessica Case at Pegasus carefully read the ensuing drafts. Jennifer McCartney did a masterful job in editing and any remaining weaknesses are my own. Showing how life works in its serendipity, Nathaniel plucked me after reading the Op-Ed pages of *The New York Times*, where I've had the good fortune to be edited by Clay Risen, a former colleague at *The New Republic*. I thank Frank Foer, the editor at *The New Republic*, for publishing some of my work on Texas as well as Ray Walker, the opinion editor at the McClatchy-Tribune syndicate in Washington, D.C. Each stoked some angle of this story over time, whether they knew it or not.

Speaking of editors and colleagues, there have been many over the years but I have to thank a few of them and some colleagues who may, or may not, ever read this thanks: Erroll Laborde in New Orleans; Kent Walz, Steve Mills, Bill Hume, Joanne Angel and Chris Mora at the Albuquerque Journal; Kathleen Carroll, now running the Associated Press in New York; Dave Garlock and Lorraine Branham, formerly of the University of Texas at Austin; Greg Marx and Liz Barrett at the *Columbia Journalism Review*; my friend Kate Galbraith formerly of the *Texas Tribune*; my friend Bryan Bender of *The Boston Globe* and my buddy Michael Zielenziger, formerly of Knight-Ridder Newspapers. Among family and friends, I'd like to thank my former father-in-law and mother-in-law, John and Suzanne Stowe of Abilene and Suzanne's dear sister, Cindy; my old friends Mark Seiler and Steve Evans; photographer, close friend and fellow traveler Erik Hildebrandt; writer and friend Jeff Connaughton; James Hyde, who encouraged me to devote myself to writing again. My sister, Janet Collins is my sweet younger sibling, confidant, and very best friend. All these people inspired, critiqued, encouraged, cajoled, supported and improved me along the way. I owe a particular debt to my parents, Josefina and James, for supporting the uncertain adventure in journalism, particularly in its very shaky beginning. I am grateful for the love of my daughters, Olivia and Isabel, and the enduring kindness of their mother, my former wife, Laurie.

There is one final note to Laurie's grandfather, the late Mac McCarty. Gone some years now, Mac was all the things God loves: A fisherman, an Episcopalian, a newspaperman, and an unrepentant yellow dog Democrat in the heart of the Catclaw Country of Abilene. His black, portable Remington Rand typewriter, made in 1932 and still in shiny, mint condition, stood vigil over me as I wrote this manuscript. In his later years, Mac and his beloved Essie enjoyed retirement by traveling the scenic highways and byways of their beloved Texas in their Chevy station wagon. At 5:00 P.M. precisely, wherever they were, they would pull over religiously—for happy hour. They would've gotten a kick out of this book.

All of these people made my Texas possible.

May 15, 2014
Wimberley, Texas

REFERENCES AND WORKS CONSULTED

Aaronson, Becca and Park, Minjae. "On the Record: Expanded Nursing Could Boost Economy." The Texas Tribune, May 14, 2012.

Aasen Eric. "75 Years Later, Texas Centennial Exposition Has Enduring Impact on Dallas." *The Dallas Morning News*, June 11, 2011.

Abernathy, Francis E. "Dobie, James Frank," *Handbook of Texas Online.* June 12, 2010. Published by the Texas State Historical Association.

Ahmed, Aamena. "Report: Texas Public School Enrollment Tops 5 Million." The Texas Tribune, April 1, 2014.

All About Ann. Directed by Keith Patterson and Phillip Schopper. New York: HBO, 2014. Television documentary.

"American FactFinder." United States Census Bureau. Washington, D.C., Philadelphia demographic information retrieved January 31, 2013.

"Annual Estimates of the Population for the United States, Regions, States and Puerto Rico: April 1, 2010 to July 1, 2013." *2013 Population Estimates,* United States Census Bureau. Washington, D.C. December 2013.

"Austin Population, 2013," World Population Statistics, accessed September 15, 2013.

Balli, Cecilia. "What Nobody Says About Austin: Is Austin the State's Most Segregated City?" *Texas Monthly,* February 2013.

Bandieray, Oriana, Rasulz, Imran and Viarengox, Martina."The Making of Modern America: Migratory Flows in the Age of Mass Migration." University College London, October 2012.

Barnes, Donna. "People's Party." *Handbook of Texas Online*. Texas State Historical Association, accessed June 15, 2013.

Barr, Alwyn. "Late Nineteenth-Century Texas." *Handbook of Texas Online*. Published by the Texas State Historical Association. Accessed June 18, 2013.

Barron, James. "Nation Reels After Gunman Massacres 20 Children at School in Connecticut." *The New York Times*, December 14, 2012.

Batheja, Aman. "Report: Panama Canal Expansion Will Aid Texas Exports," Texas Tribune, January 7, 2013.

Bennhold, Katrin. "Proud Scots, Wherever They're From." *The New York Times*, April 8, 2014.

Bissinger, H.G. Friday. *Night Lights: A Town, A Team, and a Dream*. New York: Da Capo Press, 1990, 2000.

Blank, Joshua and Albertson, Bethany. "Polling Center: Texan First, American Second." The Texas Tribune, April 3, 2014.

Burka, Paul. "A Generation of Republican Leadership." *Texas Monthly*, February 10, 2014.

Burka, Paul. "The Battle Over UT: An Inside View of the Fight for the Soul of the University." *Texas Monthly*, October 2012.

Burnett, John. "Texas Banks Draw On Lessons From the S&L Crisis." National Public Radio, Washington, D.C., October 29, 2008. Radio broadcast.

Burns, Alexander. "Democrats Launch Plan to Turn Texas Blue." *Politico*, January 24, 2013.

Burns, Alexander. "GOP Big City Mayors Vanish." *Politico*, October 20, 2013.

Busby, Mark. *Larry McMurtry and the West: An Ambivalent Relationship*. Denton, Texas: University of North Texas Press, 1995.

Busby, Mark and Heaberlin, Dick, eds. *From Texas to the World and Back: Essays on the Journeys of Katherine Anne Potter*, Fort Worth: TCU Press, 2001.

Calvert, Robert Al, Cantrell, Gregg and DeLeon, Arnoldo. *The History of Texas: 4th Edition*. West Sussex, United Kingdom: John Wiley & Sons, 2014.

Campbell, Randolph B., *Gone to Texas*. Oxford University Press, 2003.

Camia, Catalina. "Texas Gov Hopeful Likes to Sue President Obama." *USA Today*, July 15, 2013.

Cardona, Claire. "Texas College Tuition Up 55% Since 2003 Deregulation, Analysis Shows." *The Dallas Morning News*, September 22, 2012.

Caro Robert A. "Lady Bird." *Texas Monthly*, April 1990.

Caro, Robert A. *Means of Ascent*. Alfred A. Knopf: New York, 1990.

"Case-Shiller Indexes," CoreLogic, San Francisco, Third Quarter, 2013.

Chait, Jonathan. "The Conservative Fantasy History of Civil Rights." *New York*, May 22, 2012.

Chavez, Stephanie."Texas Wildfire in Bastrop County the Worst Ever Single Fire in the State." *The Los Angeles Times*, September 5, 2011.

Christie, Les. "The Fastest Growing U.S Cities." CNN, Atlanta, July 24, 2008. Television news report.

Cody, Carl. "Luci Baines Johnson: Vietnam War 'Lanced' LBJ's Gut Every Night," National Public Radio, Washington, D.C., April 10, 2014. Radio broadcast.

Collins, Gail. *As Texas Goes . . . How the Lone Star State Hijacked the American Agenda.* New York: W.W. Norton, 2012.

Combs, Susan. "The Texas Economy: Economic Outlook," Texas Comptroller of Public Accounts, Austin, Texas, 2010.

Coulter, Ann. "Bush's America: Roach Motel." *Human Events*, June 6, 2007.

Cox, Patrick. *The First Texas News Barons.* Austin: University of Texas Press, 2005.

"Databank," World Bank, Washington, D.C., Retrieved November 22, 2013.

"Death Takes James M. Dobie, Pioneer Cattleman of Texas," *The Lubbock Avalanche Journal*, May 22, 1929.

Davidson, Chandler. *Race and Politics in Texas*, Princeton, New Jersey: Princeton University Press, 1990.

DeLeon, Arnolodo and Calvert, Robert A. "Civil Rights." *Handbook of Texas Online.* June 12, 2010. Published by the Texas State Historical Society.

Dobie, J. Frank. *The Flavor of Texas.* Austin: Jenkins Publishing Company, 1975.

Dobie, J. Frank. *Guide to Life and Literature of the Southwest.* Dallas: Southern Methodist University Press, 1952.

"Dobie Paisano Fellowship Program," website of the University of Texas at Austin Graduate School, accessed November 15, 2013.

Dugan, Andrew. "Texan Hispanics Tilt Democratic, But State Likely to Stay Red." Gallup Politics, February 7, 2014.

Dunham, Richard. "Texas' Ten Top Republican and Democratic Political Money People," *Houston Chronicle*, November 3, 2012.

"DC 10 to Drop Fire Retardant Starting Friday," KXAN, Austin, Texas, September 11, 2011. Television news report.

"Economy at a Glance: Texas 2013-2014," Bureau of Labor Statistics, U.S. Department of Labor, Washington, D.C., 2014.

"Employees and Salaries," Texas Politics, retrieved January 2, 2014.

Egan, Timothy. "Rick Perry's Unanswered Prayers." *The New York Times*, August 11, 2011.

Emerson, Michael O., Bratter, Jennifer, Howell, Junia, Jeanty, P. Wilner and Kline, Mike. "Houston Region Grows More Racially/Ethnically Diverse With Small Declines in Segregation." Kinder Institute for Urban Research and Hobby Center for the Study of Texas, Rice University, Houston, Texas, March, 2010.

Fehrenbach, T.R. *Lone Star, A History of Texas and the Texans.* Da Capo Press, New York. 1968, 2000.

Ferber, Edna. *Giant.* HarperCollins: New York, 1952, 1980, 2000.

Florida, Richard. "How the Creative Class Is Reshaping America's Electoral Map." *The Atlantic* City Lab, September 24, 2012.

Florida, Richard and Johnson, Sarah."What Republicans Are Really Up Against: Population Density." *The Atlantic* City Lab, November 26, 2012.

Fisher, Richard W. "A Conversation About Longhorns, Longnecks and Liquidity: The Economy and the Course of Monetary Policy." Remarks by the chairman of the Federal Reserve Bank of Dallas before the 9th Annual Alumni Business Conference, University of Texas at Austin McCombs School of Business, Austin, Texas, February 21, 2014.

"Former A&M Assistant and Houston Oilers Coach Bum Phillips Dies at 90," Associated Press, October 18, 2013.

Foster, Robin. "Houston Mayor Anise Parker Touts Progress, Plan to Protect Human Rights." *Your Houston News*, April 3, 2014.

Frambach, Hans A. editor. *The Liberation of the Serfs: The Economics of Unfree Labor.* New York: Springer, 2012.

Gardner, Amy. "Rick Perry's Response to Texas Wildfires Offers Glimpse of Leadership." *The Washington Post*, September 6, 2011.

"Geographic Identifiers: 2010 Demographic Profile Data (G001): Missouri City, Texas." United States Census Bureau, Census 2000, Washington, D.C., February 12, 2012.

"Geographic Comparison Tables—State—Place and County Subdivision." *American FactFinder*, Census 2000, United States Census Bureau, Census 2000, Washington, D.C.

"Geology of Texas," Bureau of Economic Geology, The University of Texas at Austin and the Texas State Historical Association, Austin, Texas.

Gonzalez, John Moran. *Border Renaissance: The Texas Centennial and the Emergence of Mexican-American Literature.* Austin: University of Texas Press, 2010.

Grieder, Erica. *Big, Hot, Cheap, and Right: What American Can Learn From Texas.* New York: Public Affairs, 2013.

Grieder, Erica. "What Do You Think of Ted Cruz Now?" *Texas Monthly*, February 2014.

Gugliota, Guy. "New Estimate Raises Civil War Death Toll." *The New York Times*, April 2, 2012.

Gwynne, S.C. *Empire of the Summer Moon.* New York: Scribner, 2010.

Hamilton, Reeve. "Panel Votes That Grounds For Impeachment Exist for Hall." Texas Tribune, May 12, 2014.

Hennessy-Fiske, Mollly. "Wealthy, Business-Savvy Mexican Immigrants Transform Texas City." *Los Angeles Times*, March 24, 2013.

Hart, Patricia Kilday. "Little Did We Know . . ." *Texas Monthly*, November 2004.

"Henry B. Gonzalez," *Biographical Directory of the United States Congress 1774-Present*, Washington, D.C., 2014.

Hoffman, Charles. *Depression of the Nineties: An Economic History.* Westport, Connecticut: Greenwood Publishing, 1970.

Holley, Joe. "Former Texas Governor Ann Richards Dies." *The Washington Post*, September 14, 2006.

"Home Values in WISD Skyrocket," *The Wimberley View*, May 1, 2014.

Hoppe, Christi. "David Dewhurst Earns His Spurs." *The Dallas Morning News*, March 27, 2009.

Hudson, Wilson M. "Bedicheck, Roy." *Handbook of Texas Online*, June 12, 2010. Published by the Texas State Historical Association.

"Incorporated Places of 100,000 or More, Ranked by Population, 2000," Census 2000 Redistricting Data, United States Census Bureau, Washington, D.C., April 2, 2001.

Ivins, Molly. "The Man Never Sold Out to Anyone," Molly Ivins, Creators Syndicate, November 30, 2000.

Johnson, Tim. "Widening of Panama Canal Will Remake World Trade Patterns." McClatchy Newspapers, August 6, 2012.

Karl Rove: The Architect. Directed by Michael Kirk. Washington, D.C.: PBS Frontline, April 12, 2005.

Kever, Jeannie, "Census Shows Galaveston Smaller As Demographics Shift." *Houston Chronicle*, March 4, 2011.

Kofler, Shelley and Aasen, Eric. "Ted Nugent Appearing With Greg Abbott An 'Insult To Every Woman,' Wendy Davis Says." KERA, Dallas, Texas, February 18, 2014. Broadcast television report.

Knagges, John R. *Two-Party Texas*, Eakin Press, Austin, Texas 1986.

Kumar, Anil. "Globalizing Texas: Exports and High-Tech Jobs." *Southwest Economy*, Federal Reserve Bank of Dallas, September/October 2007.

Kuta, Sarah. "Texas Governor's Mansion Done." Associated Press, July 18, 2012.

Lane, Dorothy E. "Kirkpatrick, Alice Glass." *Handbook of Texas Online*, June 15, 2010. Published by the Texas State Historical Association.

Lavendera, Ed, Pearson, Michael and King, John. "50 Years On, Nation Pauses to Remember John F. Kennedy's Death." CNN, Atlanta, November 22, 2013. Television broadcast.

Lawrence, Vallerie. "O'Henry," Writer's Camp, June 18, 2011.

Lederman, Josh. "Obama Marks 50th Anniversary of Civil Rights Act," Associated Press, April 10, 2014.

"Lieutenant Governor David Dewhurst," official website, retrieved January 28, 2014.

Lipscomb, Carol A. "Comanche Indians," *Handbook of Texas Online*. June 12, 2010. Published by the Texas State Historical Association.

Long, J., *Weird City: Sense of Place and Creative Resistance in Austin, Texas*. Austin: University of Texas Press, 2010.

LoPalo, Melisssa and Orrenius, Pia M. "Texas Leads Nation in Creation of Jobs at all Pay Levels." Federal Reserve Bank of Dallas, First Quarter 2014.

Maher, John."Giving It Another Go." *Austin American-Statesman*, November 15, 2013.

Maher, John. "Set to Chase History." *Austin American-Statesman*, November 17, 2013.

Maron, Dina Fine. "Firefighters From 43 States Battle Far-Flung Texas Wildfires." *The New York Times*, April 26, 2011.

Mashood, Farzad. "Current Drought Pales in Comparison With 1950s 'Drought of Record.'" *Austin American-Statesman*, August 3, 2011.

May, Stephen J. *Michener, A Writer's Journey*. Norman Oklahoma: University of Oklahoma Press, 2005.

Mchann, Clinton and Clark, Bedford William, eds. *Katherine Anne Porter and Texas: An Uneasy Relationship*. College Station, Texas: Texas A&M University Press, 1990.

McMurtry, Larry, *In A Narrow Grave: Essays on Texas*. Simon & Schuster: New York, 1968, 1996.

McNichol, Elizabeth and Johnson, Nicholas. "The Texas Economic Model: Hard for Other States to Follow and Not All It Seems." Center on Budget and Policy Priorities, Washington, D.C., April 3. 212.

Mealer, Bryan. "South Texas Goes Bananas." *Texas Monthly*, November 2013.

Minutaglio, Bill and Davis, Steven L. *Dallas 1963: The Road to the Kennedy Assassination*, Twelve: New York, 2013.

Minutaglio, Bill and W. Michael Smith, *Molly Ivins, A Brief Life*. Public Affairs: New York, 2009.

Bill Minutaglio, Davis, Steven L. and Kirk, Chris. "The City That Killed Kennedy." Slate, November 18, 2013.

Mingus, Jade and Vess, Jessica. *Austin Remembers Leslie*. KVUE, Austin, Texas, March 8, 2012. Television news report.

"Mexico's Well-to-Do Move North," *Global Perspectives*, National Association of Realtors, Washington, D.C., April 2012.

"Missouri City QuickFacts From the U.S. Census Bureau," U.S. Census Bureau, Washington, D.C., Retrieved February 10, 2013.

Moran, Lee. "Flight From the Inferno." *The Daily Mail*, September 6, 2011.

Moroney, James III. "What Will the News Be At 150?" *The Dallas Morning News*, October 1, 2010.

Nickell, J.K. "The New—and Rich—Immigrants From Mexico: How Their Money Is Changing Texas." January 14, 2013.

"'No Containment' of Texas Wildfire, Associated Press, September 6, 2011.

Novak, Shonda. "Roof Raiser: Home Sales Hit All-Time Local Record" *Austin American-Statesman*, January 18, 2014.

"Oil and Texas: A Cultural History." *The Texas Almanac*, Published by The Texas State Historical Association, Austin, Texas.

Orrenius, Pia M. "*Gone to Texas*: Immigration and the Transformation of the Texas Economy." Federal Reserve Bank of Dallas, March 2011.

Parker, Richard. Author interviews with: Alex Prud'homme, author of *The Ripple Effect*, Texas Book Festival, C-SPAN, October 22, 2011; Matt Glazer, executive director of Progress Texas, July 7, 2012; Daron Shaw, University of Texas professor, July 15, 2012; Laura Kilcrease, venture capitalist, December 15, 2013; Regina Lawrence, University of Texas professor, October 8, 2013; Ron Marks, actor, musician and entrepreneur, December 16, 2013; Ray Perryman, economist, August, 7, 2011; Interview with Vanessa Parker, 5th generation Texan, May 14, 2014; Carla Ramos, student, December 17, 2013; Randolph Lewis, University of Texas professor, various; Even Smith, journalist and publisher, April 7, 2013; Holly Regan, new arrival in Texas, May 14, 2014; Nicholas Frankl, entrepreneur, December 12, 2013; Lisa Newton O'Neill, public relations executive, February 17, 2014; Rebecca Fenby, singer-songwriter, December 13, 2013; Joel Shuler, entrepreneur, December 12, 2013; Mark Seiler, entrepreneur, December 14, 2013; Jake Silverstein, journalist, December 7, 2012; Manoj Saxena, technologist, October 7, 2012; December 4, 2013; Esteban Dorantes, pseudonym of undocumented migrant, August 15, 2013; various subjects, 2012-2014.

Parker, Richard. "Becoming the Texas Tribune." *Columbia Journalism Review*, April 15, 2013.

Parker, Richard. "Can Austin Stay Weird?" British Airways *High Life*, March 2014.

Parker, Richard, "A Laurel to Univision 41's Arantxa Loizaga." *Columbia Journalism Review*, February 27, 2013.

Parker, Richard. "As Texas Dries Out, Life Falters and Fades." *The New York Times*, August 13, 2011.

Parker, Richard. "Back to the Basics on Immigration." *Columbia Journalism Review*, July 12, 2013.

Parker, Richard. "Can Austin Keep Itself Weird?" *The New York Times*, October 25, 2012.

Parker, Richard. "Fighting on Fumes." *The New York Times*, March 28, 2012.

Parker, Richard. "Houston, We Have No Comment," *Columbia Journalism Review*, December 17, 2013.

Parker, Richard. "How West Was Spun." *Columbia Journalism Review*, May 24, 2013.

Parker, Richard. "In Texas, A Filibuster For the Digital Age." *Columbia Journalism Review*, June 27, 2013.

Parker, Richard, "John Bell Hood's Great Adventure." *The New York Times*, July 3, 2013.

Parker, Richard. "Lone Star Blues." *The New York Times*. February 19, 2013.

Parker, Richard. "Lone Star Politics: Anything But Dull." *Columbia Journalism Review*, January 28, 2013.

Parker, Richard. "Rick Perry, Please Come Home: Why Texas Needs Its Governor Back." *The New Republic*, October 20, 2011.

Parker, Richard. "Sam Houston, We Have A Problem." *The New York Times*, January 31, 2011.

Parker, Richard. "Seriously Slick." *Columbia Journalism Review*, December 5, 2013.

Parker, Richard. "Still, Water." *Columbia Journalism Review*, June 4, 2013.

Parker, Richard. "Taking Stock in Texas." *Columbia Journalism Review*, October 4, 2013.

Parker, Richard. "Texas Catches Fire." *The New York Times*, May 18, 2011.

Parker, Richard. "Texas Voter More Than Bubba Stereotype Courted by Voters." *Albuquerque Journal*. March 8, 1992.

Parker, Richard. "The Great Recession: A Small-Town Portrait." *The Denver Post*, June 23, 2011.

Parker, Richard. "The Lone Star State Turns South." *The New York Times*, February 28, 2011.

Parker, Richard. "The Newspaper Columnists of the Lone Star State," *Columbia Journalism Review*, March 19, 2013.

Parker, Richard. "Voting Wars Redux in Texas." *Columbia Journalism Review*, August 22, 2013.

Parker, Richard. "The War Comes to Galveston." *The New York Times*, July 1, 2011.

Parker, Richard. "What's to Come in West, Texas: After Wednesday's Fertilizer Explosion, the Town Is Still Picking Up the Pieces." *The New Republic*, April 18, 2013

Parker, Richard. "Who is Greg Abbott?" *Columbia Journalism Review*, July 24, 2013.

Parker, Richard. "Why the Middle Class Is In Trouble." *St. Paul Pioneer Press*, September 28, 2012.

Parker, Richard and Boyd, Emily. "Massacre On the Nueces." *The New York Times* Disunion, August 11, 2012.

Parker, Richard and Boyd, Emily. "The Great Hanging at Gainesville." *The New York Times*, October 16, 2012.

Parker, Richard and Craun, Lindsey. "Blood and Sand." *The New York Times*, February 22, 2012.

Parker, Richard and Guest, Hardy. "A Few Bad Apples." *Columbia Journalism Review*, February 18, 2013.

Parker, Richard and Posgate, Natalie. "Go West, Young Confederacy." *The New York Times* Disunion, August 23, 2011.

Parker, Richard and Smithson, Cate. "Time for Washington to Get Serious About Mexico." *The Deseret News*, October 20, 2010.

Potter, Lloyd B. and Hoque, Nazrul. "Texas Population Projections: 2010-2050," Office of the State Demographer, Austin, Texas, January 2013.

"Profile of General Population and Housing Characteristics, 2010, Demographic Profile Data (DP-1): South Houston City, Texas," U.S. Census Bureau, *American FactFinder*, retrieved June 26, 2012.

Perry, Rick Governor, Letter to President Barack Obama Requesting Federal Disaster Relief, April 16, 2011.

Ramsey, Ross. "Analysis: In the Legislature, Race and Party Line Up." The Texas Tribune, May 5, 2014.

Perez Joan Jenkins Perez. "Dealey, George Bannerman." *Handbook of Texas Online*. June 12, 2010. Published by the Texas State Historical Association.

Perryman, Ray. "Long-Term Forecasting for the Texas Economy," The Perryman Group, Waco, Texas, August 16, 2013.

Perryman, Ray. "The Long-Term Forecast for the Economies of Texas Metropolitan Areas," The Perryman Group, Waco, Texas, October 10, 2013.

Price, Asher. "Drought Conditions Expected to Worsen," *Austin American-Statesman*, January 17, 2014.

Ragsdale, Kenneth. *The Year America Discovered Texas: Centennial '36*. College Station, Texas: Texas A&M University Press, 1987.

Ramos, Mary G. "Cattle Drives Started in Earnest After the Civil War." *Texas Almanac.* Texas State Historical Society: Austin, Texas.

Rogers, Will. "Ma' Feguson Is Given Lead In Texas Vote," *The Evening Review (Liverpool),* August 30, 1932.

Ronner, Claire. "Memorable Quotes From Barbara Jordan." *Texas Highways,* August 2012.

Root, Jay. "Perry Baptized Anew in Historic Creek." The Texas Tribune, April 29, 2014.

Rossi, Victoria. "Celebrating Eyeore: Young and Old Gather for Traditional Tribute to Fictional Character." *The Daily Texan,* May 2, 2005.

Saslow, Eli. "Too Much of Too Little." *The Washington Post,* November 9, 2013.

"Save Our Springs Alliance" official website, accessed February 17, 2014.

"State Area Measurements and Internal Point Coordinates." *2010 United States Census,* United States Census Bureau, February 11, 2011.

"Tanker 10" official website, retrieved October 7, 2013.

Seager, Richard and Celine Herweijer. "Causes and Consequences of Nineteenth Century Droughts in North America." Lamont-Doherty Earth Observatory, Columbia University, 2011.

Schwartz, Jeremy. "Austin Beginning to Compete With Other Texas Cities for Wealthy Immigrants From Mexico." *Austin American-Statesman,* June 6, 2011.

Schwarz, Mimi. "Are You a Woman?" *Texas Monthly,* August 2012.

Segura, Gary and Texeira, Ruy. "The Myth of the 'White' Latino," *The New Republic,* June 19, 2014.

Slater, Wayne. "South Texas Newspaper Scolds Greg Abbott for Comparing the Hispanic-Rich Region to a 'Third-World country.'" *The Dallas Morning News,* February 7, 2014.

Steinbeck, John. *Travels With Charley: In Search of America.* New York: Penguin, 1962, 2002.

Steinberg, Kaitlin. "100 Favorite Dishes 2014: A Love Letter to Houston Food." *Houston Press,* April 9, 2014.

Stone, Rob, *The Cinema of Richard Linklater: Walk, Don't Run,* New York: Columbia University Press, 2013.

Stoney, Sierra and Batalova, Jeanne. "Mexican Immigrants in the United States." Migration Information Source, Washington, D.C. February 28, 2013.

Sweany, Brian D. "The Gov: Who Is Greg Abbott? How Would He Lead?" *Texas Monthly,* October 2013.

"Taumalipan Mezquital," *Terrestrial Ecoregions.* Word Wildlife Fund, retrieved November 26, 2013.

"Texas Centennial," *Handbook of Texas Online,* accessed October 22, 2013. Published by the Texas State Historical Association.

"Texas Fire Destroys 1,554 Homes, 17 People Missing," Associated Press, September 11, 2011.

Texas Politics, University of Texas at Austin, 3rd Edition, Revision 66.

"Texas Triangle," *America 2050,* New York, New York, 2014.

"Texas Statewide Survey," University of Texas-Texas Tribune, Austin. June 2014.

"The Changing Face of Texas," Tierra Grande, Texas A&M University, Vol. 1938, College Station, Texas, July 2013.

"The Natural Law Tradition in Ethics," First published September 23, 2002; substantive revision Tue. Sep 27, 2011, *Stanford Encyclopedia of Philosophy.* Stanford, California, 2011.

"The Potential Economic Benefits for Texas of a Free Trade Agreement Between the United States and the European Union," The Perryman Group, Waco, Texas, February 2013.

"The Savings and Loan Crisis and Its Aftermath," Appendix to Chapter 11, Federal Deposit Insurance Corporation, Washington, D.C.

"The Savings and Loan Crisis and Its Relationship to Banking," Chapter 4, *An Examination of the Banking Crises of the 1980s and Early 1990s,* Vol. 1, pp. 167-187, Federal Deposit Insurance Corp. Washington, D.C.

"The University of Texas at Austin Releases Preliminary Enrollment Data," The University of Texas at Austin, September 19, 2012.

"The World in 2050," HSBC Global Research, New York, January 2013.

"The 32nd Kinder Institute Houston Area Survey," The Kinder Institute, Rice University. Houston. 2013.

Tilove, Jonathan. "Greg Abbott Holds Double-Digit Lead Over Wendy Davis, Who Is Viewed Unfavorably By Almost Half the Electorate," Jonathan Tilove, *Austin American-Statesman,* April 15, 2014.

Tilove, Jonathan, "Dallas Feels Indebted to JFK."*Austin American-Statesman,* November 17, 2013.

Tinkle, Lon. *An American Original.* Boston: Little, Brown & Co., 1978.

Turner, Allan. "City to Offer Information In English, 5 Other Languages." *Houston Chronicle,* July 31, 2013.

"United States and Texas Populations 1850-2012," Texas State Library and Archives Commission, Austin, Texas, February 19, 2013.

"United States by Places and (in selected States) County Subdivisions with 50,000 or More Population and for Puerto Rico (geographies ranked by total population)," *American FactFinder,* United States Census Bureau, Washington, D.C., 2000.

Van Sickle, James. "2014 Democratic Primary: Dallas Contested Races." Burnt Orange Report, December 10, 2013.

Villareal, Angeles M. "U.S.-Mexico Economic Relations: Trends, Issues, and Implications." Congressional Research Service, Washington, D.C. August 9, 2012.

Walker, Tim. "Austin: The City That Lance Armstrong Built." *The Independent,* January 12, 2013.

Wallace, Chris, Rove Karl and Megyn Kelly. "Barack Obama Re-Elected President." Fox News, November 7, 2012. Television news broadcast.

Weise, Karen. "Austin Or Bust: America's Biggest Cities Lose People to the Urban B-List." *Bloomberg Businessweek,* April 8, 2014.

"Welcome to the New Frontier," Report for Christian Science Monitor Publishing Company. Parker Research, Austin Texas. 2013.

Welsh, Jennifer. "Prehistoric Texans May Have Been First Humans in U.S." *LiveScience*, March 24, 2011.

Wheeler, Anne. "LBJ Library Opens New Exhibits After Multi-Million Dollar Renovation," LBJ Presidential Library, Austin, December 5, 2012.

Witliff Collections, Texas State University, San Marcos, Texas.

Worcester, Donald E. "Chisholm Trail," *Handbook of Texas Online.* June 12, 2010. Published by the Texas State Historical Association.

Yago, Glenn, and Barth, James. "The Savings and Loan Crisis: Lessons From a Regulatory Failure." Milken Institute, Santa Monica, California, January 6, 2005.

Yergin, Daniel. *The Prize: The Epic Quest for Oil, Money & Power.* Free Press: New York, 1991, 1992, 2008.

Zehr, Dan. "Austin Jobless Rate Down to 4.7%." *Austin American-Statesman*, December 21, 2013.

Zehr, Dan. "Hiring Surge Cuts Austin Jobless Rate." *Austin American-Statesman*, April 19, 2014.

Zheng, T.C. "Developer Calls Sienna Plantation 'A Passion Fulfilled.'" March 23, 2009.

"83rd Lege's Regular Session: What Happened, What Didn't," The Texas Tribune, May 28, 2013.

"2010 Census: Texas Profile," United States Census Bureau, 2010.

FAMOUS TEXANS:
THE TEXAS 300

AUTHOR'S NOTE

When I set out to compile this list I began merely out of curiosity. There just seemed at nearly every turn to be famous people who were, as fate would have it, from Texas. The resultant list was very long. But it was interesting to me how many personalities who called Texas home at some point were household names to most Americans.

This could be ascribed to the size of the population, the energy of the people or the desperate desire to get out of Texas and see someplace else, accomplishing something of note as the price of passage. So, I decided to winnow what would have been a list, literally, of thousands to a list of 300, spanning nearly two centuries now.

Here is the resultant disclaimer. This list is in no way comprehensive, let alone scientific; there are plenty of Texans who were and are accomplished, but not famous, whatever that means, today, to most Americans, who are not included here. And for that I apologize.

I strove to include people who are well-known to most Americans and who had some level of accomplishment or simply recognition that was national or international in scope—beyond the borders of Texas. In some cases, just outrageous celebrity mattered, from a burlesque dancer to a television personality. Notorious criminals and murderers are on the list. Some people were excluded, namely because they were simply the spouses and children of famous Texans. In the case of early settlers I do not include their home states or countries; it should be noted that they all migrated to Texas. In the case of Native Americans I have made a similar choice, whether they were born in Texas or not.

Only later, in the lists of the 20th century, do I denote those who were born in Texas and those who may have been born elsewhere but spent substantial early, formative, or significant years in Texas. People who came late in life, say the novelist James Michener, are not on the list. Michener spent his final years in Austin, but Texas was not his home either for the preponderance of his life or his formative years. Dwight D. Eisenhower, for example, was born in Texas but raised in Kansas from the age of two; he is not on this list. The Oscar-winning actor, Forest Whittaker left Texas when he was just four years old so he is not on the list, either. George W. Bush was born on the East Coast but was most decidedly raised in Texas. In these cases, each is noted with a parenthesis, as are other figures.

As for the other people not on this list, these rather arbitrary criteria of mine do not in any way detract from their individual achievements or notoriety. By my count, more than two dozen Texans, for example, have been astronauts but for the reasons above just a few are on this particular list. All, of course, are or were hugely accomplished individuals. There are dozens and dozens of football players and baseball players not on this list.

The list is organized by era and alphabetically, not in order of importance. My point here is that there are a lot of Texans and to paraphrase the late Walter Cronkite, what happens in Texas changes the world. And, yes, I'm aware that's a deeply Texan and chauvinistic statement, one to which, yes, Texans are consistently prone.

Even so, with all that winnowing, the list is nonetheless epic and, moreover, entertaining, just like Texas, I suppose.

—Richard Parker

EARLY 19TH CENTURY

Moses Austin, founder of the Austin Colony, settler, 1761–1821

Stephen F. Austin, Father of Texas, 1793–1836

James Bowie, frontiersman, 1796–1836

Jesse Chisholm, namesake of Chisholm Trail, 1806–1868

David Crocket, politician and adventurer, 1736–1836

Sam Houston, president of the Republic of Texas, senator, and governor, 1793–1863,

Emily West Morgan, Yellow Rose of Texas, 1815–1891

Jose Angel Navarro, rebel against Spanish rule of Mexico, 1784–1836

Juan Seguin, soldier and politician, 1806–1890

William Travis, adventurer and soldier, 1809–1836

LATE 19TH CENTURY

Sam Bass, train robber, 1851–1898

Roy Bean, justice of the peace, 1825–1903

Sitting Bear, Kiowa warrior, 1800–1871

Ten Bears, Comanche Chief, 1792–1872

Santos Benavides, Confederate colonel, 1823–1891

Little Bluff, Kiowa chief, 1780–1886

Juan Cortina, rancher, renegade and Mexican general, 1824–1894

John "Rip" Ford, Texas Ranger, 1831–1897

John Wesley Hardin, gunfighter and outlaw, 1853–1895

John Bell Hood, Confederate general, 1831–1879

Buffalo Hump, Comanche chief, birth unknown–1870

George Jackson, slave and Republican politician, 1850–1900

Albert Sidney Johnston, Confederate general, 1803–1862

Mifflin Kenedy, rancher, 1818–1895

John B. Magruder, Confederate general, 1807–1871

Samuel Maverick, rancher and politician, 1807–1870

Benjamin McCulloch, Confederate general, 1811–1862

Jose Antonio Navarro, revolutionary and politician, 1795–1871

Peta Nocona, Comanche war chief, birth date unknown–1860

Cynthia Ann Parker, Comanche captive, 1825–1870

Quanah Parker, Comanche warrior and chief, 1850–1911

Soapy Smith, confidence man, 1860–1898

Belle Starr, bandit, 1848–1889

Libby Thompson, aka Squirrel–tooth Alice, dance hall girl, prostitute, and madam, 1855–1953

Louis T. Wigfall, Confederate general and senator, 1816–1874

Ignacio Zaragosa, Mexican general and Cinco de Mayo hero, 1829–1862

EARLY 20TH CENTURY

Jessie Daniel Ames, suffragette, 1883–1972

Gene Autry, singer, 1907–1998

Candy Barr, burlesque dancer, 1935–2005

Clyde Barrow, bank robber, 1909–1934

Sammy Baugh, football player, 1914–2008

Raul Perez Benavidez, Medal of Honor Winner, 1935–1998

Fred Bipson, novelist and author of *Old Yeller*, 1908–1973

Tom Blasingame, cowboy, 1898–1989

Harlon Block, Marine at Mt. Suribachi, Iowa Jima, 1924–1945

Cyd Charisse, actress and dancer, 1922–2008

Claire Chenault, Flying Tigers commander, 1893–1958

Douglas "Wrong Way" Corrigan, aviator, 1907–1995

Joan Crawford, actress, 1908–1977

Joseph Cullinan, founder of Texaco, 1860–1937

J. Frank Dobie, folklorist and writer, 1888–1964

Ira C. Eaker, commander U.S. 8th Air Force, 1896–1987

Dale Evans, actress and singer, 1912–2001

William Stamps Farish II, president of Standard Oil, 1881–1942

Miriam "Ma" Ferguson, first female governor, 1875–1944

John Nance Gardner, American vice president, 1868–1967

Alfredo Cantu Gonzalez, Medal of Honor Winner, 1946–1968

Charles Goodnight, cattle baron, 1836–1929

Woody Guthrie, singer and songwriter, 1912–1967

Conrad Hilton, hotel heir and businessman, 1926–1969

Jim Hogg, first native–born governor, 1851–1906

Howard Hughes, aviator and filmmaker, 1905–1976

Howard R. Hughes, Sr., oil executive, 1869–1924

H. L. Hunt, oil executive and businessman, 1889–1974

Blind Willie Johnson, singer and guitarist, 1897–1945

Jack Johnson, first African American heavyweight champion, 1878–1946

Scott Joplin, musician and composer, 1867–1917

Elmer Kelton, journalist and novelist, 1926–2009

Fred Koch, founder of refinery that became Koch Industries, 1900–1967

Dick "Night Train" Lane, football player, 1927–2002

Herbert Marcus, co–founder of Neiman–Marcus, 1878–1950.

Ann Miller, actress and dancer, 1923–2004

Doris Miller, first African American recipient of Navy Cross, 1919–1943

Tom Mix, actor, 1880–1940

Audie Murphy, decorated soldier, 1924–1971

Byron Nelson, golfer, 1912–2006

Chester Nimitz, admiral and Allied commander, 1886–1966

Bonnie Parker, bank robber, 1910–1934

Charles F. Pendleton, Medal of Honor winner, 1931–1953

Katherine Anne Porter, author, 1890–1980

Wiley Post, aviator and first to solo around the world, 1898–1935

Sam Rayburn, House speaker, 1882–1961

Debbie Reynolds, actress, 1932–

Sid W. Richardson, cattle baron and oilman, 1891–1959

Ginger Rogers, actress, 1911–1995

Willie Shoemaker, jockey, 1931–2003

Ozzie Simmons, first African American all–American football player, 1914–2001

William H. Simpson, commander of U.S. 9th Army, 1888–1980

Oliver P. Smith, Marine general, 1893–1977

Katherine Stinson, aviator, 1891–1977

Edwin Walker, ideologue and cashiered Army general, 1909–1993

Walton Walker, commander of U.S. 8th Army, 1889–1950

Walter Prescott Webb, historian, 1888–1963

Smokey Joe Williams, baseball player, 1886–1951

Boxcar Willie, singer (aka Lecil Travis Martin) 1931–1999

Bob Wills, singer, 1905–1975

LATE 20TH CENTURY

F. Murray Abraham, actor, 1939–

Red Adair, oil field firefighter, 1915–2004

Joe Albritton, banker and media owner, 1924–2012

Lance Armstrong, disgraced cyclist, 1971–

Mary Kay Ash, businesswoman, 1918–2001

James Baker, lawyer, politician and Cabinet member, 1930–

Joe Don Baker, actor, 1936–

Ernie Banks, baseball player, 1931–

Edward Bass, businessman and philanthropist, 1945–

Alan Bean, astronaut, 1932–

George R. Brown, businessman, 1898–1983

Michael Stewart Brown, Nobel Prize–winning geneticist, 1941–

Carol Burnett, actress and comedian, 1933–

Gary Busey, actor, 1940–

George H. W. Bush, American president (born Massachusetts), 1924–

Charles Butt, businessman, 1938–

Earl Campbell, football player, 1955–

Liz Carpenter, journalist, 1920–2010

Vikki Carr, singer, 1941–

Lauro Cavazos, Cabinet member, 1927–

Mark David Chapman, John Lennon's killer, 1955–

Pat Choate, economist and author, 1941–

Henry Cisneros, politician and Cabinet member, 1947–

Sandra Cisneros, author and poet, 1954–

William Ramsey Clark, lawyer and attorney general, 1927–

Roger Clemens, baseball player, 1962–

Randall "Tex" Cobb, boxer, 1950–

Dabney Coleman, actor, 1932–

John Connally, governor and Cabinet secretary, 1917–1993

Dash Crofts, musician, 1940–

Walter Cronkite, broadcast journalist, 1916–2009

Christopher Cross, singer, 1951–

Trammell Crow, businessman and developer, 1914–2009

Robert B. Cullum, founder of Tom Thumb Food & Pharmacy, 1912–1981

Robert Curl, Nobel Prize–winning chemist

Price Daniel, governor and senator, 1910–1988

Jimmy Dean, singer and television personality, 1928–2010

Michael DeBakey, heart surgeon, 1908–2008

Tom DeLay, House Majority Leader, 1947–

Michael Dell, businessman, 1965–

Sam Donaldson, broadcast journalist, 1934–

Sandy Duncan, actress and singer, 1946–

Linda Ellerbee, broadcast journalist, 1944–

Ron Ely, actor best known as Tarzan, 1938–

Morgan Fairchild, actress, 1950–

John Henry Faulk, blacklisted broadcaster, 1913–1990

Farah Fawcett, actress, 1947–2009

Gloria Feldt, feminist, 1942–

Freddy Fender, singer, 1936–2006

O'Neill Ford, architect, 1905–1976

George Foreman, boxer, 1949–

A.J. Foyt, race car driver, 1935–

Larry Gatlin, musician, 1948–

Phyllis George, broadcaster and Miss America, 1949–

Joseph Goldstein, Nobel Prize–winning geneticist and biochemist, 1940–

Alberto Gonzalez, attorney general, 1955–

"Mean" Joe Greene, football player, 1946–

Oscar Griffin, journalist, 1933–2011

Larry Hagman, actor, 1931–2012

Jerry Hall, model, 1956–

Angie Harmon, actress, 1972–

Charles Harrelson, hit man, 1938–2007

Grant Hill, basketball player, 1971–

John Hinckley, would–be assassin, 1955–

Buddy Holly, musician, 1936–1959

Kay Bailey Hutchison, first female senator, 1932–

Molly Ivins, journalist and commentator, 1944–2007

Stephen Jackson, basketball player, 1978–

Leon Jaworski, attorney and special prosecutor, 1905–1982

Waylon Jennings, musician, 1937–2002

Jimmy Johnson, football coach, 1943–

Lyndon Johnson, American president, 1908–1973

Michael Johnson, Olympian sprinter, 1967–

Janis Joplin, singer, 1943–1970

Barbara Jordan, congresswoman, 1936–1996

Robert Earl Keen, singer and song writer, 1957–

Larry L. King, novelist and playwright, 1929–2012

David Koresh, cult leader, 1959–1993

Kris Kristofferson, singer and songwriter, 1936–

Jim Lehrer, broadcast journalist, (born Kansas) 1934–

Lisa Loeb, singer and songwriter, (born Maryland) 1968–

Lyle Lovett, singer and songwriter, 1957–

Natalie Maines, musician, 1947–

Barbara Mandrell, singer, 1948–

Louise Mandrell, singer, 1954–

Jane Mansfield, actress (born Pennsylvania), 1933–1967

Steve Martin, actor and comedian, 1945–

Delbert McClinton, singer and songwriter, 1940–

Billy Joe "Red" McCombs, billionaire businessman, 1927–

Larry McMurtry, author, 1936–

Willie Nelson, singer and songwriter, 1933–

Oliver North, Iran–contra figure and commentator, 1943–

Sandra Day O'Connor, Supreme Court justice, 1930–

Norah O'Donnell, broadcast journalist, 1974–

Shaquille O'Neal, basketball player, 1972–

Selena, aka Selena Quintanilla Perez, singer, 1971–1995

Ross Perot, businessman and politician, 1930–

Bum Phillips, football coach, 1923–2013

Stone Phillips, broadcast journalist, 1954–

T. Boone Pickens, businessman and philanthropist, 1928–

Jonathan Pollard, convicted spy, 1954–

Dennis Quaid, actor, 1954–

Randy Quaid, actor, 1950–

Anthony Quinn, actor 1937–2001

Dan Rather, broadcast journalist, 1931

Julia Scott Reed, journalist and columnist, 1917–2004

Rex Reed, film critic, 1938–

Ann Richards, second female governor, 1933–2006

Jiles Perry Richardson, aka The Big Bopper, musician, 1930–1959

Tex Ritter, singer and actor, 1905–1974

Frank Robinson, baseball manager, 1935–

Gene Rodenberry, creator of *Star Trek*, 1921–1991

Dennis Rodman, basketball player, 1961–

Jack Ruby, killer of Lee Harvey Oswald, 1910–1967

Nolan Ryan, baseball player, 1947–

Bob Schieffer, broadcast journalist, 1937–

Bobby Seale, co–founder of Black Panthers, 1936–

Billy Joe Shaver, singer and songwriter, 1939–

Amarillo Slim, aka Thomas Preston, Jr., poker champion, 1928–2012

Jacquelyn Smith, actress, 1947–

Sissy Spacek, actress, 1949–

Aaron Spelling, television producer, 1923–2006

Ken Starr, solicitor general and independent counsel, 1946–

Sly Stone, (aka Sylvester Stewart) singer and songwriter, 1943–

George Strait, singer, 1952–

Sheryl Swoopes, basketball player and Olympian, 1971–

Sharon Tate, actress and victim of Manson family, 1943–1969

John Tower, first Republican senator since Reconstruction, 1961–1985

Lee Trevino, golfer, 1939–

Tanya Tucker, singer, 1958–

Janine Turner, actor, 1961–

Gene Upshaw, football player, 1945–2008

Brenda Vaccaro, actress, 1939–

Stevie Ray Vaughn, musician, 1954–1990

Richard Viguerie, influential conservative, 1933–

Jerry Jeff Walker, singer and songwriter, 1942–

Charles "Tex" Watson, Manson Family murderer, 1945–

Virginia Whitehill, women's rights activist, 1928

Charles Whitman, mass killer, 1941–1966

Jo Beth Williams, actress, 1938–

Jim Wright, House speaker, 1922–

Jeana Yeager, aviator, 1952–

Zig Ziglar, salesman, 1926–2012

Marvin Zindler, broadcast journalist, 1921–2007

21ST CENTURY

Lauren Anderson, ballet dancer, 1965–

Jim Angle, broadcast journalist, 1946–

Marcia Ball, singer and pianist, 1948–

Paul Begala, political consultant and commentator, 1961–

Drew Brees, football player, 1979–

George W. Bush, American president (born Connecticut) 1946–

Jeb Bush, governor of Florida, 1953–

George Cantu, baseball player, 1982–

Kelly Clarkson, singer, 1982–

Michael Crabtree, football player, 1987–

Mark Cuban, sports team owner, 1958–

Hillary Duff, singer, 1987–

Billie Sol Estes, businessman and swindler, 1925–2013

Carly Fiorinna, businesswoman, 1954–

Jamie Foxx, actor, 1967–

Melinda Gates, philanthropist, 1964–

Woody Harrelson, actor, 1961–

Ethan Hawke, actor, 1970–

Don Henley, musician, 1947–

Jennifer Love Hewitt, actress, 1979–

Larry Hovis, actor, 1936–2003

Millie Hughes–Fulford, astronaut, 1945–

Rick Husband, astronaut and commander of shuttle *Columbia*, 1957–2003

Alex Jones, conspiracy theorist and radio host, 1974–

Jerry Jones, football team owner, 1947–

Mike Jones, rapper, 1981–

Norah Jones, singer and songwriter, (born New York City), 1979–

Tommy Lee Jones, actor, 1946–

Mike Judge, television producer, 1962–

Beyoncé Knowles, singer, 1981–

Bob Lilly, football player, 1939–

Richard Linklater, film director, 1961–

Eva Longoria, actress, 1975–

John Mackey, founder of Whole Foods, 1953–

Matthew McConaughey, actor, 1969–

Nina Mercedes, adult film star, 1979–

John Olivas, astronaut, 1965–

Joel Osteen, preacher and televangelist, 1963–

Bill Paxton, actor, 1955–

Scott Pelley, broadcast journalist, 1957–

Robin Wright Penn, actress, 1966–

Piper Perabo, actress, 1976–

Usher, aka Usher Raymond IV, musician and entertainer, 1978–

John Rich, musician, 1974–

LeeAnn Rimes, musician, (born Mississippi), 1982–

Robert Rodriguez, filmmaker, 1968

Jessica Simpson, singer, 1980–

Anna Nicole Smith, model, 1967–2007

Matt Stone, television producer, 1971–

Chesley "Sully" Sullenberger, airline pilot, 1951–

Patrick Swayze, actor, 1927–2009

Tila Tequila, television personality, 1981–

Rip Torn, actor, 1931–

Luke Wilson, actor, 1971–

Owen Wilson, actor, 1968–

Lawrence Wright, journalist and author, 1947–

Vince Young, football player, 1983–

Renée Zellweger, Academy award–winning actress, 1969–

TEXAS IN QUOTES

"Anybody who wanders around the world saying, 'Hell yes, I'm from Texas,' deserves whatever happens to him.'"
—Hunter S. Thompson

"If I owned Texas and Hell, I would rent out Texas and live in Hell."
—Philip Henry Sheridan

"Next time I tell you someone from Texas should not be president of the United States, please pay attention."
—Molly Ivins

"There are parts of Texas where a fly lives ten thousand years and a man can't die soon enough."
—Katherine Dunn

"I like it here in Austin. Anybody got a room?"
—Keith Richards

"Texas girls have an amazing sense of purpose when they lose it. They're the best girls in the world—they're loyal and fun, but when they get mad, they'll try to kill you."
—John Cusack

"It's fun telling you tall Texas tales. You always look like a little girl who's hearing Cinderella for the first time."
—Edna Ferber

"That's right, you're not from Texas. But Texas wants you anyways."

—Lyle Lovett

"You may all go to Hell, and I will go to Texas."

—David Crockett

"Texas has yet to learn submission to any oppression, come from what source it may."

—Sam Houston

"I'm from Texas, and one of the reasons I like Texas is because there's no one in control."

—Willie Nelson

"Texas, to be respected, must be polite. Santa Anna living can be of incalculable benefit to Texas; Santa Anna dead would be just another dead Mexican."

—Sam Houston

"Give me an army of West Point graduates and I'll win a battle . . . Give me a handful of Texas Aggies and I'll win a war."

—George S. Patton, Jr.

"You know the good part about all those executions in Texas? Fewer Texans."

—George Carlin

"You can imagine me as a kid growing up in redneck Texas with ballet shoes, tucking the violin under my arm. I had to fight my way up."

—Patrick Swayze

"I'm always going to live in Texas. Texas is my home. It'll be my home forever."

—Kelly Clarkson

"Texas is okay if you want to settle down and do your own thing quietly but it's not for outrageous people, and I was always outrageous."

—Janis Joplin

"Everybody thinks the Bushes are from Texas. I've been there twice."

—Billy Bush

"If English was good enough for Jesus Christ, then it's good enough for Texas."

—Ma Ferguson

"I made more money yesterday than I ever thought I'd make in an entire lifetime. But it's like somebody's going to take it all away from me and I'll be back in Texas, installing them damned irrigation wells. I didn't like that when I was sixteen. And I know I wouldn't like it when I'm 80."

—Jimmy Dean

"News events are like Texas weather. If you don't like it, wait a minute."

—Jessica Savitch

"Texas is as odd as it is vast."

—Henry Rollins

"There is a growing feeling that perhaps Texas is really another country, a place where the skies, the disasters, the diamonds, the politicians, the women, the fortunes, the football players and the murders are all bigger than anywhere else."

—Pete Hamill

"I'm super laid-back. I'm from Texas."

—Selena Gomez

"If God isn't a Longhorn then why is the sunset burnt orange?"

—Unknown

INDEX

INDEX

INDEX

INDEX

INDEX

ABOUT THE AUTHOR

R ichard Parker is an award-winning journalist.

His work has appeared in the Op-Ed and Sunday Review sections of the *New York Times*, the *New Republic*, the *Columbia Journalism Review* and his commentary is syndicated by the Tribune Content Agency to leading news outlets in the United States and around the world. His commentary in the *Times* won a 2013 prize from the National Society of Newspaper Columnists. He has been appointed twice as the visiting professional in journalism at the University of Texas at Austin.

He was the associate publisher of the *New Republic* in Washington, D.C. As a newspaper correspondent, he previously covered conflict and crisis in the Balkans, the Persian Gulf, and Latin America, as well as reported on the Pentagon, the White House, Congress, and presidential politics in America. He has won numerous awards and fellowships for his journalism. Raised in El Paso, Texas he received a B.A. in political science from Trinity University and an M.A. in political science from Tulane University.

He lives in the Texas Hill Country outside Austin.